HOME FROM THE HILL

HOME FROM THE HILL

BY

FRED WEBB

Safari Press Inc.

P.O. Box 3095, Long Beach, CA 90803-0095, USA

Webb, Fred

Second edition

Safari Press Inc.

1997, Long Beach, California

ISBN 1-57157-153-1

Library of Congress Catalog Card Number: 96-070047

10 9 8 7 6 5 4 3 2

Printed in China

Readers wishing to receive the Safari Press catalog, featuring many fine books on big-game hunting, wingshooting, and firearms, should write to Safari Press Inc., P.O. Box 3095, Long Beach, CA 90803, USA. California and worldwide (714) 894-9080, or visit our Web site at www.safaripress.com.

HOME FROM THE HILL

DEDICATION

To Irene, who has devoted her life to raising our family and supporting my dreams. She has followed when I was right, and helped me even when I was wrong. From the Atlantic to the Pacific to the Arctic, despite our nomadic existence, she has kept it all together.

PREFACE

Not all that long ago there was a group of men probing their way in the strangest parts of the world, making some kind of sense of the places on the old maps called terra incognita.

There are a few of this sort still around. One such is the professional North Country outfitter: part guide, part teacher, part adventurer, and part whatever is needed. These are the heirs of the explorers and their like, the men who straddled the great mountains and died seeking the Northwest Passage.

Fred Webb is one of this breed. I can easily see him with Byrd or Peary or Scott, and I can say with great sincerity that if I were down to my last match in some barren waste, there's absolutely no one I'd rather see!

I can't tell you how much I've enjoyed being at Fred's campfires, listening to his tales of a life spent in the North Country. Why not pour yourself a cup and sit with us?

Gene Hill

TOM HENNESSEY

REMEMBERING GENE HILL

It is hard for me to put much into this without a lot of maudlin malarkey. Of all the "famous" people I ever guided, Hilly was, hands down, the finest sport of them all. Unlike some of the younger writers whose careers depend on making *themselves* marketable (and believe me, there is nothing wrong with that), old Hill was the most relaxed guy in the world.

I half-believe in predestination and the fact that everything that happens to a person is leading them somewhere, for better or worse. Probably the Indian side of the family. However, Hill's influence was instrumental in getting me out of the woods in northern New Brunswick, where havoc is being wrecked by logging, mining, and hydro-exploitation, and convinced me to find new places to hunt. This took us from New Brunswick to Newfoundland, Labrador, Ungava Bay, Quebec and eventually to the Northwest Territories and the Arctic. Through Hill, I met Jim Rikhoff and the rest of the Fraternity, got involved in SCI, became a member of Game Coin and wrote for them, right on down the line.

My last note from Hilly was a shakily hand-written note written while I was up North in the spring of 1997. It says, in effect, that we will have to put off our trip to the Central Arctic for now.

We will make it one of these days.

ACKNOWLEDGMENTS

My deepest appreciation to our immediate family. To my son and partner, Martin, who has spent his life running hunting operations from New Brunswick, to Ungava, to the Central Arctic; without him our business would be at a standstill. To Derek and Cindy, who have helped in our various operations, and to Janice, our company bookkeeper, who put my ravings into shape for the publisher. I am proud to be your father.

To Rick Fitch, John Hancock, and Porter Hicks old friends who have helped us for a quarter-century. You are part of the Outfit.

To Eleanor, Coleman, Leigh, all the many, guides and cooks, pilots, packers, and boatmen; to those who have saved my life and those who have made it interesting: A heartfelt "Thank you" to all.

To my Inuk friends in the East, *"Nakomik!"* and in the West, *"Koanamik!"*

To all the companions who have shared life's campfires and trails, I will treasure the memories until we meet again.

Foreword

Many moons ago—October 1979—we ran our very first National Sporting Fraternity trip. It was a combined grouse-woodcock hunt at Fred Webb's Nictau Lodge in the Tobique Valley, New Brunswick, Canada. There were sixteen of us, counting Fred and myself. We brought our own dogs but had guides, good food and lodgings, a fairly well-stocked refreshment stand (later Fred bought an icemaker which he dubbed the "Rikhoff Memorial Ice Machine," for some reason). As it turned out, we all made some new friends to match a couple of old ones.

We had a magnificent time and decided to widen our horizons and look for new adventures. Well, we sure have . . . we've been to Alaska, Costa Rica, Botswana, Zimbabwe, Zambia, Argentina, Mexico, Scotland, the Bahamas, Tennessee, China, New Zealand, the Florida Keys, Québec, and a lot of other spots since, but we have never forgotten Fred or Nictau, where we spent several more years both hunting and salmon fishing.

I just went back and looked at the original roster and found that ten of the original sixteen are still members! Unfortunately, we lost two who left us early.

A few years ago—1991—Fred Webb was at the Game Coin conference in San Antonio, and we got to talking about the old days, as old geezers are wont to do, and once again we opined that it would be great to have another NSFL–Webb combined shebang. Fred's interest in the Tobique Valley lessened in direct relationship to that area's development and loss of sporting opportunities. He was connected with Arctic Adventures for some years, and through him we opened up our fine salmon fishing on the George River each year. The past few years, however, he has really gotten involved in the Northwest Territories, mostly for hunting, but with some fishing.

Well, if there was one place that I wished to visit back then, it was the Northwest Territories, so off we went in September of 1992. Unfortunately, I was recovering from a bad malaria siege, so Fred and I couldn't match our past exploits, which is probably just as well for all concerned.

As most can guess, certain letters from special people attract more than a bit of interest in an office devoted to the outdoor sports. It would be an understatement to say that Fred's letters rank somewhere near the top of the list for most people. . . . but a few of a more refined sensitivity have been known to recoil from his communications as if reacting to either the anti-Christ or the Marquis de Sade. I have even remarked that sometimes people carry his letter in tongs. I can't understand why, but I'll give you a mild sample (somewhat censored) that just happens to be part of the letter we wrote setting up that Northwest Territories trip mentioned above.

"If the Fraternity members want this type of trip we can satisfy them. I will endeavor to get in a couple of bottles of bingo; they bring their own bottle of hard stuff. We cannot fly tons and tons of beer and soda pop but can get in some for sure. Flying costs here are a (blank). It isn't like hopping from Chimo over the Falls; this is two hundred miles and a *lot* of money. Same with their baggage. I will supply them with lists, etc. They just can't bring the (blanking) kitchen sink. They can leave their tuxedos in Yellowknife. Going out they are covered for forty pounds of meat, if they want it; hotel will store overnight, etc. All of this (blank) is covered and arranged. I would hope to be able to meet you in town and show you a little bit of the local culture. There are two kinds: One for gentlemen and the other for you and Hennessey and me."

Well, that gives you a fair sampling of his literary style, which—to be fair—is both refreshingly frank and full of ribald wit. All I can say is that you haven't lived until you have experienced the storytelling abilities of Fred Webb. He is a classic! What? I don't know—but a classic. I am reluctant to tell any more stories about Fred or repeat any of his tales, as I know he has covered all the pertinent ground in a better, certainly more original, fashion in this book.

Well done, Old Friend, and may our paths cross a few more times. Here's to absent comrades!

Jim Rikhoff
Speakeasy Hill
October 3, 1996

EDITOR'S NOTE

I haven't hunted with Fred Webb nearly as much as I would like to—nor hopefully as much as I will in the future. But I've enjoyed a long association with him, not only in various hunting camps, but through all-too-many long hours on the floors of various conventions. In my business of writing about hunting and guns, one hesitates to go too far out on a limb; the chances of someone chopping it off in your rear increase exponentially the farther out on the limb you go. However, when pressed, I have described Fred Webb as one of the best outfitters I know.

This is not because his camps are the fanciest. They aren't. Nor is it because he's put me onto particularly huge trophies. He's done that for a lot of folks, but never for me. I've said this—and meant it—about "Uncle" Fred Webb for a lot of reasons, but a couple of key ones.

First, he's honest. Sadly, in this business of dream fulfillment (whether you're providing trips to directly fulfill your customers' dreams or, in my case, simply writing about the stuff dreams are made of), I'm not certain this is the best way to be successful. At the various shows I routinely hear some of the most outrageous promises—and often enough that I've come to wonder whether "pie in the sky" is what prospective clients *want* to hear. But you won't hear it from Fred Webb. Just the facts, ma'am.

Second, he's consistent. Dealing with far-flung situations all across Canada and laboring under some of the worst weather conditions and most difficult logistics in the world, Fred Webb finds a way to make things work. Or he doesn't outfit it. Perfect? Rarely. But reliable, consistent, and "as advertised."

When I heard that this book was in the offing, I got hold of Safari Press publisher Ludo Wurfbain and *demanded* that I be allowed to edit it. Ludo acceded, and then I began to wonder exactly what I'd let myself in for, again for two key reasons.

The first is a repeat: Fred is honest, straightforward, and outspoken. The more I thought about it, the more I worried I became about what I might find in a Fred Webb manuscript. And what I might do about it. For instance, how would I feel about a completely honest and unabridged account of one of our own hunts together? On that score I needn't have worried. Master storyteller that he is, he apparently found the material from our own hunts together too boring for inclusion. (*Whew, dodged that bullet!*) Some of the stories I'd heard before, well, Fred had already changed the names to protect the innocent—and the guilty.

I was also worried because, well, Fred Webb possesses the most creative use of the English language that I have ever been a party to. When Fred Webb says something, you generally know exactly where you stand . . . and it's said in such a way that you're unlikely to forget it. It isn't necessarily that Fred swears a lot; it's just that he swears, well, *creatively.* Although I had read several of his straightforward, to-the-point articles in *Safari* and other magazines, and had admired his style, I had never actually seen any of his raw copy. I had, however, received a great many letters from Fred. As Jimmy Rikhoff says in his foreword, a Fred Webb letter is a treasure . . . but you generally can't leave one laying around. In the case of personal correspondence, "raw copy" is an apt phrase, and I feared I would feel compelled to, well, "dilute" some of Fred's prose.

I didn't. You will find herein some number of words and phrases that you may not find in most outdoor magazines. But I left them simply because, as Fred told me when we discussed the book, they were there not for shock value or for their own sake, but because they offered the best way to tell the story and get the point across. Which, of course, is what skilled use of the language is all about. You will not find herein the "unabridged Fred Webb." You'll need to share some campfires for that. But you will find herein the life and times of a great outfitter, a great outdoorsman, and one of our sport's greatest spokesmen. He tells his own story far better than anyone else could, with a mixture of understatement and emphasis that also marks him as a great storyteller. Uncle Fred, honest, I didn't change a thing!

Craig Boddington
Paso Robles, California
December, 1996

I'M SCARED OF IT ALL

by Robert Service

I'm scared of it all, God's truth, so I am;
It's too big and brutal for me.
My nerve's on the raw and I don't give a damn
For all of the "hoorah" I see.
I'm pinned between subway and overhead train,
Where automobillies swoop down;
Oh, I want to go back to the timber again
I'm scared of the terrible town.

I want to go back to my lean, ashen plains;
My rivers that flash into foam;
My ultimate valleys where solitude reigns;
My trail from Fort Churchill to Nome.
My forests packed full of mysterious gloom,
My ice-fields agrind and aglare:
The city is deadfalled with danger and doom
I know that I'm safer up there.

I watch the wan faces that flash in the street;
All kinds and all classes I see.
Yet never a one in the million I meet
Has the smile of a comrade for me.
Just jaded and panting like dogs in a pack;
Just tensed and intent on the goal:
God, but I'm lonesome—I wish I was back,
Up there in the land of the Pole.

 I wish I was back on the Hunger Plateaus,
And seeking the lost caribou;
 I wish I was up where the Coppermine flows
To the kick of my little canoe.
I'd like to be far on some weariful shore
In the Land of the Blizzard and Bear;
Oh, I wish I was snug in the Arctic once more,
For I know I am safer up there.

REQUIEM

by Robert Louis Stevenson

Under the wide and starry sky
Dig the grave and let me lie:
Glad did I live and gladly die,
And I laid me down with a will.

This be the verse you grave for me:
Here he lies where he long'd to be;
Home is the sailor, home from the sea,
And the hunter home from the hill.

THE DAY THE GUN JAMMED

I have always noticed that tabloids next to the supermarket checkout make most of lurid titles to ensnare the prospective reader. Now that I have your interest, I can tell you that the following episode from my spotted career does not involve a muskox charge or a polar bear mauling. It is, in fact, not a big-game hunting tale at all, but rather an account of a pleasant summer canoe trip with two charming ladies.

Back then, as I now realize too late, I was at the peak of my physical prowess. Guiding for our own budding outfit, for some of the other outfits, or for the big fishing clubs, kept us busy between the spring log drive and the fall hunting seasons. Staying at various camps up in the woods and in tents along the rivers, we seldom enjoyed a night at home.

With the construction of hydro dams on the rivers, the great era of big Atlantic salmon clubs had ended, but at least the streams offered good brook trout fishing. One major club remained in the country. The Nictau Fish and Game Club, which controlled a group of lakes in the interior, still provided employment for guides, cooks, and wardens.

On this particular trip, Tommy Everett and I were guiding a party for one of the outfits in Riley Brook. The operation was based in the village, and this allowed us to stay home most nights, running various sections and branches of the Tobique River on day-long trips.

The term "day-long" meant exactly that. We were packed up and ready to haul canoes in the early morning clouds of midges. Breakfast, two lunches, and all the daylight hours were spent on the river. The client, a repeat guest of many years, was an automobile dealer from over the border in Maine, and like most Maine Yankees he wanted his money's worth.

Days were never long enough, nor bag limits generous enough, to suit this gentleman. Fortunately, his son, his wife, and two daughters were a bit easier to work with, but the old man paid the bills and called the shots. Guiding for my own outfit, I would have soon educated this gentleman as to game laws and sportsmanship or sent him packing. (With this attitude, needless to say, I am still not rich and retired). He was the guest of the outfit we were working for, however, so Tom and I bit our tongues and plied our canoe poles, as good guides are expected to do.

On some days, when we were running the upper, low-water branches, the boss would come himself, with another guide to lighten the canoes on the rough spots. Sometimes the old lady

would wish to remain in camp to sit on the veranda and knit, and sometimes one of the girls would want to go to town, instead of upriver, so no two days were ever the same.

This suited Tom and me, as long as we got our eight dollars a day and our share of the lunch. In this we were lucky because, regardless of how cheap the "old sport" might be, the outfitter's wife was one of the best cooks on the river and packed a mighty grub box for each day's expedition. No can of sardines and dry noodle soup in those days. The box would be packed with good homemade bread and biscuits, butter, jam, and molasses. Main courses might be chops, or hamburger or chicken to cook, with the makings of bannock, potatoes and onions. In other words, we had full-course campfire meals to be prepared and enjoyed along the shore.

On the fateful Day The Gun Jammed, Tom and I were taking the old man and the two daughters up to Red Bank on the Little Tobique, planning to run down to the forks at Nictau. This is a good long day's straight canoeing with decent summer water. With fishing along the way, the old sport would get his money's worth today.

In those days I used to drink a bit, probably more than a bit. We all used to drink whatever we could get, whenever it was available-but always within the bounds, so we could get up and be ready to go to work on the river. Drinking on the job when firearms, boats, trucks and guests were involved, was definitely out. We lived by a rule: "Any of the boys can whoop it up all night, but the men get up in the morning."

Driving up that morning, I was having a hard time keeping my eyes open in the predawn light. Two canoes rode on top of the truck, the two girls were in front with me, while Tommy and the old man dozed comfortably on top of the gear in the back. After a hard day's poling the canoes the day before, Tom and I had sort of spun out on a batch of homemade beer in the evening. Now the nagging headache, the dry mouth, and the roiling in my lower guts reminded me that I should have known better.

Half-an-hour after daylight, we arrived at last at Red Bank, a log landing used for stream driving earlier in the season. It

3

afforded one of the few points of access to the river. Here was the chance to stretch cramped muscles, as we unloaded the canoes and geared up for the trip. My cramped guts refused to limber up, despite discreet sorties away from the guests.

Tommy, likewise afflicted, made the only complaint I had ever heard him utter about anything to drink. "Jesus, what do you think was in that beer? I'm bloated up like a poisoned pup, and my mouth is drier than popcorn."

I could only suggest that one way or another we had to go down the river. Maybe if we had breakfast right off, before starting, it would clear our heads and make us face the day with a more positive attitude.

On this day, the boss's wife had outdone herself in packing a gigantic feed. For breakfast we had two dozen hard-boiled eggs, homemade bread to toast over the fire, and two jars of preserves. Soon tucked full and with an extra cup of coffee under our vests, we loaded up and set sail. Tom would haul the old man in the eighteen-foot canoe, and I would take the two grown daughters in the twenty-footer. We were off and sailing for Nictau by about seven o'clock. Now if we could keep the old man from extracting every single trout from every single pool, we should hit the landing at LeRoy Johnson's house late in the evening.

What followed was typical of a beautiful sunny day on the Little Tobique. Once the sun burned the last of the fog away and put the midges ashore in the shade, we had hours of delightful drifting along on a winding scenic river. The young ladies soon tired of catching and releasing trout, and just sat back to relax and enjoy the ever-changing panorama, as we turned one bend after another. It had been decided that, as the old man enjoyed seeing lots of fish in his cooler, we would let him keep enough to fill all three twenty-five fish quotas.

Although not totally compatible with the Fisheries Act, from a conservation standpoint it made little difference to the river whether seventy-five people took one fish each, or one old fish hog caught all seventy-five. For once, he wouldn't be pressing for "just one more, Tommy"—a plea we had endured all week. My main aim in life just then was to survive the day and get home safely without blowing up from the ever-expanding gas in my guts. Breakfast, far from helping matters, had only added fuel to the problem.

At lunch time we arrived at a great spot to boil the kettle, just below the mouth of Little Cedar Brook, where the lumber company had bridged the river. This landing place, made by removing gravel to build the road, provided a safe location to build a fire for tea and relax awhile.

In the grub box, we found that the cook had provided us with one of my very favorite lunches. Wrapped carefully in dish towels was a stone crock of homemade beans, and in another dish was cold potato salad. With generous slices of cold ham and baking powder biscuits, this was a traditional Tobique country feast, albeit not one designed for gas-free digestion.

On the pretense of going to check on a bear clawing tree, where we intended to hunt in a couple of months, I at last got out of earshot of the guests and attempted with not much success to alleviate the distress in my distended abdomen. As in all such occasions, when you can, you can't, and when you shouldn't, it takes the strength of Samson to hold it back.

Back at the landing, though barely able to bend over, I managed to get the canoe loaded and everyone settled, and we headed downriver. At least, I thought as we sailed along, if I don't die within the next few hours, I will be able to do it at home in the arms of my loving family.

River running, as we do it, means placing your passengers and baggage so that the canoe is slightly bow heavy, for downstream travel. The guide stands erect in the stern, with a setting pole, and pushes or sculls along, depending on the water. On long, easy stretches, he may occasionally sit down and steer with a paddle, but mostly he will dangle along with the pole. When negotiating rough, shallow water, the pole is used to snub up on one side or the other, allowing the bow to swing onto a new course by the action of the current. The term "setting pole" comes from the act of "setting" the stern aside so the bow must follow. To set a boat across the river, you steer from the stern, at such an angle that the current carries the boat across the river. This is the way ferries are operated.

On the subject of local jargon, the terms "canoeing" or "canoeist" were totally alien until amateur recreation-seekers began traveling down our rivers, leaving nothing in the country except their garbage. Our working guides and steam drivers, whether operating the traditional wood and canvas canoes, the big plank scows used as cook boats, horse boats, wannigans, or sacking boats on the lumber drives, were universally termed "boat runners." To be known as a good boat runner on the wild rivers of the Northeast was right up there with being known as a good guide.

The trip down from Little Cedar to the Forks at Nictau, in good water and without stopping to fish too often, can be accomplished in three or four hours without pushing. By this time you have passed the tight turns of the upper Little Tobique, which have you fighting out from under the sweepers and alders every few hundred yards, and you are on a mostly straight, decent-sized river.

There are only a few minor rough spots to contend with, "rough," as always, being in the eye of the beholder. I have heard the most horrific tales of paddlers rushing to oblivion at the "falls" or at the more dreaded "ledges." Sufficient to say that anyone, with a pole in his hands, even with gas in his guts, can slip through these places standing on his head. Naturally, as with all legendary local rapids, in really high spring water it is fast, with great standing swells that one must hit right to avoid being swamped. In low summer water, it is harder picking around the rocks.

That day, despite the charming company, my intestinal problems were rapidly turning what should have been a pleasure into a nightmare. As usually happens on sunny days on the river, by mid-afternoon we had a wind blowing straight in our faces. Poling and picking along, my mind went over every possibility as to how I could relieve my suffering without embarrassing both myself and my genteel passengers.

6

There was no doubt in my mind that, should I relax my hold on things, an explosion of great proportions would result. This time my guts were *ready*. How to do it occupied my entire attention, as I picked around the turn above the ledges. *A ha, perhaps as we take the plunge over the little falls, there will by enough noise and confusion to get away with letting go the gas.* Coming down the middle, setting over to the right-hand side, I clenched every muscle to hold on, until we dashed down through the run and leveled out. Alas, somehow in the confusion, my body betrayed me, and once again we sailed serenely onward; I however, was still unrelieved.

The next few miles went by in a blur. I was aware of the girls chatting away, content to view the scenery and enjoy the ride. With the occasional glance astern on the straight stretches, I could see that Tom had finally broken off the last of the old man's million lures. With the seventy-five trout securely in the cooler, Tom was more than content to follow me downriver.

By the time we had passed Whitefish Brook, I knew that it was do or die. I had long abandoned the last hole in my belt; my jeans were cutting me in half. If I could not find a solution, I would die an ignominious death. Into my mind popped the Ultimate Plan. In the stern rested the means of my salvation.

Many guides in those days carried a shotgun, taking advantage of a special game license that allowed the shooting of such "vermin" as crows, porcupines, groundhogs, and mergansers. Upon the back of the lowly merganser, or fish duck as we called him, rested the blame for the decline of Atlantic salmon stocks. Everyone, including the fisheries biologists, were convinced that the smolts, or young salmon, were all being devoured by the mergansers. Of course it never occurred to anyone that the turbines of three power stations, making fish chowder of everything headed downstream, might have something to do with the problem.

Having left my trusty old single-shot 12-gauge in one of the canoes back at camp, I had that morning grabbed the outfitter's worn-out pump-action Remington from behind the seat of the truck. Now with the barrel pointing skyward, and with three loads of No. 4s stuffed into the magazine (but none in the breech), the

Remington rested in the stern of the canoe. Coming up around the next turn was the mouth of the bogan on the left, just above Sisson Branch. "Eureka," I muttered as The Ultimate Plan continued to form. I knew from experience, that every time I passed the mouth of this bogan, a pair of mergansers would burst from the water and take to the air. All I needed to do was to precisely coordinate events so that upon the report of the shotgun, I could discreetly relieve the pressure building up under my heart.

We sailed down, and I line up for the turn, sculling smoothly with the pole, my eyes alert for the mergansers. As we made the approach, I quietly rested the pole in the boat, bent to pick up the pump gun, and as gently as possible worked the action. In the next two seconds, exactly as I expected, there was a splashing and a whirring of wings; the birds were airborne like rockets, straight overhead. Swinging in a high arc I simultaneously pulled the trigger and released the sphincter! *Click, Ka Roar!* But, the explosion came not from the mouth of the weapon, but from the depth of my distended bowels.

The traitorous bastard of a shotgun, not having been slammed back with sufficient force, had failed to chamber a round. I was stricken. Thoughts flashed through my mind. *Should I try the gun again with the muzzle under my chin? Should I just jump overboard with the anchor, or should I brazen it out? With the wind blowing hard in our faces, perhaps my guests had failed to witness my disgrace.*

No such luck. In a second I saw the reddening back of their necks and the hunching of their shoulders. One of them turned to the other, and both burst into gales of howling laughter. I stood there with the shotgun still in hand, drifting along, at last relieved enough to wiggle my toes without it hurting. Every time one of the girls stopped strangling in mirth, the other would raise her arms as if with a gun and shout *boom*, and they would become convulsed again.

We almost capsized as they waved Tom alongside to reenact the entire scene for the benefit of their doting parent. As we sailed on to the landing, I began to see the humor of the situation myself. I came out of my sulks and once more gave thanks for a job in the great outdoors, where the occasional indiscretion can be forgiven.

However, to this day I have never trusted any shotgun more complicated than a break-open single or double, remembering always The Day The Gun Jammed.

WORKING WITH A PROFESSIONAL

In a lifetime of guiding, I have been fortunate enough to have enjoyed the outdoors with many fine people. Most have been "ordinary sportsmen," but a good percentage have been professional writers, artists, photographers, and filmmakers. With very few, but notable, exceptions the experience has been extremely rewarding, and has led to treasured friendships that endure long after the trip has ended. One of the finest projects ever, was the making of an Atlantic salmon film with Joan and Lee Wulff, on the Tobique River in the late 1970s.

To all who knew him, Lee was the man who had done it all. His exploits as a hunter, fisherman, filmmaker, and pilot, will never be equaled. As he explained it, he was lucky enough to live in an era when many northern parts of North America were still relatively unexplored, while, at the same time, the use of light aircraft was becoming possible. When still a young man in Alaska, Lee pioneered many of the fly-fishing techniques being used today. His innovations in equipment include a series of flies that bear his name and the fishing vest now in common use. Lee, whether the inventor or not, was one of the first fly fishermen to use the so- called "riffling hitch," by which the fly, hitched from the side, skitters over the water to make a different sort of presentation to the fish. The fact that it became known as the "Portland Hitch," after a river and a fishing camp Lee operated in Newfoundland, says a lot as to its origins.

The acquisition of his first Super Cub opened the door to the exploration of countless lakes and streams in Labrador and on the island of Newfoundland. Many of these places have long since been developed into internationally known destinations. A few of the smaller lakes, in the depth of the Labrador wilderness, have probably never had another set of floats on them since Lee's departure.

Besides some of his books and articles, which remain as current today as they did the day they were written, his legacy includes an extensive library of outdoor films. They endure as classics, not only for the era in which they were produced but in an age that has seen such immense improvement in equipment. Lee as filmmaker was known as a perfectionist, sparing neither time nor effort to bring the finest examples of the outdoor cinematographer's art to the sporting public.

I first became acquainted with Lee and his wife, Joan, through Jack Hegarty. Jack had spent a good part of his life as a cinematographer, serving as Lee's chief of photography on many of his finest productions. To anyone engaged in the sport of Atlantic salmon angling, whether guests, guides, or camp owners, Lee and Joan Wulff were well known, warmly regarded and, above all, respected as true professionals.

When I was contacted by an old and mutual friend, Bob Cook, to see if I was interested in hosting Lee and Joan, plus another half-dozen people who were considered the "movers and shakers" in the Atlantic salmon conservation world at the time, I didn't have to think about it too long.

As fate would have it, we had previously arranged with an outdoor filmmaker, George Klucky, to produce a documentary based on the recovery of the Tobique River as a salmon river. The Tobique, previously world-renowned, had through the years been just about ruined by the series of hydro dams perceived as "progress" by the politicians of the time. Now, having destroyed the resource and closed the salmon camps and clubs, with resultant loss of local employment, the government was spending millions trying to recover what had been thrown away. With Lee's kind permission to cooperate in the project, we hoped to bring back some of the "good old days" to the image of the river.

On that particular summer, the salmon run, such as it was, reached its peak in mid-July. Now at least two weeks later, we would be attempting to film a successful salmon angling trip, with water levels and temperatures far from ideal for productive fishing. However, to be modest, we had the best guides on the river, two of the best-known anglers in the world, at least a few fish in the pools, and a photographer who would stand on his head all day if that's what it took to get the right shot. Now we would see if it would all come together in a decent film.

I was to guide Lee. Noah Ruff, one of the finest veteran salmon guides on the Tobique, would accompany Joan. Salmon fishing on the main river is best accomplished by canoe, although some pools allow wading. Boats and equipment vary from one river to another. On the Tobique, the traditional rig is the locally built cedar and canvas poling canoe. When anchored from the stern by way of a pulley and line, and weighted properly by the position of the occupants, it will set straight and true in the water. The "sport" sits in a low folding seat with a comfortable cushion, just ahead of the first crossbar. The guide, who runs the boat with a pole, stands in the stern when running, but moves up to sit just behind the guest and then drops the anchor by use of the rope and pulley.

In most cases, one starts fishing at the head of the pool, and descends by a series of short drops, so the angler can cover all the possible spots in which a fish might be holding. These holding positions, called "lies" or "lays" depending on the local jargon, might change from year to year due to ice action, or even by the day, depending upon the rise or fall of the water level. One might pretend to be an expert on just exactly where a fish is located, but it paid to hedge one's bets and cover all the available water. Besides, there was always the possibility of fish moving up from below.

The guide tries to take into account all the many natural variables. Then he proceeds to apply what wisdom he can in the use of his guest's tackle. The selection of just the proper artificial fly, destined to tempt a strike from the "King of Fish," holds by far the greatest mystique connected with the sport. No two anglers, perhaps, will ever agree on just the "right fly," and to some extent this applies to guides as well. However, one belief held by both guides and sports of long experience is that the fly that catches the fish is the one currently on the end of the line. There are also strong indications that a fish that is in the "taking" mood may just take whatever is presented, if it is presented in the proper fashion.

Most people assume that the guide himself must be an accomplished fisherman. This is, indeed, the ideal and many guides are proficient anglers in their own right. On the other hand, some of us were never particularly expert at handling the rod ourselves, having spent our lives running boats and watching other people fish. This was especially true on rivers where the fishing rights were solely owned by the big companies and the clubs, and the chance to legally "try a few casts" was usually at the invitation of the paying guest. (However, by one means or another, we did know what salmon tasted like.) The true measure of a guide in this or any other sport is in his ability to look after his client, to place him where his chances of success are the greatest, and to make his trip enjoyable and rewarding.

How does one go about guiding a person who is acknowledged around the world as the ultimate authority? Noah and I were not long in finding out that we were working with true professionals. Although between them they had probably more experience in Atlantic salmon angling than all the guides on the river, Joan and Lee were eager to listen to our suggestions and to show respect for our knowledge of the local situation.

Our cameraman, Klucky, from daylight the first morning, was geared up and ready to go. I felt confident that given even the slightest break with the fishing, we would have a great week and would produce a fine movie. One may make all the noble denials that success is not always measured by results in any outdoor sport, but it is still nearly impossible to present a "fishing film" in which no one catches a fish.

It was going to be difficult in the extreme. Two weeks at least beyond the peak of the run, the water remained low and warm. Fish were in most of the pools, but not in the taking mood. As Noah put it, "Any self-respecting fish was laying under the bank, panting in the shade." We urgently needed a change in weather, rain and the resultant cooling of the water to bring new fish moving up from downriver. It was at least beautiful weather for filming, and George ground out thousands of feet of scenic background shots, fill-in shots, cutaways, picnics, canoeing, casting, and sitting around the lunch fire, but no one catching a fish.

We fished all the main river pools from the Forks to the Kingfisher, twenty-five miles' worth. We trucked up and fished the Serpentine River pools—the Salmon Hole, Pup Falls, Big Falls, McArty Falls, Clyde Brook, and the Narrows. We took a day and ran the Right Hand Branch and fished Britt Brook Pool, Cedar Pool, Jimmy Brook, Half Way and Mouth of Serpentine. The next day we came back up and finished the trip down past Seven Mile Pool, Rocky Pool, Right Hand Branch Falls, Rocky Bend, Rocky Brook, head of Grassy Island, Half-Mile Pool and back again to the Forks. Lots of fishing, no fish. Lots of filming, no fish.

All of this required a considerable amount of effort, expense and arrangement, with canoes to truck around, special meal hours and shore lunches. Every night we returned to our main Nictau Lodge well after dark to eat a late evening supper, compare notes with the other guests, and get ready to go again before dawn. A few fish had been taken by the other guests, but altogether, it was a bitterly disappointing period of fishing for all concerned.

Difficult yes, and disappointing for sure, but to Noah and me, it was one of the finest weeks we had ever enjoyed on the river. Not for even one second did Lee or Joan, by word or deed, show anything except interest and enjoyment. Every suggestion by me or Noah was greeted with consideration and assurances that "we are having a marvelous time, the fish are here, now all we have to do is catch them."

Having always held the belief that the biggest damn fool in the guiding profession is the one who thinks he knows it all, I have always tried to be the old dog that is smart enough to learn new tricks. Believe me, with these people, I learned plenty. The one true gem, the one that sums it all up as far as the Atlantic Salmon Hopeful is concerned, and comes closest to Lee's Secret for Success is contained in the statement, *"Fish every single cast as if you think you are going to catch something."*

Simple enough? This one statement separates the professionals in any situation from the "would like to be" experts. Present the fly properly with no big gobs of line falling all over the pool. Do not stand there with a mile of line wrapped around your feet while you tramp the finish from your expensive shooting head. Do not use poor knots between leader, casting line, and backing. And most importantly of all, check that you haven't disabled your hook by smashing it on the rocks while back casting and never, but never, forget to check your leader frequently for wind knots. The infinite distance between a rise and actually landing a fish depends about 95 percent on the foregoing. The distance between a professional angler and a bumbling hopeful is soon apparent.

During the hot midday on what was to be the last day, we decided to return to the lodge to have a sit-down lunch, to rest a few hours, and to give Lee a chance to tie up a few new flies for the final evening's effort.

The grossly under-appreciated, unsung heroes in any "sporting camp" operation are the cooks and camp staff. In this, as in most of my ventures, my wife and partner, Irene, is responsible for anything good that happens around the camp. Salmon fishing is especially hard on the cook as hours are irregular and subject to change on short notice. Taking one more surprise arrival in stride, Irene once again provided us with an excellent lunch, working smoothly and efficiently with no more than the occasional glare for me, the culprit, out of sight of our guests.

After lunch, over in the Sleeping Lodge front room, we were treated to a unique demonstration, as Lee proceeded to tie up a number of dry flies of the White Wulff Series, totally by hand and without the use of a fly-tying vise. I have never before or since heard of anyone else capable of doing this, and George made sure to film it for posterity.

I will not go into the entire explanation of how most people tie flies; if you are an angler you already know. What is unique in Lee's method is that with no vise, holding the fly in his fingers and at some stages in his lips, he is able to whip up these dry flies in virtually minutes. Put a drop of dope on the heads and they are ready to fish. This is one more aspect of Lee's tremendous ability when it comes to anything concerned with the sport of angling.

Leaving camp for an evening on the main river, we hauled the canoes and gear once again up to the Forks Pool. In the Maliseet language the name of our community, Nictau, means literally the "meeting of the waters." Here, within a half-mile or so, the Little Tobique and Sisson Branch combine with the Mamozekel and the Right Hand Branch to make up the main Tobique River. At the Forks Pool, the camps of the former Tobique Salmon Club, are a reminder of the "good old days," before dams, roads, clearcuts, and pollution reduced the mighty Atlantic salmon runs to their present dismal level. As usual, now that the rivers are open to the public, an assortment of trailers, campers, and miscellaneous resident scroungers littered the banks. After a few half-hearted attempts to fish in these surroundings, I pulled anchor and with Noah and the camera canoe following, we sailed for downriver.

Noah and Joan dropped down to fish the Miller Pool at the foot of the long, straight stretch beginning at LeRoy Johnson's house. LeRoy at one point was the gatekeeper on the lumber company road, and he later guided for us at the lodge. His wife, Eleanor, still worked for us, as assistant cook and waitress, one of our rock-solid good friends and helpers.

Out in front of LeRoy's, just below the mouth of the "Run-Around," is a salmon pool that is sometimes productive. I cannot remember what the original name was, but LeRoy had named it the Welfare Pool, in honor of a local resident. Although this fellow's bad back would never allow him to accept a job, it didn't seem to hinder him from coming up from Riley Brook every evening, unloading a canoe from the top of his car, and casting for six hours. The Welfare Pool is indeed well named.

However, tonight was not the night for the Welfare Pool. With only about an hour's filming light remaining, I motioned over the camera boat and told the boys we were going to drop down to Little Nictau Pool to finish up. For better or worse, it would be the last attempt at taking a fish for the camera. As I slid past Noah and Joan at anchor, Noah started pulling up to follow.

16

Little Nictau was always one of my favorite pools. You go around a gentle bend in the river, drop down over a long bar, and you are into the top of the pool. Gravel, without big rocks, makes it nice to fish either by canoe or by wading. This beautiful evening, a slight breeze kept the "no-see-ums" at bay, and the fact that the pool is a quarter-mile walk from the road meant that we had it to ourselves.

We put ashore on the west bank and took the seats out of the canoe to sit and rest a minute. A cold beer from the cooler was exactly appropriate to the company and the setting, as we quietly discussed our experiences of the week and our tactics for the last attempt. Although the sun was rapidly going behind the mountain behind us, George decided to push the film a couple of stops and set up to have what light we would have over his left shoulder.

Taking his time, Lee tied on the White Wulff dry fly that we had filmed him tying at lunchtime. "Now," he said softly, "enough for the practice. Time to catch a fish."

Joan, Noah, and I sat and watch him wade out, full of respect for a gentleman in what is supposed to be the twilight years of life, stepping up to the pool once again after such a strenuous and discouraging week of endless, fruitless casting.

Klucky has the camera focused and rolling, filming another of the endless series of shots, that without a fish, will mean exactly nothing.

Lee makes a false cast, and another, and then the White Wulff drops like thistle down onto the surface of the pool. The water erupts to meet it. Now comes the exultant cry, dear to the heart of the guide, "Fish on!" Fish on for sure—no missed strike, no broken hook, no wind knot or parted leader. Fish on, to be played with the finesse only obtained by a lifetime of experience, to be brought, not to net, but to be tailed and picked from the water by hand, in the classic Lee Wulff manner.

And through it all, the camera kept rolling, handled, as had been the rod, by a true professional. No excuses for poor lighting, bad angles and long hours, just a terrifically good piece of film.

Rolling into camp that evening, to the applause of the other guides and guests, I knew that this week would remain forever a highlight of my life as a professional guide. On other days, on other rivers of the North East, we would encounter much more spectacular fishing, but we would never best this experience. Long after all of us have gone on to the land where all the fish are fresh-run and takers, someone will view this film and appreciate how it was made by a little band of professionals.

CAMPFIRE HUMOR, PROFOUND OR PROFANE?

A few years ago, at Game Coin, one program on the agenda was an afternoon get-together in which "campfire stories" were to be told for the entertainment of the mixed audience.

It was one of those ideas that probably sounded great when conceived; after all, some of the greatest storytellers around were on the program. I must say they did extremely well, under the circumstances, but being put on the platform cold sober, in daylight, and told to be funny just isn't conducive to great yarn-spinning. Analyzing the situation later, I realized that it is damn near impossible for any of us "outdoor artists" to clean up our act and expect to retain the humor; the two extremes just cannot be reconciled. If one eliminates all the stories that are racist, sexist, or obscene, there just isn't a hell of a lot left. If, for example, you remove all the "four-letter" words from the vocabulary of most guides—myself included—then our range of adjectives would be limited to "nice," "good," "bad," and the three primary colors.

Oh yes, I know there are guides who don't swear. There is one in Texas, one in Alaska, two in Africa, and a booking agent in Pennsylvania who will quote you the Scriptures—while picking your pocket. There are exceptions to everything.

The same applies to the use of alcohol. Ninety-five percent of the people whom I know enjoy the occasional libation; for some, it is not so occasional. The other five percent consists of reformed drunks, for whom I have the greatest respect; and a few who claim that Demon Rum has never passed their lips. The guy who coined the phrase, "never trust a man who doesn't drink," must have been a sportsman.

So let's agree that "sporting humor" can rarely be applied while politely sipping ginger ale and nibbling cucumber sandwiches, and admit that most of us work hard while hunting, party occasionally in less than moderation and sprinkle our speech with words and phrases not often found in the "Christian Ladies Guide to Social Conversation."

In defense of our vocabulary, however, it must be pointed out that outdoor humor rarely descends to the level of the programming your four-year-old kid sees and hears daily on television. We guides couldn't start to compete with the daytime talk shows that expose every perversion known to the species, nor the tasteless sex jokes aired on one popular show by a bunch of little-old-lady animal rightists, who make a most considerable amount of money dealing in deviant innuendo.

No, we simple souls from the outback can never aspire to stardom by being obscene; we just sometimes happen to be that way in the normal course of our conversation. With that in mind, I hope you won't be too offended the next time you sit around one of our campfires, or listen to our stories.

A QUARTER-CENTURY OF BLACK BEAR HUNTING

I n the spring of 1990, we carried out the last of twenty-five sea-sons, guiding black bear hunters from our base in Nictau, New Brunswick. It left a hole in our business and in our memories. As Martin remarked when May 1991 rolled around, "It's the first time in my lifetime we're not getting ready for bear hunting."

Based on the game department surveys in the sixties and seventies, the records we kept for them in the eighties, and my personal diaries over a period of 25 years, we killed approximately 750 bears, hunting spring and fall. Some may dispute this record, but none can prove better in that part of the country.

In the 1950s and early 1960s, when I was guiding for other outfitters, we had two ways of hunting bears: absolute chance encounter, or the universally accepted method of simply setting a bear trap to be tended occasionally throughout the season. This last method was accepted as the way of doing things, by the guides and "sports" alike, and many were the hair-raising and heroic tales.

I will not bother going into all the sickening details involved in bear trapping. I am happy to say that a few of us, with some inkling of what "sportsmanship" was supposed to involve, harassed the Game Department until, around 1970, the practice was outlawed. Other techniques, a bit closer to fair chase hunting, were developed.

Depending on the jurisdiction and geographical consider-ations, various methods are used to hunt this North American trophy. If you are fortunate enough to work an area where you can travel by boat, hunting tidal flats, or by truck, glassing moun-tain slides and clear-cuts, then you will see a good number of bears. You will be highly successful if you are in physical condition to stalk within shooting range.

In small woods and farm country, interspersed with roads a mile apart, hunting with hounds offers a great deal of excitement, at least for the guides and dog handlers. With radio and direction-finder equipped 4x4s in hot pursuit, some of the out-of-shape clients, if they're lucky, will get to see the bear while it is still breathing.

Although decried by the uninformed as not "sporting," the method that offers the most one-on-one, direct involvement, between the animal and the hunter is hunting on strategically placed baits. In flat, thick, big woods country, this offers the only realistic expectation of success, but with results still far from being assured.

When encountering some snob who looks down upon "waiting to kill the animal when he comes to dinner," I have always pointed out that people put worms on fishhooks. It is also considered correct to sit for deer in corn fields, and hunt ducks, geese, grouse, and woodcock where they are known to be feeding. In terms the big-game hunter can understand; the difference between hunting black bear in New Brunswick and leopard in Zambia is that in one case, the bait is on the ground with the hunter in the tree, and in the other, the hunter is on the ground and the bait in the tree. This and about ten thousand dollars.

The spring bear hunt, while exhausting in the extreme, was always anticipated and enjoyed by the guides. From the early weeks in April, when we used snowshoes to reach the stands, to the long evenings of late June, it was a delightful time to be in the woods.

Naturally, throughout the years, we gained experience, impressions, and plenty of bear stories. We can tell you about our own personal observations, but as everyone knows, the animals don't always read the script. One should always remember when hearing bear stories, the old guides say, "Any bear story wants lots of big bears in it."

There has been much discussion about which particular species of bear is most dangerous to man. These arguments are easy enough to settle. Statistically, the black bear annually accounts for more maulings than the rest of the bears put together. I hasten to add, that this is based primarily upon the fact that more black bears come into intimate contact with humans, than do polar bear or grizzlies, who reside a lot farther away from town. Needless to say, the one chewing on your leg at the time is the one to worry about the most.

Usually, if one could hear the bear's side of the story, most conflicts happen when the bear is threatened or cornered. Just as valid is the situation when he *thinks* he is threatened or cornered. The grizzly, especially the barren ground variety, the polar bear, and on rare occasions the black bear, may at times simply consider you a tender morsel. Although the least likely, this provides the ammunition for the very best bear stories.

So how about the attacks by wounded bears or sows protecting their cubs? Well, maybe this happens, sometimes, somewhere, but I would have to consider such incidents quite rare.

For all those years, we routinely tracked wounded bear into the woods in the dark, armed with a flashlight and sometimes an ax to mark the trail. As you may deduce, we were always more concerned with being shot in the kidneys by some nervous client's .300 Magnum than being devoured by a bear. We never, however, lost sight of the fact that, should he so desire, that old bear had the weapons and the strength to rend the boldest guide limb from limb, and then some. As I sometimes warned the younger guides, just because grandfather died home in bed from cirrhosis of the liver doesn't mean that you will enjoy the same. Someday you might meet some resentful old bear who, having been shot in the ass, is lying in a brushpile waiting for you to step on him.

Are the woods full of bears waiting to pounce upon the unwary traveler? Naturally, any outfitter in the bear business would hardly be dumb enough to dispel all the mystique and challenge, as perceived by the visiting dude. However, when pressed on the point, I would usually tell people that sitting out in the evening woods was a hell of a lot safer than walking, day or night, around their cities in the south.

What about the oft-heard claim that the most dangerous thing in the animal world is a female bear with cubs? Again, keep in mind that there are exceptions to every rule, and for damn sure one should not mess around in the thick brush where things may get confused. I can, however, tell you of a dozen occasions when Mother Bear had no intention of saving anyone's hide except her very own.

As the greatest cause of mortality among bear cubs is from being eaten by their own kin, the mother is indeed well-tuned to rush to their defense. However, most attacks upon man seem to me to be cases of mistaken identity. In our experience, whenever the bear had time to get our wind and identify the dreaded human, she would circle, she might huff and puff, but invariably she simply took off for parts unknown, leaving her dismayed kids behind.

One time my chief guide, Coleman McDougall, and I were guiding Gene Hill and his wife on a salmon fishing trip. On our way down the Riordan Gulch road, headed for the river, we saw a bear with two cubs cross the road in front of the truck. The cubs scrambled up the first tree, a spruce right beside the road. Telling our guests to stay in the truck, from which they could safely take pictures, Coleman and I did everything possible to entice that old bear out of the bushes to have her portrait taken. As they say in the TV auto commercials, "Don't try this on your own at home," but there was no way in hell she would come out and pose for pictures.

We have seen basically the same thing on many occasions.

My sons, Martin and Rick, were brought up around bear guides, and they inherited some very casual attitudes. They needed reminding once in a while to not forget the exceptions to the rule when dealing with wounded bears or sows with cubs.

Once they were walking in to check a bait in the middle of the day, when they were startled by scratching and whining noises right over their heads. Two bear cubs had scrambled up a big leaning cedar beside the trail. A big sow came bounding up the trail right at them just as Rick hollered, "Let's get the hell out of here!"

If you have seen a bear carrying on, chomping its teeth, woofing and snorting, while it pounces up and down on stiff front legs, you know you are looking at one trying to make up its mind about attacking. When they do come for real usually it will be like an ugly terrier, flat out and close to the ground. Very rarely will they walk upright like the Gentle Bens and other Hollywood bears.

This one sure looked like the real thing! However, backing out, as soon as the boys passed the tree, the cubs slid down and all the bears were happy to depart. As were the boys, as a matter of fact. It was a subtle reminder of what just might happen in certain circumstances, and for the next few days at least we all looked around a bit before barging into the bushes near a bait.

While perhaps not enjoying the glamour, or the high expense, of a grizzly or polar bear hunt, black bear hunting remains extremely popular across most of North America.

Game departments and outfitters should advocate a strict limit of one bear per license holder, unless in exceptionally high populations. Over the years we have had plenty of experience moving into new "virgin" hunting areas that were full of bears. Believe me, whether dealing with black bear, barren ground grizzlies or even the more widely traveled polar bear, you are not long in knocking off the big old male bears, with even moderate hunting pressure. Initially the total population in a given area will actually increase as these old boars are taken out. However, before long the average size of the bears encountered will decrease and the whole concept upon which trophy hunting is dependent will become untenable.

While the antihunting industry continues to fill its coffers in crusades to end bait hunting, hound hunting, and indeed all hunting, the truth is that the black bear remains prolific across most of its traditional range. As with any wildlife, urbanization and human expansion present the only real threats to its existence.

Good management, through selected sport hunting, will ensure future generations of the opportunity to hunt this traditional North American trophy.

"EESUMANHAIVIK"

"THE PLACE WHERE PEOPLE COME TO BE FREE"

W*e were sitting on the rocks above Number Six Pool at Helen Falls, on the mighty George River. I was trying to put into words that my friend would understand my feelings for this magnificent land he calls home and that I am privileged to visit as often as possible. Sandy Annanack is what southerners have known as an Eskimo. In his culture and his language he is Inuk, meaning simply a Man; member of the race Inuit, the People. During his lifetime, Inuit have moved from the Stone Age of the nomadic Arctic hunter into the present.*

Now, Sandy Annanack is a northern businessman. He and his wife, Maggie, operate one of the finest Atlantic salmon fishing camps in the world and have recently opened an immensely successful trophy caribou hunting camp up on the shores of Ungava Bay. They still retain a foot in each world, as much at home with the traditional ways of their ancestors as when Maggie shops in Montreal and Sandy accompanies me on big-game hunting trips to other parts of Canada.

"*Eesumanhaivik,*" he muses, "The place where people come to be free." Sandy realizes, as do I, that we are part of a vanishing time. Now we rest by the thundering rapids, as his People have done for eons. But how long have we left before modern man with his greed for more minerals, oil, and hydroelectric power, alters forever this eternal vista?

I have been "going north" since the 1950s. Sometimes I have lived like a dog and at times like a king, but I have never lost my love and appreciation for this unique part of Canada. During the past decade, I have worked with the People of George River, helping to establish tourist fishing and hunting camps. These camps, operating under the umbrella of the Federation of Co-operatives of Northern Quebec, not only offer the southern sportsman the finest enjoyment, they are also valuable to the Inuit as a means of making a living while instructing their children in the ways of the land.

The George River, draining an immense area of Northern Quebec and Labrador, empties into Ungava Bay. Inland a few miles, George River Village, the major community on that part of the coast, provides a base of operation and a winter home to many of the People. Salmon coming into the George migrate pretty well as they have since the beginning of time. There is no pollution, as yet no power dams, no organized fishery beyond a few gill nets set mainly for char, and no known offshore interception by any commercial fishery. There may be early and late seasons and years of high or low water, but few, if any, man-made obstacles impede the annual migration of fish up this mighty river system. About twenty miles above head of tide, at the first major resting water on the salmons' upstream journey, the lucky guest at the Helen Falls Camp enjoys angling hard to beat anywhere in the world today.

The origin of the name Helen Falls eludes me. I have run down various theories, and have researched governmental departments and the priceless archives of the Hudson Bay Company, but it remains a mystery. Names for nearby rivers and lakes and for the George itself can be traced to everyone from King George of England to the various clerks and factors of the Bay Company, but nothing on "Helen." When Mrs. Mina Hubbard, first white woman to descend the river crossed the watershed from Labrador in the early years of the century, the falls had already been named. Perhaps someday we will find out.

The first recorded instance of a sports angler taking salmon with a fly on this part of the George, and indeed on a number of Ungava rivers, was in the late 1940s. Bill Littleford was a helicopter engineer, designer, and avid angler working at the time with the government on the first accurate survey of the Ungava coastal region. Falling under the spell of Ungava, he later established the first sports camps in the area, in partnership with Bob May, then manager of the local HBC post. Bill, always the innovator, developed a system of fly casting based on his mini rod. A film exists of Bill casting, and then hooking and landing a twenty-pound-plus salmon, using this fourteen-inch rod tip with the reel tucked into his belt. This is quite an achievement in water where plenty of experienced anglers, using nine and ten-foot rods, still lose fish along with their fly line and backing.

The camp was operated very successfully for many years under the name "Arctic Anglers" until political considerations in Quebec brought about changes. At the close of the 1970s, owner- ship of the camp was transferred to the people of George River and Sandy Annanack became the new owner-manager. While the camp previously could only be reached by float planes land- ing on the river, Sandy was able to accommodate modern Twin Otter aircraft by cutting out a runway and a trail connecting to the camp. Other improvements continue to be made; each year more permanent log cabins appear at the falls and more refinements are added for the comfort of the guests. Sitting on a high esker like a miniature village, it is a landmark to the wilderness traveler. The magnificent view from the dining room windows, overlooking the Little Rapids and the mountains guarding the river, is one unexcelled anywhere in the Northland.

Although many "fishing greats" have visited the area, there has never been any real effort to tell the world about the fabulous salmon angling, the brook trout, lake trout, and char available. The season is short, basically six good weeks. Less than fifty guests are accepted yearly and spots have been booked by people returning through two generations. Only once in a while, through attrition, does space become available at the falls. The deaths of major members of a party that had visited for over fifteen seasons made it possible for us to enter a new group in 1983. They have now become another "traditional party," one that we all look for- ward to seeing each year.

Jim Rikhoff and his National Sporting Fraternity, otherwise known in camp circles as "Rikhoff's Rangers," had been guests of mine on various bird shooting and Atlantic salmon angling expe- ditions to our camps in eastern Canada. First introduced by Gene Hill, Jim and I had hit it off fairly well, probably because as Ernie Schweibert once told me, "You are the two most irreverent bastards of my acquaintance!"

When I declined to continue pursuing two vanishing species; woodcock and Atlantic salmon in New Brunswick and
renewed my love with the subarctic, it was with the understanding
that when space became available, the Fraternity would be ready
to shift its northern boundaries. With only a few minor hitches, it
has been a distinct pleasure to all concerned, and the fishing has
far outdone anything the Fraternity had been exposed to when
fishing with me elsewhere.

Every visit by Jim and the Rangers has had its highlights.
Some members change, some remain the same but fond memories are harbored by all of us at the camp. In the 1985 season,
Sandy and I, sitting at Number Six, were talking over other years
and watching Jim patiently casting a hitched Blue Charm to the
edge of the fast water.

We were remembering past triumphs, as in the 1983 season
when John Obrecht achieved the "Helen Falls Grand Slam" by
taking in one week two caribou, a black bear, numerous salmon,
two species of trout, and arctic char. We talked of the 1984 season, when Doc Howard, missing his flights north with the gang,
had proceeded on his own, first to Fort Chimo, then to George
River Village, and finally arriving at camp, having come sixty-five
miles upriver by canoe.

How could we forget the two world-traveling "sportsmen"
who had become ill when Sandy and I had killed a couple of
caribou for camp meat and coat skins for the People, but who
delighted in finishing off every single fish that had the misfortune to fall into their hands? "Selective Sportsmanship" is an
invention of the civilized South, amusing to the Northerner who
realizes that he is part of the Creator's scheme of things. We
reminisced about the early morning downriver caribou hunts,
when we would stop at the "char hole," take a couple of silver
beauties to feast on later, foil-cooked in the fire as we glassed
the mountains. We joked about the fact that my birthday is
always celebrated in the northern latitudes and that this, my
fiftieth, was to be shared with old friends, both southern and
Arctic. What more could one ask? And we talked of how my
son, Martin, first coming north four years ago, had been adopted

29

into Sandy's family and had formed friendships that would last forever.

Now in this third year of the Fraternity trips, we had run into a few rough spots. The water in the river was the lowest in the memory of the oldest Inuk on the coast. The fishing, while far better than anything elsewhere, was just not up to our highest standards. At least four of the most productive pools on the West Side did not even exist and normally excellent pools on the East Side had been unproductive. Although Tom Hennessey had pioneered a brand-new pool that will henceforth bear his name, going up the East side was pretty well just a nice scenic walk. A couple of other matters added to the complication. One member of the party had recently been hospitalized and could not walk more than a few yards, so one boat crew and two pools that could be easily reached had to be taken out of the regular rotation. To add to our frustration, we were attempting, in this of all years, to produce a film about the excellence of the fishing, and had apparently incurred a bit of resentment because we couldn't all be stars in one short movie.

As a guide for nearly thirty-five years, I maintain my sense of humor most of the time. Inuit have a saying, "*Ahnaiatsuk*," which roughly translates as, "Don't worry about things which can't be changed," or, I suspect, something considerably earthier. So Sandy and I were relaxing, knowing that we had done everything over which we had control over and if it wasn't the best in the world, it was at least the best that could be provided. Our reverie was broken by Jim Rikhoff's shout of, "Fish On!" We could see instantly that he was into a good salmon, and in trouble. The movie cameraman came running, destined, I thought, to record disaster as the condition of Number Six made landing a leaping salmon just about next to impossible. Number Six, as past guests will recall, is normally a good-sized pool, circular in shape, whirlpool in nature, lying between two of the major drops in the rapids. In this dry year, it was mainly a straight hard run through and misfortune was certain if the fish was allowed to escape even twenty yards downstream. We have seen many fish lost here at the best of times. Jim had his work cut out for him. Out ran the fish—it

30

jumped in the fast water, back into the sight eddy, then out again and again, as Jim maintained the delicate balance between letting him get over the falls, breaking off, or straightening the slim shank of the No. 8 hook. It was with relief and joy that at last Sandy was able to slip the net under the river warrior and settle the issue. For once things conspired to our satisfaction, and the piece of film made of this effort will become a major part of our proposed movie. Even in this, one of our "off" years, we will be able to show people a bit of what we enjoy: fishing with Rikhoff, Hill, and Hennessey and other members of the Fraternity on one of the last truly wild rivers on earth.

Even the medium of film can never capture all the memories; some things work and some don't, some end up on the editing room floor. The images, the memories, the tales retold around the campfire wherever guides gather, are what will remain forever. Harry Tennison, acting as Rikhoff's ghillie on Number One, tangling in the line, falling in the river but emerging triumphant with the fish in the net, at least as good as 95 percent of the ghillies of the world ... the traditional Fraternity party, where honors are bestowed, friendships sealed over refreshments generously donated—the only party at the falls where guests and staff mingle as friends . . . the perilous journey back to one's cabin, along the walkways under the northern lights . . . the friends like Whit Smith, Wayne Grayson, and Willy Payne, who became fishers of note under the tutelage of more expert members like Bob Devito . . . Of guiding a lady like Donna Grayson, as much at ease with the "bad boys" of the Fraternity or gunning for ptarmigan with the Inuit in the Ungava winter as she is playing the classic southern belle with husband Dr. Wayne, back home in Virginia.

These are the memories that last with Sandy and me, after the season is over, after the few less-than-pleasant experiences are long forgotten. This may be the reason that many of us remain in the profession. While we will never be rich, the good times outweigh the bad by far, and "*Eesumanhaivik*," the place where people come to be free, is our home.

31

CAMPFIRE PHILOSOPHY

"Freedom"

Do you city dwellers, sometimes have a dream,
Is your soul ever filled with the frustrated scream,
"Oh God, turn me loose, like some men I know,
To wander the North where the free winds still blow?
I wonder.

Do you factory workers, as you stand on the line,
Ever think of what's out there in this land of mine,
Where horizons are wider, where water is pure,
Where my job is different from yours I am sure?
I wonder.

Do you long-range truckers, toiling over the hills,
Ever think beyond schedules and "wake me up" pills,
Of unions and log books and payments on trucks,
Can you say to the Boss Man, "Buddy, this sucks?"
I wonder.

Do you bankers and brokers, accountants and such,
Ever feel that the suit and the tie is too much,
Ever think about space that's not bounded by walls,
Of a night on the Barrens when the Arctic wolf calls?
I wonder.

Do you other captives, wherever you are,
Ever stand out at night and look North to the Star,
Will you stick to the safe life, the regular pay,
Or will someday you wake up and just walk away?
I wonder.

I am of the wild bunch, I'm one of the free,
My life as a Hunter guarantees it for me,
I'll never be settled, for sure never Rich,
But I swear that I envy no Son-of-a-bitch.
No wonder!

UNGAVA BAY CARIBOU

"*Akuliak*" *is one of those words like Denali, Serengeti, and Altai; words that bring to mind visions of wilderness beyond the reach of present-day pressures and frustrations. To the serious trophy hunter, Akuliak, on the shores of Ungava Bay in Arctic Quebec, will become known as one of the most unusual and successful camps now hunting the Quebec-Labrador caribou.*

A lifetime as a guide should teach a person a few lessons, but apparently I am a slow learner. Regardless of how many trips I have made in the North, I can never convince myself to dress warmly enough. On a starlit evening last summer, with a couple of Eskimo guides, I had left George River and was heading up the Ungava coast to our new caribou camp at Akuliak. The wind was blowing from the ice just offshore, and the northern lights were streaming across the sky, reminding us that, August or not, this was the Arctic. It is always hard to believe that you can leave Montreal in sweltering summer weather, then twelve hours and fifteen hundred miles later be dozing and shivering your way up the coast of a land that hasn't changed much in the last few thousand years.

I first came to the North in the mid-fifties and worked from Labrador to the High Arctic as a guide and radio operator on various scientific expeditions. The Ungava Bay country in particular has always appealed to me. The terrain varies from flatland tundra to the spectacular beauty of the Torngat Mountains, with a mix of Arctic and subarctic environment, being just at the limit of the tree line. Most of all, the character of its native Eskimos, or Inuit, help to make this one of my favorite places. The word "Eskimo" is a semi-derogatory term applied to them by others. They much prefer their own name "Inuit" meaning simply "the People." Until fairly recently they had every reason to believe that they alone inhabited the planet. These are truly remarkable people, moving in one generation from the Stone Age into the Space Age. Within the lifetime of those now working at Akuliak, they lived as nomadic Arctic hunters. They traveled inland in small family groups to seek the caribou, out on the coast for fish and seal, and across the sea ice for walrus and bear in a never ending journey.

Increasing contact with the outside world brought many changes. The emphasis shifted from subsistence hunting to trapping the fur that could be traded for food and implements from the south. Missionaries, traders, and various government agencies urged the People to settle in more permanent villages. Some of this has undoubtedly helped the Inuit. One can hardly argue against the benefits of medical care, education, and other social services. However, permanent settlement brought some negative aspects as well such as the loosening of traditional family ties, and the loss by the younger generation of the very skills that allowed the People to exist for eons within this unique and sometimes hostile environment. For a while it looked as if most of the old ways would be lost, as if the future of the Inuit was to be stuck between two worlds. They could not return to the ways of their fathers, nor could they participate fully as citizens of Canada.

In the late 1950s, the people of the Ungava region began to recognize the need to develop a way of life that would allow them to take advantage of the benefits of the South, while retaining their culture and independence. With their tradition of helping one another, establishing a cooperative venture seemed the logical course. The first cooperative was formed at George River in 1959, and from that beginning, the movement has spread across the entire Canadian Northland. This crucial turning point in the history of an entire race was brought about to a great extent by the very people with whom we are now working at Akuliak. In 1967, all the cooperatives of northern Quebec joined in a federation. It combines efforts to supply trading stores in the communities and to market the craftwork, furs, and other products of the area. The tourism arm of the federation, known as Arctic Adventures, operates six of the finest hunting and fishing camps in the world.

Not content only to run present operations, Arctic Adventures also aims to develop further areas of interest to the sportsman tourist. The importance of these ventures to the economy of the North is obvious. Just as important is the opportunity they present for the Inuit to get back to the land, to instill in coming generations the skills and values of their ancestors.

At the time I became involved with Arctic Adventures, I was busy promoting my own bear hunting business in New Brunswick, as well as moose and caribou hunts I was working with elsewhere. The federation was already running an excellent caribou camp at Tunulik Lake, under the able management of Bobby Snowball and his family. This camp enjoyed a wide reputation as the source of many of the record book entries for the newly classified Quebec-Labrador caribou. With Tunulik constantly booked to capacity, it seemed the time had come to establish another camp. This could work in conjunction with Tunulik, as hunters might wish to progress from one camp to the other. The best way of achieving this would be to open another facility fairly distant from the existing one, preferably in an entirely different type of setting. Just such an area existed, sixty-five miles to the northeast of George River village, up on the shores of Ungava Bay in a location known to the natives as Akuliak.

According to the people in George River there were "always caribou at Akuliak." Throughout repeated interviews, we were told that the bulls were present throughout the summer and early autumn months, and the Game Department confirmed that this segment of the herd apparently moved within a limited area. This should mean that the population would not be subject to the wide fluctuations encountered farther south, where the annual migration must be relied on to bring caribou into the country.

In September 1981, we went up the coast on what was to be an exploratory trip. In George River we met our host, Stanley Annanack, who would become the Inuit manager of the new camp. Mr. Annanack, in his early sixties, is one of the founding members of the cooperative movement, a leader in his community, a man eager to take on new ventures and capable of seeing them through.

Arriving at the proposed site, we found it just as promised. High ground right on the edge of the bay, on the point of land known as Akuliak, provided clear, level space for building a camp. Farther up the slope was plenty of room for what would become the airstrip. Here we would be able to operate Twin Otters on wheels, insulating ourselves from the troubles associated with using float planes in tidal water. Most important, it took very little scouting to confirm that the country was full of good big bull caribou. Within three days, seven bulls had been selected. Five of them had double shovels and three rough-scored above the minimum for the book. Dropped antlers all over the place confirmed that indeed the animals stayed here until well after the normal hunting season. This looked like the place to establish a caribou camp, and within another year it would come into being.

During the winter, plans went forward for setting up the operation. While we headed south on the promotion trail, Stanley and the gang were busy cutting poles for constructing the camp and for firewood for the tents of the guides and their families. This was done in Arctic winter weather, by dog team and snowmobile, sixty-five miles from their permanent homes in the village. Once the snow was off, early in the summer, work commenced in earnest on the tourist cabins, cookhouse and the all-important airstrip. In August, a couple of weeks before the opening of the season, we were to put on the final touches and await the first hunters from the South.

Any arrival at an Inuit camp is an event. That night, landing at Akuliak, it was like coming home, hearing the welcoming: "Ai, Fred!" and then shaking hands with everyone from Stanley to the youngest grandchild. Warming by the wood stove in Stanley's tent, enjoying hot sweet tea and bannock, I wasn't long finding out that these people were eager and ready to go. Later in the sleeping bag, I had time to think ahead to the season that confronted us. Logistics are immense problems way out here on the Arctic coast. Uncertainties are connected with any new venture that brings together clients from the high-pressure, industrialized South and people of an entirely different culture. Would the airstrip be adequate, would the camp be completely ready in time, and most of all, would the caribou stay in the country? As it turned out, I was worrying for nothing.

We had all agreed on the concept of a camp that would offer the client a different kind of hunting trip at Akuliak. It is the most northerly camp hunting this particular species, and by accepting only eight to ten hunters at a time, we also planned to make it the most exclusive. Rather than just another of the million trips patterned after the legendary deer camp, this would be life with one of the last true hunting cultures on earth.

Tom Hennessey—

No attempt has been made to transpose a deluxe hotel atmosphere to the Arctic coast—just the opposite. It is a traditional Inuit hunting camp, with only as many benefits of modern technology as are needed to assure comfortable accommodation and good meals. The guides and their families live in the old-time round tents, as they have for generations, right at the edge of the high tide. These are coastal, sea-loving people. Turned-up freighter canoes; racks for drying fish and meat; and a stakeout area for the dog teams, idle at this time of year, complete the picture.

The tides of Ungava Bay, highest in the world, range from a normal forty-five to an extreme sixty feet, bringing to the coastline an ever-changing panorama. At high tide, you land your canoe beside the tents at Akuliak. Until you experience it, you will never believe just how far it goes out.

By late August, the camp and crew were ready. One plane had already been in to deliver groceries, propane and fuel oil for the guests' cabins. Although not exactly up to the standards of Kennedy or Heathrow, our strip, which had been handmade with a wheelbarrow, two shovels, and a caribou-antler scraper, had proven adequate. Ongoing improvements, later to include oil drum approach and boundary markers and a homemade wind sock, qualified it for the name Akuliak International Airport.

All of the people at camp are related to Stanley, directly or thorough marriage and adoption. In the best tradition of the North, the place is run as a community effort. In this society, the hunters come first; the guides, therefore, are the top men in the village. I had attempted to prepare them to a certain extent for the idiosyncrasies of trophy hunting with southern guests, in contrast to everyday killing caribou for meat. But they are the finest caribou hunters in the world, and only had to be taught what cuts should be made to properly cape a trophy bull, and that the license allowed each guest only one caribou, so they had best be a bit selective. The rest would come with exposure to clients. Guides are mostly born, not made, and aside from basic skills, attitude and experience are most important. Like hunting guides anywhere in the world, each is a character in his own right. One of the keys to running a happy hunting operation is knowing how to match guides to guests.

With an expected guest list of eight persons per hunt, Stanley and I had worked out a plan of operation. The four crews would each consist of an older guide who did not speak English and a younger one to help with communications. Depending on weather, tide, and other variables, some would hunt on foot directly from camp, while others would cruise the inlets by motor canoe, glassing the slopes.

Incidentally, anyone who has any doubts as to the practicality of hunting caribou with either bow or muzzleloader should remember that these people have harvested the animals traditionally with arrows, spears, and more recently with what we would consider quite marginal firearms. If you are in decent physical shape, even semiskilled as a stalker, and smart enough to do as the guide instructs, then you will be brought within range of the animal you seek.

Slightly lower in status than the guides are the crew of younger boys who take care of camp chores, such as hauling wood and water, bringing guests' luggage to the strip, and, of course, getting in on as much of the hunting as possible. They anxiously await their turn as the guides of tomorrow.

Some of the girls work in the cook tent, some help and serve, and some work as maids, looking after the guests' cabins. A couple are delegated to do the camp washing. Some do sewing and other crafts, and a most important crew prepares the capes and trophies. Women of the Inuit, brought up on generations of working with furs, turn out skins that are the envy of any southern taxidermist lucky enough to receive them.

Throughout all of our preparations, there had been caribou every day within sight of the camp. Each evening Stanley and I had taken the binoculars up the hill to look the country over. At this season, the animals do not congregate in large herds, but a few minutes' glassing would always turn up solitary bulls, a pair of bulls, or small groups of bulls. Any big, mature Quebec-Labrador caribou is acceptable as a worthwhile representative trophy. Some of these were really outstanding, and I could only hope that they would stick around until the hunters arrived.

On 24 August, an hour before the Air Inuit plane was to deliver the first party, three bulls strolled through the tents and proceeded to browse on the airstrip. They finally bedded down on the side of the mountain in plain view of the arriving guests.

This was an indication of how the season would go at Akuliak. While other areas languished throughout the early season doldrums, here on the coast, as the Inuit had promised me, there were "always caribou at Akuliak." Each and every week of the season produced a full house of good bulls.

As I write this in midwinter, the land is under snow at Akuliak. Stanley and all the crew are back in George River, and we are already looking forward eagerly to next season. Some refinements will be made, and more improvements to our airstrip. Spike camps are planned for even more variety and enjoyment. We will once again be striving to show our guests the trip of a lifetime.

It is hard to improve on 100 percent success, but we will be trying, as that is the way of my friends, the Inuit of Ungava.

THE GREAT CERTO ESCAPE

There's one story I must tell you. It's not a tale about hunting and fishing, but about a man who wished he could. It's a true story, one that our friend Jim Rikhoff has insisted I repeat around many campfires from the Arctic to the Marriott Riverwalk in San Antonio. It's about my Uncle Murray.

It is said that every man has at least one talent, perhaps not always apparent, but bound to come out sooner or later. My Uncle Murray possessed such a talent. Outwardly, he was the model urban commuter, long broken to the white shirt and tie in an office-bound career of quiet desperation; yet he harbored within his soul the seeds of rebellion and a talent for escape and evasion.

You might understand his situation better if you knew my Aunt Helen. Not that she wasn't a kind and generous person to those she approved of, it's just that she had the knack of putting people, Murray included, under her own particular brand of microscope. If you passed inspection, you had a friend for life; if found wanting, you were bound for hell with no hope of redemption. My brother, in one of his less generous observations, referring to Helen's piercing stare, claimed that when they produced the movie *Jaws*, they used her eyes for the shark.

As a youngster, I recall speculation that perhaps Uncle Murray had what was then termed a "drinking problem," and that perhaps was why he disappeared every so often. Personally, I never witnessed anything more outrageous than an occasional cold beer or a drink at a family wedding. What drew him most to my attention and admiration was his ability to escape periodically from the shackles of urban domesticity. To what, to whom, or to where, I did not care. He was a hero to me.

There were probably some breakouts over the years that didn't filter down to the whole family, but every once in a while we heard whispers of the more classic examples of Murray's talent. One time, when working in the office of a mining company in the coal mining section of New Brunswick, he went off to work one day and simply didn't come back. The office, the town, and eventually all of the company's mines were searched, but to no avail. Murray turned up in his own good time. Later he moved the family to Montreal, where the offices were bigger, the buildings higher and the lifestyle even more fenced in. This job, with its greater financial rewards, was undoubtedly a step up for Aunt Helen, but even more confining for Murray. Finally, on a vacation back to the lakes and woods of New Brunswick, when it came time to return to the big city, they looked around and Murray had escaped again. Helen, by now holding an important job herself, had to fly back to Montreal, leaving behind an all-points fugitive warrant to locate Murray. He was discovered three weeks later, when a zealous customs officer at the U.S. border opened a trunk of a car, to find, to the utter dismay of its driver, Murray, a complete stranger, inside.

There were other minor lapses, I am sure, but standing in my memory as the absolute best, for planning, timing and execution, was "The Great Certo Escape." It was the summer of 1958, and I was assigned as a communications specialist and guide on an exploration party bound for the high Arctic, to establish Canadian sovereignty in some doubtful areas and to carry out scientific projects. I was to sail from Montreal. As with anything to do with the government, someone screwed up and I found myself in town a week too early, and broke. Fortunately, Helen and Murray lived in Dorval, a western suburb of the city, so at least I could flop with them, instead of fighting the bedbugs and the deviates at the Mission to Foreign Seamen while I awaited the arrival of my ship.

Treated with the kindest hospitality by Aunt Helen, as she perceived my job to be one of some importance, I also enjoyed getting better acquainted with Murray. Over a couple of beers one evening, while not actually complaining about his lot in life, he became a bit wistful about how, for medical reasons, he had not "gone overseas" as my father and most of the male adults of

42

the family had done during the war. He had always felt that he had missed the only chance for high adventure presented to his generation. At my age then, pretty cocky and callous, maybe I didn't fully appreciate his longings as I can now, thirty years later. Now I see that perhaps he was wishing to escape on a venture such as I was facing in the Arctic. Perhaps he was feeling some regret that his life of respectability still chained him to the daily trip to the office towers, while the North beckoned with space and freedom.

For her part, Helen was at last content with her position in the scheme of things. They had achieved the dream of a "respectable steady job," a nice house in the English section of Montreal, and a daughter safely launched with a good education, and she believed that Murray was at last sufficiently domesticated to forgo any more efforts to escape. Murray, as it turned out, had other plans.

Through phone calls, I was finally advised of when and where to report to my ship, the CGS *Labrador*, famous as the first modern ship to successfully navigate the fabled Northwest Passage. She was docked at the foot of Pie Neuf, or Pius the Ninth Street, in the east end of Montreal. Leaving from Dorval, in those days before the cross-city expressway, it was a couple of hours of driving through the Paris of North America. We left early, right after supper, as I had to be aboard by 10 P.M. in time to run up the radio equipment before we sailed at midnight.

Helen elected to drive, being the expert, with Murray riding shotgun and me jammed with my gear in the back seat. As we left the house, Helen mentioned that she had purchased a case of strawberries that day from the farmer's market, and she wanted to stop somewhere to pick up some Certo, to make strawberry jam. To you who are unfamiliar with country lingo and jam-making, Certo is a product that takes the place of natural acids usually found in green apples or something. It makes your jelly jell and your jam jam. I'm not a cook either.

As we wound our way through Old Montreal that Saturday night, it became apparent that probably we would just make it on time. At every grocery store we passed, we debated about stopping for the Certo, but parking was impossible. Finally, we spotted a big Steinbergs store, which at that time was the "supermarket of all supermarkets" in that part of the world. As usual, there was no place to park. "Don't worry," said Murray, "I'll jump out, run in and get the Certo. You go around the block and pick me up when you come by." No problem. Out he went, and we proceeded to the next street where we could turn left, and after a bit of back street maneuvering with more left turns, we were back on St. Catherine's again, heading east toward Steinbergs.

As we cruised by, Helen hugging the curb lane with me watching, we saw people coming out and people going in, but there was no sign of Murray. "No sweat," I told her, "There are lots of people in there. He hasn't had time to get the Certo and pay for it."

So around we went again, and ten minutes later, back by Steinbergs, there was still no Murray. "Well," I said, "no doubt there's more people in there than we figured. Not to worry, I still have half an hour." So around we went again, and still no Murray. Helen by now was sweating and muttering, and even I was wondering how long it takes to find Certo, get it paid for and get back out on the street? How long was it going to take us to find the pier at Pie Neuf? What did they do to guys who screwed up and missed the ship, especially when it was sailing north for half a goddam year? I started to sweat too.

"Well, I've got it figured out," I said. "I'll jump out this time and run in and find Murray. You go around again and pick us up." Out I sprang, into the store, a big store, with lots of aisles. I ran up one aisle, down another, and even found the Certo section. I checked all the aisles, washrooms, all the checkouts, but still no Murray. By now, Helen was creeping up the curb lane with traffic lined up behind her and drivers blowing horns, Frenchmen shaking fists and cursing *"Maudit Anglais."* I dove into the car. "Well, shit," I said, "He's gone, he's disappeared." He had pulled off "The Great Certo Escape."

That winter, I was informed through the family that Murray had been located in a town out west, but by then was back at home, on the job again, apparently resigned to the rut. Over the next decade I heard occasionally that Murray was doing well, had achieved success and prosperity and hadn't attempted to top "The Great Certo Escape." Everyone was content that he had settled down, happy to toil away toward his retirement. I wondered.

Finally one fall, when I was up north working with some Eskimos running a caribou hunting camp, I was saddened to learn that Murray, just recently retired, had taken sick and died. He had crossed the "Long Swamp." I figured he had pulled his last great escape.

When I got home, my mother, who attended the funeral, told me how they waited for the casket coming by train from Montreal, but it didn't arrive. Finally they discovered that the remains, supposedly shipped to Minto, New Brunswick, had ended up instead in the lost freight office in Moncton, a hundred miles away. They finally got it straightened out and a couple of days later, by then in winter weather, they got Murray established in the small town cemetery. Murray had made his last escape, this time for sure.

The following May, when I was busy with our spring bear hunters, I got a call from my mother. "You're not going to believe this," she said. "You remember I told you how we finally got Murray buried?" "Oh God," I thought, "he's done it again." She continued, "Well, when the snow went off, they came in and surveyed the graveyard, and wouldn't you know it, Murray hadn't been put in his own lot at all. They had to shift him over to another."

Late that night, I stood out alone in the camp yard with a beer in my hand. Behind me, from the dining room, came the noise of celebrating hunters. A couple of them had taken good bear and they wanted to let everyone within hearing know about it. Across the sky streaked a falling star, carving its way toward the far horizon. It may have been the beer, but I felt the pull of

45

that star, a presence and a yearning toward the unknown reaches below Polaris, the guardian of the North. Glad to have had no witness, I whispered to the night sky, "Attaboy Murray. That last one was a dandy, but the best ever was 'The Great Certo Escape.' We'll see you down the trail somewhere."

FAMOUS LAST WORDS IN TRANSLATION

T*he outfitter or professional hunter who has been in business for a while has heard quite a few lines from clients and has managed to figure out what they really mean. Here are a few that are pretty well standard across Northern Canada.*

From the client to the outfitter, upon arriving in camp:

"Don't worry, our guys don't measure success by whether we kill an animal or not. We want a real trophy buck, or nothing at all."

Translation: "By Thursday, we will shoot anything from a fawn to our grandmother. If it is brown it is *DOWN*. Then we will complain to the outfitter every time we meet him at a sports show for the next ten years."

—

"You don't have to worry about our gang getting lost. We are all accomplished woodsmen."

Translation: "We will totally disregard everything the guide tells us, and will take off promptly in the wrong direction. You and your crew will be out all night in the rain shooting and shouting to get us rescued."

—

"Don't worry about looking after us. We will help the guide with all the camp chores."

Translation: "We will stick matches through the last gas light mantle in camp, drive your best sharp ax into the rocks, kick over the tea pail into the fire and burn holes in your new tent."

—

"Don't worry, all of our rifles are sighted in. Any one of us can hit a dime at a thousand yards."

Translation: "We are going to shoot a bear in the guts, paws, ears or ass and the guides are going to be out trailing drops of blood with a flashlight."

"Don't worry, we are all experts in the safe handling of firearms."

Translation: "We are going to shoot a hole in your truck, boat, airplane, or packhorse."

—

"Don't worry, we are all in great physical condition, and we will get there if we have to crawl."

Translation: "We are fifty pounds overweight and plead bad knees from high school football injuries. We're going to huff and puff, load our pack and rifle on the guide, and then piss and moan to the outfitter because the sheep insist on living so high up the mountain."

—

"Don't worry about me not wearing the life preserver in the boat, I was an Olympic swimmer in college."

Translation: "After using up your time and resources to recover my body, my widow's boyfriend, the lawyer, is going to sue you into bankruptcy."

—

"Don't worry about our baggage being a problem. We are all accomplished travelers. We always travel light."

Translation: "I am going to bring everything I possess. I expect every packhorse to carry four hundred pounds, every Super Cub to handle a Beaver load, every 185 to handle a Twin Otter load, and every Twin to handle a Herc load."

—

"Don't worry, our gang will just love to have a lady hunter in camp with us."

Translation: "We are going to start off making condescending remarks, go downhill to the sulks when the lady outshoots us at the sighting-in session, and be totally pissed when she walks farther, works harder, and brings in the best trophies."

—

"Don't worry about me bringing my non-hunting wife to camp at half-price. She will be no trouble at all and just loves the outdoors."

Translation: "I can't make the bitch stay at home, so she will take up the space of a paying client, keep trying to herd the

48

guides into the bushes, and hang around the kitchen driving the cook insane."

—

"Don't worry about our gang getting along with your northern guides. They haven't a racist bone in their body, they just love to meet people from other cultures."

Translation: "We will ask your Inuit guides if it is true that Eskimos let strangers sleep with their wives, and call your Dene Dogrib and Chipwyan guides 'Hey, Chief" or 'Tonto'."

—

"Don't worry, all of our guys are sportsmen to the core."

Translation: "Buddy, if we don't kill something soon, you can bet your ass that the weather will be bad, the food lousy, the tents leak, the guides lazy, and the outfitter the biggest goddam crook this side of New York City."

—

The list is endless, but we have to stop somewhere.

DANGEROUS GAME

Every once in a while, someone is bound to ask me about dangerous encounters with bears. Some people, apparently, want to believe that they are in grave and imminent danger every time they take a walk in the woods, but the truth is somewhat less colorful. While we have hunted for polar bear and barren ground grizzly and continue to guide hunters for both, by far the most numerous hunts we have guided over a quarter-century and more have been for black bear. Out of literally hundreds of "bear stories" we can relate, only a few of them stand out as being even remotely approaching what I would term dangerous. However... if really hard-pressed, sufficiently late at night and perhaps with some liquid persuasion, I might tell them about the time I was painfully injured while following up on a client-wounded bear.

Merle Everett, a good friend and good guide who is long gone to the Happy Hunting Ground, and I were guiding a couple of hunters up on the ridges around the head of Red Brook. Spring bear hunting in that part of the world is best accomplished by placing your client on a stand, usually a tree stand, overlooking an area where bear have been coming to a bait. This is the only method that offers the client even a marginal chance of success, and in my experience, is the technique that truly places the client and the bear in a one-on-one situation. Merle and I had placed the hunters in their stands hours previously and were waiting back on the ridge, hoping to hear a shot. We were discussing one of the hunters, a young man from Chicago, who the previous evening had let a large bear stroll right through without shooting.

"The only thing I can think," Merle was saying, "is that he has read too many books or heard too many bear stories. I bet right now he is sitting up there, safety off, half-scared to death that a bear will actually appear."

"Yes," I agreed, "and no matter how many times I tell them not to release that safety till they are ready to shoot something, some of them still don't listen. It worries the hell out of me, I can tell you. We have insurance against everything except stupidity."

Merle gets a chuckle out of this. "Remember the guy who told us he was a colonel in the Marines, but he shot a hole up through the brim of his cowboy hat climbing down with the rifle loaded?" "I sure do," I said. "And when we asked him what he shot at, he claimed he was 'just clearing his piece.' I remember that guy all right!"

Just then, "*KA-BOOM*," way over on the right-hand tongue of the ridge. We were on our way, hoping it was lying dead in the open, as it was getting dark pretty fast.

As we came into the clearing we spotted the hunter, still up in the tree stand.

Scrambling down as we got out, I can see he was just about frantic. "Now cool down," I said, "and tell us what the hell happened. Did you kill the bear, and where is he?"

"Oh my God," he blurted out, "he was a monster. He came in right over there, walked across here, went under my stand and didn't even look up."

"Well, Jesus," Merle asked, as impatient as I am, "did you hit him, or did your gun go off, or what?"

"He just started into the woods, right there, when I shot at him."

Merle and I have the same thought: another screwed-up deal. We work for a month getting stands built, getting bear coming to baits, sit the guy up with a comfortable seat, with a rest for his rifle, listen to his stories about hitting a dime at a thousand yards, and now he has missed or scratched a bear as big as a boxcar at thirty feet. Guess we shouldn't complain, because his check passed at the bank. But it sure gets discouraging sometimes.

By this time it was full dark in the woods, and we were barely able to see across the clearing. We were out on the end of a ridge that drops off into thousand-foot gulches in three directions. The only thing to do is look for sign, follow it as far as possible with flashlights, just in case he might have hit it fatally, and come back in the morning if we had to.

"Okay," I told the client, "you wait here in the truck. Merle and I will follow it as far as we can and see what happened."

"Oh my goodness," he said, shaking, "I couldn't stay here alone. I'd go crazy."

I relented. "Unload that rifle and put it in the truck, I'm a lot more worried about getting shot up the ass with a .300 magnum than I am of getting bitten by any bear."

In a case like this, one guide with a flashlight does his best to pick up and follow any blood trail. The other guide will mark the trees, usually with an ax, so that if you have to abandon the trail, you can pick it up easily the next morning. In no case do we carry a firearm. Besides being illegal in that particular jurisdiction, in our following up of wounded bear we have found out that 99 percent of the time they are either dead or long gone. Naturally, someday we might run across one who hasn't read the script.

We find a drop of blood, about as big as if you squeezed a pimple. Now we will have to go on with an all-out effort until we either find the bear, or know there is no chance that he is left with a major wounding. As someone who makes his living hunting, who knows that accidents happen and are inevitable, there do come occasions when you are more in sympathy with the critter than the client.

After an hour, we were down over the side of the ridge, Merle on his hands and knees, turning up leaves to find that one more drop of blood. I was a couple of steps behind with the ax, marking a bush, aware of the client almost tramping my boot heels off, he's so scared of being left behind.

All of a sudden, apparently a bush snapped up and hit him. He thought the bear had him, lets out a scream "*AAHHGH.*" He startles me so bad I almost leaped on old Merle's back.

"Jesus," Merle roared. "What in hell happened?"

My heart pounding, his scream was echoing in my ears, and I was coldly furious, "Chummy," I told him, "take this flashlight, follow that spotted trail back to the truck and lock your ass inside of it, or you'll want to trade places with this goddam bear."

52

Merle had seen me throw a few fits before, all minor alongside this one. We went along in silence, drop of blood here, broken twig there, stepped on a log here. Slow half-hour's going. I heard strangling noises, and saw my partner's shoulders shaking.

"What's so goddam funny?" I demanded, and then it hit me, too.

There we were in the middle of the woods, in the middle of the night. Two guides who should have known better, rolling on the ground, laughing our guts out. Every time I tried to speak, Merle came in with, "Did you see the way that poor bastard's eyes bugged out? I wouldn't be surprised if he's up there cleaning out his underwear with the wooden knife."

"If he is, then he'll ride on the back of the goddam truck."

I laugh so hard I take a pain in my chest. "Let's get the hell out of here. That bear is only scratched and long gone, not hurting half as much as I am."

After a sleepless night, with the wife's pushing me, I went down to the local hospital for X-rays. I had torn the cartilage between three of my ribs; taped all around, I was three weeks getting over it. Sometimes in bad weather it bothers me still today. A wound suffered in the line of duty.

If you hear someone ask about hair-raising encounters in pursuit of dangerous game, you might hear me say, "Well, yes, one time Merle Everett and I were hunting up around Red Brook, and . . . ."

HOW TO READ THE OUTFITTER'S BROCHURE

(Definitions—The Inside Dope)

F or the novice sportsman, about to engage upon his first great adventure, the following is presented in the spirit of edification.

Tom Hennessey—

PROFESSIONAL HUNTER

As with the professional athlete, and the professional ladies who hang around the bar in Reno, we must somehow make a living at our chosen line of employment. I therefore claim with pride that we are "professional hunters," in that we are the people who do it for money.

As with the other two professions, we are distinct from the happy "amateurs" who do it for fun and give their services for nothing.

GUIDE

Used proudly by all "professional hunters," but equally valid when used to describe Girl Guides, tour guides and Seeing Eye dogs.

OUTFITTER

The word many of us use to describe our "professional hunting" services. However, the same term is used to describe any guy with an airplane, selling cheap do-it-yourself hunts in Alaska, the bane of professional hunters, who there call themselves Master Guides. "Outfitter" may also denote an English shoppe selling gentlemen's clothing and accoutrements.

CLIENT

Known variously as the guest, sportsman, sports hunter, the dude, the old sport, and other terms in descending order of endearment. Usually dependent on individual personalities and the duration of the trip.

CAMP

Any collection of tents, shacks, or buildings, which it is hoped will provide at least minimal shelter from the elements, in a location where the game pursued is rumored to exist.

THE LODGE

Same as above but more pretentious. Often refers to the fact that while there is indoor plumbing, no serious game has been seen in the area for at least a decade.

SPIKE CAMP

Any relatively level, and ideally rock-free piece of mountain, tundra, ice, or snow. Sometimes covered by a pup tent or a tarp.

HOME-STYLE MEALS

Usually fairly tasty, hearty, and clean.

CAMP-STYLE MEALS

Same as above, but perhaps slightly less so.

CUISINE

Same as above, but prepared by some snotty Frog who doesn't wash his hands after going to the bathroom.

HORSES

Well-trained and gentle. . . . May refer to big, fat plow horse, or the family pet. Old enough to be on a one-way trip to a bear bait. Make alternate arrangements for return journey.

Spirited mountain horse. . . . One that will buck, kick, strike, bite, or run away with the dude. One which, upon any pretense, such as a grouse flushing or the scent of a bear eight miles away, will come totally unglued at every seam.

Well-trained packhorse. . . . Much like the above except with a holy mission to rub against every tree, roll over in every swamp, tear off the tarp, and crush cast-iron pack boxes. If trusted with your rifle, no matter how well secured, is guaranteed to break the stock or the scope, or both.

Any of the above. . . . Will limp along all day, but during the night, with all four feet hobbled, will run all the way home to southern Alberta.

AIRCRAFT IN CAMP

Can mean that the highest level of service and efficiency in travel, camp supply, and meat recovery is at your disposal.

Can also be a code for, "We will fly your fat ass around until you kill a critter, disregarding the fact that it is both unethical and illegal."

OUTFITTER-OWNED AIRCRAFT

In most cases, refers to the fact that the outfitter, who should have a million other things on his mind if he is doing his job, is also your pilot. Pay up your insurance, and good luck.

OTHER OFTEN-ENCOUNTERED PHRASES

Expert trophy handling. . . . Denotes the fact that the greater portion of the animal will be removed from the skin, which will then be shipped to some unlucky taxidermist, in a bag dripping blood and salt water.

"Our Country Abounds in Game". . . . Phrase invented by the writer of the first hunting brochure, State of Maine, circa 1803, and copied by about two million outfitters since that time. Usually means that back in grandfather's time, someone shot a deer.

Highest standards of fair chase. . . . If no one is looking except the guide, who can be bribed easily.

Immense wilderness area. . . . Any strip of woods you can't see through, between the power line and the Interstate.

We cater to an exclusive clientele . . . basically means that we take anyone whose money is green and whose deposit check clears the bank.

Addendum: *Everyone knows that I'm joking. Don't they?*

PERSPECTIVE

A PROFESSIONAL HUNTER'S REFLECTIONS

T*hings aren't always as they seem in the hunting business. Some clients are not out of shape, and some guides can't leap over mountains in a single bound.*

As a professional hunter, I was intrigued with an article in the January/February 1989 issue of *Safari*. In it, the writer set forth his six, excuse me, seven, rules for us poor, misguided guides to follow.

Whether you call us outfitters, guides, or professional hunters, we are all in the business of fulfilling dreams and expectations, some of which are attainable and some not. When asked just what a professional hunter is, I point out that the answer has its parallel both in a baseball player with a million-dollar contract and in the ladies who hang around the bars in Las Vegas.

A "professional" means that we hope to make a living at it, in contrast to the enthusiastic amateurs who do it for fun.

Fortunately, even for us hardened pros, there remains a certain element of enjoyment, or we would have left our profession years ago.

There may be no other business on which success rests to such a large degree on such variables as game populations, weather, economic and political considerations and blind luck. But most of all, success depends on the personality and ability of the customer.

Working nine months a year, hunting various critters across northern Canada—and the other three months pursuing clients in the United States—I don't have much time to read magazines. When I do, it is usually *Safari* or the publications of the other hunting clubs because I seem to know a lot of the people involved. In more than thirty years of guiding in one place or another, I have had the pleasure of sharing camps with a considerable number of sportsmen. I am always interested in the hunting reports, the "how-to-book-an-outfitter" articles, and critiques about our industry.

After all, our aim is to serve the hunting public, and even an old dog can pick up a new trick or two. With that in mind, I studied the Seven Commandments pretty carefully.

Let's start, as the gentleman did, and paraphrase him as he paraphrased Will Rogers, by saying that even if we did meet an occasional client that we didn't initially like, the vast majority of them were made likable during their stay with us. Considering that we have hosted, in one place or another, virtually thousands of adventure seekers, the fact that I have had to actually fight with only a half-dozen in over a quarter-century says a lot for hunters as a group. Even the six outstanding cases were sorted out by various means, and their names remain forever enshrined in my memory so they will never again darken the doorway of my tent.

So let's take that list of commandments and see how they look from the professional hunter's perspective.

Commandment Number One appears to be "Never laugh at the client's physical shortcomings." If we are in the business of dispelling myths, we can start right here. Not all guides are seven feet tall, in top shape, and run up mountains all day. Personally, there was a time when I smoked two bags of "roll your owns" a day, drank anything that would pour, could snowshoe thirty miles dawn to dusk and make love all night standing up. Nowadays, I am over the half-century mark, short, fat, lazy, and I use my brains more than my feet when hunting.

Most problems with a client's physical condition stem from a lack of communication about the facts. By that, I mean the facts as laid out by the guide as to what to expect, and the client's equally true appraisal of what he is capable of doing.

In my experience, I have found that it is usually the guy who is least equipped physically to really hunt hard who expects to take eight record book animals on a six-day mountain hunt and is bitterly disappointed when it doesn't turn out that way. Our company offers hunts in areas for which you should be in reasonably good shape. We have other hunts on which we are immensely pleased to host the more senior hunter and those in less-than-great shape—including those with mild handicaps.

These people are told the truth. If they tell me the truth, we can handle it, or advise them to seek a different type of vacation. However, this only works if both sides are frank and honest.

I had one case in which the client had been told everything possible in the English language and he still showed up for a snowshoe mountain bobcat hunt, seventy-eight years old, seventy pounds overweight and with an old-fashioned wooden leg. Fortunately, he was a good companion as we drove around the roads hoping for a hot track. And we did manage to tree a cat within hollering distance of the truck. It doesn't always turn out that pleasantly.

Another client, having promised that he was in great shape for what usually is a strenuous hunt, showed up in Newfoundland looking for a record moose, but totally unable to put out the required effort. Finally, in despair, my partner, Gerry, and I flew him to a pond where we only had to walk a mile up a small creek to where we knew a moose resided. With terrifying effort, we finally got him to where he managed to kill the mediocre bull.

Sitting back, wheezing over his tenth cigarette, while Gerry and I wrestled around in the tuckamores to cape his animal, he boasted, "Boys, I sure fooled the hell out of you. I have had major heart surgery and could drop dead any time, and then what would you do to get me out of here?"

I was mad enough to sulk, but Gerry, in his true Newfie fashion, said, "Well, sir, my good man, you sees that tuft of grass yonder? Well, if you croaks, I'll jam that up your rectum, and after you had bloated a bit, me and Fred will jump upon your rotten old carcass and paddle you down to the pond."

Now that probably violates Commandment Number One about not commenting upon the client's physical condition, but it seemed appropriate at the time.

Commandment Number Two deals with the problem that some clients, with the help of less-than-scrupulous operators, will book a hunt based upon unrealistic expectations or prices, and then not take even a little bit of blame upon themselves. Yes, we have all seen the ads, but like most ads we don't necessarily believe them. One hundred percent success is achievable on some species—when everything goes right. But that is not always the case. Anyone expecting no kill—no pay, or guaranteed hunts, has either done all his hunting at Pete's Piggery or has very little knowledge of the variables encountered on a real wilderness hunt.

I hasten to assure you that I have nothing whatsoever against preserve or exotics hunting, if that is what turns you on. However, don't go on a two-day Texas vacation, kill ten assorted heads of game from all over the world, and then complain to me because you thought you were booking a two-month safari in Tanzania.

As to the veracity of outfitters, I would hazard a guess that in general they are about par with people in other professions. Come to think of it, probably a notch or two above a couple I could mention.

Having spent a great deal of my life standing around sports shows and conventions may have made me a bit cynical, so you will have to forgive me, but it has been my observation that there is a definite percentage of hunters who want to be lied to. They actually crave a screwing, and worse, only about half of them even know when they are getting it. Not one of the honest, straight-arrow guides I know has ever become rich, but we can point out the crooks who have made it big.

Personally, I loathe using kill ratios as the sole criteria by which a hunting experience is judged, but we are forced into it by circumstances. When I point out that we have had a particular success figure, I can only guarantee to tell people the truth about what has happened in the past.

Obviously, if I could predict the future, I would be at the gaming tables in Reno or Vegas, not stuck behind a booth trying to sell hunts. As for the record book statistics that the gentleman mentioned, I quote them all the time because they are genuine. I assume that if you have the financial resources to book a hunt with me that you probably can read, so I don't see much sense in lying about it.

The reason I continue to enjoy the booking game as well as the hunting game is simple. By telling people the truth, I sort out 99 percent of the problems before they get to camp. Although this hasn't yet made us rich, it has led to innumerable happy memories and it allows me to look forward to each coming season as eagerly as the first one.

In *Commandment Number Three,* based upon the complaint that the guide sometimes sees game that the client doesn't, I again suspect that something must be lacking in the way of communication.

In our operations, a guide who insists upon continually outrunning the client definitely has a career problem. In defense of over-eager guides, it is easy to see how they may occasionally let the spirit of the chase override their judgment. However, there are a few things the client can do to rectify this problem before coming to the boss with it.

Start with sitting the guide down and explaining that regardless of the joy he takes in seeing game, it does not mean diddly (or lead to great tips) if the man paying the bill can't be let in on the secret.

If this doesn't work, then perhaps you can trailbreak him as we used to do with cat hounds. Tie one hundred feet of nylon line around his neck and occasionally step on it to slow him up. This only works, of course, if you can keep within a hundred feet of him. Under no circumstances should you let him carry your rifle. Without it, you can't even threaten to shoot him.

If all else fails, let me know and I will go to the final solution and sic a certain friend of mine on him.

The following incident reveals how even the most incurable ridge runner can be brought to heel.

A few years ago, we were running caribou camps up on the shores of Ungava Bay with the Inuit (Eskimos) of the area. Most of the guides were traditional old-school native hunters who couldn't speak much *Haloona* (white man) talk, but were extremely competent and very considerate of the visitors' welfare. We were also in the process of sorting through the second generation of younger, more militant smartasses, some of whom seemed to think that "tourists" were something to be endured between paydays. Most of this type had been re-educated and were excellent guides. A few had been sent back to the village to watch sex and Kung Fu movies on satellite television and smoke dope. (Yes, we have all the southern social amenities up North.)

One of the most incorrigible and hardest to fire was Billy, son of one of the local native leaders, but even he finally came around. On this occasion we were hunting with Judy and Bruce Keller, friends of mine from many northern hunts. They are eager trophy hunters, easily pleased and game to tackle anything. Though deceptively slight of build, Bruce is a real athlete, complete with a competitive nature when pushed enough. For days, and many miles, after climbing rocky slopes and glassing hundreds of caribou, we had the infuriating problem of Billy and the other young guide forging way out ahead of us.

We called them back repeatedly and explained in forceful pidgin Inuktitut that if they wanted to run the Eskimo Olympics to wait until the clients had gone home, but that had only marginal effect. Judy had taken two nice bulls, but Bruce was saving his tag for a real world-beater. Finally, late on the last day, traveling down a long, deep fjord, we spotted the skyline silhouette of "the bull." We were ashore in a minute, leaving one guide to handle the boat as the forty-foot Ungava tide was going out as we climbed to the plateau.

The bull had gone over the top, but I knew there was a long, shallow valley beyond, and I hoped he would linger there. Judy, lady that she is, waited up for old fat Fred, but Billy and Bruce, scrambling for handholds, made it over the top and disappeared after the caribou.

When Judy and I finally topped out, we were able to sit and glass the valley to observe the drama. The bull, far from pausing, had run right out of the valley and was just going over yet another ridge at least five miles distant.

Out in the middle of the plain were two figures pursuing fast. Billy, encumbered only by the clothes on his back, was in the lead, but right on his heels, carrying rifle and pack, was ol' Bruce, just picking 'em up and putting 'em down. As they disappeared over the far ridge, they started to jog into the setting sun.

Not wanting to tackle the descent in the dark, Judy and I returned to the boat, which the other guide skillfully kept clear of the rocks as the tide bay emptied the bay like a bathtub. We waited, and as we speculated on the outcome of the chase, I told Judy that in thirty years in the North, I had always wondered why an Inuit never seemed to sweat. I recalled a million times when I had panted along behind them, pushing clothing into my pack, while they never took off their parkas.

Finally, in my glasses, I picked up a minuscule figure topping the skyline and disappearing into the darkness of the cliff face. Many minutes later, another appeared. At last, out of the dusk, I heard rocks rattling and a form appeared. It was Bruce, slightly disappointed in not taking the new world record caribou, but reveling nonetheless in a great hunt.

Then in staggered Billy, damn glad to be there, although he would never admit it. He was fagged out, sweated up, shirt tied around his waist, parka dragging behind, to my disbelief, and blood running out of both nostrils.

"Well, by Jesus," I said. "Have you been on a walk, Bill?"

"Ahai," he panted, "*Tucktuk ahniook*, gone Labrador, tourist gone crazy!"

From this I determined that the big caribou ran into another country, and Bruce ran Billy's butt off—and he admired him for it.

Sometimes friends are made in easier ways; however, ones I treasure the most are the ones that come hard, upon the hunting fields. I am sure Bruce and Billy would agree.

Commandment Number Four seems to have something to do with not asking your client, "What's that brown stuff running out of your mouth?" I guess I'll have to pass on that one. After all, some of you may have witnessed me eating raw seal liver with my friends up North, with the attendant messiness. "When in Rome, do as the Romans do," they say, so if you travel in tobacco-drooling circles, I guess you just go along with the gang.

Commandment Five is about food and the gentleman's advice to stay away from fast-food restaurants while on hunting trips. I

most heartily agree. We have always, even with horrendous logistics, managed to keep the clients from starving to death. We
would never dream of flying you a thousand miles for a grease
job at some hamburger joint. However, it does occur to me that
the more I travel down South, at the mercy of airlines, hotels,
and convention menus, the more I am convinced that there still
is a place for good old Ronald McDonald and the Colonel.

Commandment Number Six: "Thou shalt not get drunk on your
client's booze," is indeed a most serious one. Many years ago, I
learned that while customers are on vacation, the guides are not.
We have tried to impart this to all the people we have worked
with. Our advice to incoming guests is always explicit: They are
not to do me any favors by treating the staff, including myself.
After all, it is a well-known fact, among clients at least, that we
natives of the bush cannot handle liquor.

In our camps, the boys are allowed a beer ration, as long
as they can handle it sensibly and pay for it. But they are left in
no doubt about what happens to anyone who boozes it up,
drinks while guiding, or fails to be on deck and ready to go in
the morning.

I am not a missionary or a baby-sitter; I figure that people
should be at least partially responsible for themselves, and that
includes the clients. In just about every problem of this sort that I
have encountered, the guests initiated the party, enjoyed the antics
of the "simple rustics" or the "colorful natives," and then were
upset when it turned out badly.

Again, I advise anyone that if you do not want the staff to
drink your liquor, then don't give it to them. To have an experience, as the gentleman apparently did, is indeed inexcusable.
Personally, I doubt if I would let a drunk soak up all my booze and
then run me out of camp, halfway through a trip I had paid for.
Perhaps in the outfits he has described, the inmates run the
asylum, but any guide who pulled that stuff on clients in our
operations wouldn't be there long enough to sober up.

In conclusion, I would hope that the author of the Seven
Commandments is as forgiving as He who put out the original
Ten, and will accept my reflections in the spirit intended. I

assume that he must have encountered other more pleasurable experiences or he would not have stayed with the sport for twenty-five years and then enjoy writing about it.

All of us, on both sides of the fence, should keep the lines of communication open. If I have one word of advice it is this: Don't book hunts based upon who gives out the biggest line of bull or quotes the lowest rates. If the gentleman would book a hunt with our organization, he would find we are sportsmen beyond reproach, keen-eyed guides, hosts without par, and we will probably even let him drink at least part of his own booze.

Oh, yes, I almost forgot. He need never worry about Commandment Number Seven, "Never tell your client 'I think we are lost.'" All of my guides are given standard instructions. They may get lost occasionally, but if they are dumb enough to admit it, they had better not bring back a witness.

THE .300 WEATHERBY MAGNUM

S ome memories may dim over the years, but I will always remember my first experience with the .300 Weatherby Magnum.
        I was home on leave from the army and guiding for one of the old-time outfitters in northern New Brunswick. At that time the hunting season lasted over two months. We started bird shooting in balmy September, and ended up buck hunting in knee-deep late November snow.

Guiding seemed to be more fun in those days, before the country was logged to death, when there were still relatively few roads. A good deal of the traveling was done by river. Guests were in less of a hurry then. The "short week hunt" had not yet been developed, most folks staying at least ten days and some of them for two weeks or longer. Up to that point, most of our guests had been from the eastern United States, and the majority of them carried what we considered "ordinary rifles." Iron sights still outnumbered telescopes by far. Occasionally we had seen a sporterized military rifle, but the most popular were the lever action .30-30s and the like. The only .300 any of us had ever seen was the venerable .300 Savage, in the good old Model 99 rifle.

Little did I know, on an early October Sunday, that shortly my experience with both firearms and clients would be expanded forever.

The outfitter had informed me that an elderly gentleman and his wife, from a "foreign country," were coming in for a two-week hunt. I would be teamed up with a senior guide named Archie to look after them. Having nearly a half-century seniority on me, Archie, a confirmed bachelor, allowed as to how he would guide the Gentleman Leader of the Party, while I could babysit the female companion.

My experience with clients of the opposite sex had been limited mainly to female salmon fisherman. We had not heard of "fisher-persons" in those days.

Most of them had been nice ladies of my grandmother's generation, content to idle along in the canoe, watching as their husbands lashed up the river. I had it figured out. All you had to know was how to pole a canoe, boil the kettle, and not use too many four-letter words until you got acquainted a little. As Archie and I went down to camp to meet the party, we thought we had the upcoming trip pretty well planned—a routine two-week hunt, no problems.

Knocking on the door of the guest cabin to introduce us, I thought the outfitter had a bit of a smirk on his face, but really wasn't prepared for just how different this party would prove to be. Bade to come in, we tossed away cigarettes, stomped off our muddy boots and entered. Arising from before the fire-place, toddy in hand, was a gentleman of advanced years, although his military bearing and neatly clipped beard, made him appear perhaps younger.

Dressed in what I found out later to be standard European hunting lodge attire, he was a far cry from the good old boys from the States that we had been used to dealing with. His over-firm handshake, preceded by a curt little bow with boot heels clicking together, impressed me, although not in a totally posi-tive manner. After all, my father, his brother, and many of my older friends had recently fought overseas for six years to rid the world of heel clickers.

Salutations from our contingent consisted of the customary eye-shifting, foot-shuffling and mumbling, common to our culture. The gentleman launched straight into it: "And how are we to conduct the hunt for trophy bear and stag?" The outfitter slith-ered out the door and left old Archie and me to earn our pay. Fortunately the gentleman did not wait for an answer. As we shuffled and mumbled, he proceeded immediately with his next directive. "At zero eight hundred hours tomorrow, we will inspect our weapons, review your plan of strategy, and you shall have the opportunity to meet my good wife, who is now resting from our journey." Good enough. We were dismissed; bows, heel clicks, shuffles and we were out the door.

Over at the outfitter's cabin I asked, "Is this old sonofabitch a U-Boat captain, or some camp commandant who has escaped the war crimes trials?"

"No," the boss assured us, "they were sent here by a booking agent, who tells me that he is a White Russian count. His passport is from Hong Kong, and his wife is apparently from that part of the world as well. He is in Canada on business, got a brand-new rifle, and figures to hunt both here and out west before returning home."

Ten years later, I learned from a book that "White Russian" referred to his political leanings, rather than his color. At the time, old Arch and I were content to label him the "Rooshian Duke."

I could hardly wait till tomorrow to meet the wife, who with my luck, would be some equivalent of the Dragon Lady.

Accustomed to starting out early on the first day of a new hunt, Archie and I were ready to go three hours ahead of the Duke's deadline. Knapsacks were packed with lots of lunch, not forgetting the tea or the grease for frying up a bird if we got lucky. Cutlery, salt, pepper, dishes, matches, all were in order. Axes and knives sharp enough to shave with, don't let the clients get their hands on them. Pack rain gear, sweaters, and cameras.

The other guides in camp dragged their feet about leaving after breakfast. They all wanted to get a glimpse of the new party as well. We drank more tea, chain smoked and watched the door of Cabin Three with all the fascination of a bobcat watching a rabbit hole in a brushpile.

Finally. Zero eight hundred hours. Door opened, out backed the Duke, green knee britches, little red tabs on long socks, queer little dingus on hat, rifle case in each hand.

Following by the proper paces, at last came the Lady of the Party. Immediately my entire outlook was transformed, my feelings of doom dispelled. In stiff new blue jeans, flannel shirt, kid-sized Bean Boots and a friendly smile, she was young and pretty. Cute as a bug's ear, as they say back home, her features and her lilting speech attested to her partial Oriental heritage.

She was presented by her formal name, something that we rustics could never pronounce. She explained it means something to do with bees and flowers. We settled on calling her "Honey." She responded with grace, her husband with stern disapproval.

We were introduced next, and with even more formality, to his arsenal of weapons. With a flourish, he whipped open the case labeled Number One. There on a red velvet lining, revealed to our lustful gaze, lay a wonder in wood and metal. Complete with high shine, fancy stock, and a 12X power telescope, it was a weapon indeed fit for royalty. It was the very first .300 Weatherby Magnum we have ever laid eyes on. We had heard of them and I had read about one in a magazine the sports left in camp. None of us thought that we would ever meet someone wealthy enough to actually own one.

".300 Weatherby Magnum," our gentleman client whispered reverently, the first emotion he has shown so far. "Oh my God," cried one of the other guides crowding around, ".300 Weatherby Magnum, finest rifle in the world, shoot a mile and never drop an inch." He was led away in a daze by his disgruntled client, who had wanted to leave camp an hour ago.

"Yes," intoned the Duke, ".300 Weatherby Magnum, kill everything."

Almost as an afterthought, I opened case Number Two, to check on what he has armed his wife with. A somewhat rusty Japanese military rifle, in one of the dozen odd 6.5mm calibers, wood clean out to the end of the barrel, weighed fifteen pounds. Probably picked up for five Hong Kong dollars in some flea market. I could see he was not much different from some of my other clients, who spare no expense on themselves but foist off some piece of junk on their lady companion.

It was time to sight in the .300 Weatherby Magnum. We solemnly paced out three times the distance we usually sight in at, and tacked a target on a butter box.

The Duke assumed the proper stance and touched her off. Kicked the piss out of him, laid a big bloody cut over his eye. He couldn't hit the box the target was nailed to. Further shooting worsened the situation.

Finally, with great reluctance, the rifle was consigned to my grubby paws. Within a few rounds and a mild headache, I had it right on the nail. I could see immediately that I had done the wrong thing. Expecting appreciation, I had instead made an enemy for life. One must remember not to out-shoot, out-drink, or out-anything, persons of noble extraction, refugee or not.

To cover the embarrassed silence, I fumbled around and tried to load the Iwo Jima Special. Naturally, the ammunition didn't fit. It never does in that assortment of military junk falling vaguely between 6 and 7mm. "Not to panic," I assured Honey, "I have my .30-30 behind the seat of the truck and we'll do just fine with that."

Dreadful glares from the owner of the .300 Weatherby Magnum.

In private, I gloated a bit to old Archie about his choice of which client to guide. Being considerably older and smarter, he allowed that he could spend two weeks with the Devil Himself, if he had to. Especially as we both knew who would hand out the tips, if any, at the end of the two weeks. I wondered.

On a year such as this was, with a good crop of beechnuts, one of the best ways of hunting is simply sitting around on the ridges, where deer and bear have been feeding. The alternative, this early in the season, was to run the rivers, hoping to catch game coming to water. Weather was balmy, Indian summer, autumn foliage in full color, leaves just starting to fall, beautiful for picnics, too warm for good hunting.

For a couple of days we hunted with Archie and the Duke, then decided to split off and go our separate ways. The lady preferred the latter and once out from under the stern eye of her husband, she became very talkative, full of enthusiasm and interest in all the new things she was seeing and doing. A few lessons with the old .30-30 and I see she was a natural shot. We would have no trouble taking game if our guest was successful.

Her knowledge of English was extensive, although with a different rhythm than we were used to, in our part of the world. Her slight difficulty pronouncing the sounds of "L" and "R," we all found charming. Addressing me, her sentences always started with, "Ah Fled," which didn't escape the rest of the crew in camp who thought it amusing, or her husband, who did not.

On the fourth day of the hunt, sailing the river, we jumped a nice little eight-point buck, which she neatly dispatched with the .30-30. Back in camp that night, we were the heroes of the gang, to everyone except the Duke, who dismissed it as a "too small stag."

Comparing notes with Archie, after supper, it was plain that he wasn't enjoying the hunt half as much as I was. As he puts it, "The old gentleman can walk okay, in fact insists upon walking ten times more than we should for the conditions. But fifty times a day, he throws up the rifle as if he's going to shoot, but he's only looking at things through that God-awful, over-powered telescope. He seems to think that we just have to walk far enough and some big old buck will keel over dead when he hears we are coming with that cannon. Every time we stop for a break, he tells me 'Just show me the stag. .300 Weatherby Magnum kill everything.'"

Three or four days later Honey and I picked up a bear. Not much of a bear to be sure, hundred and a half maybe, but she was thrilled to death with it and so was I. That night as we rolled into camp, I blew the horn on the old truck, and all the gang poured out to admire the bruin and hear the lady's bear story. The Duke went back into his cabin and shut the door, didn't come in to supper.

Later, outside having a smoke, I asked Archie, "What ails that old bastard, anyway? At the first of the week, he told us he would be pleased as hell if his wife even saw some game, let alone kill anything. Now he acts like poison."

"Well, Sir, the fat is in the fire now," says Archie, "I wasn't going to tell nobody, but three times in the last couple of days, he had good standing shots at game and missed every goddam time. He flinches so bad that now he just shuts his eyes and lets her rip. The first time, he refused to believe it was a clean miss, on a pretty decent buck, not as big as the lady killed, but nice. When I couldn't find any sign of a hit, he raged and frothed at the mouth till I was afraid he was going to have a stroke or shoot me, one or the other. Kept hollering, '.300 Weatherby Magnum, kill everything, no miss.' You can be damn sure I either carry the rifle or have him walk ahead now. Today, twice more, one on a dandy buck, the other time an old sow bear with two yearlings, standing right out on the open ridge. Never cut a goddam hair on none of it."

"Well hell," I wondered, wanting to help, "Maybe I should ask him if he would like me to try the gun out for him again."

"Not on your goddam life," Archie raged, "You best just stay well clear of him till he cools off. If Honey brings in any more game before he kills something, or keeps on bragging at the table how, 'Ah, my Fled, best guide in Canada,' he's liable to take a shot at you with that .300 Weatherby Magnum, if I don't first." I knew old Archie was kidding, or at least I thought he was.

A few more days were spent cruising the river, rifle along but mostly just enjoying the scenery, taking a few pictures, swapping stories. The lady still had a deer tag left, I was half-hopeful we would see a gigantic buck, half-afraid of what would happen if we did. She was still bubbling over with enthusiasm, happy with everything we did, said she was writing everything down at night so she will always remember her wonderful vacation in Canada.

Nice kid, I was going to miss her. Hated going back to guiding some loudmouth from New York the following week. Too bad she was married to that crabby old bastard. She had by now told me how her father, a British national, was snapped up by the Japanese early in the war, leaving her Chinese mother to somehow survive with three young children to feed. Her marriage to the Duke was arranged with the consent of her mother, she going along with it to help the rest of the family rise above the sheer survival level.

"He good man," she explains solemnly, "make much money, no time fun." Then giggled "Want velly velly bad shoot something with .300 Weleby Magnum."

Next to the last night in camp, I was helping the outfitter's wife wash up the dishes. She dug me in the ribs, "What in hell have you and that woman been up to? You should have heard her at the table tonight, it's 'Fled say this, and Fled say that.' I thought the old Duke was going to bust a gut trying to keep his hands off her neck."

"Oh, come on now," I laughed, going along with the joke. "You know me better than that, I'd never do anything so unprofessional as to get mixed up romantically with a client, especially one whose husband is toting one of them shoot-a-mile, never-drop-an-inch .300 Weatherby Magnums."

I turned to my friend Archie for a testimonial to my moral character. He was not in the mood for joking, and held up two fingers, glumly shaking his head.

"Missed again?," I shouldn't have asked. "Yes, goddam it all to hell," he nearly snapped my head off. "Twice, on two different bucks, cut down half the goddam woods and never drew a drop of blood. Tomorrow's the last day, if he doesn't kill something, we can forget about any tips from this party."

This is a serious matter; gratuities to old Archie, while certainly welcome from a financial standpoint, were even more important as a matter of pride.

"If he'd only listen to me," he went on, " and quit using the goddam enormous telescope for looking around with and save his strength to hold the rifle steady when it comes time to shoot, maybe he could hit something. That is," he adds, "if he didn't turn his head and jerk the trigger like he was tripping a goddam bear trap."

Before turning in, we decided upon a plan of action for the last day's hunt. Maybe we could work together a bit to improve the old Duke's chances. By now we were feeling sorry for him, and besides, we were desperate curious to see what would happen if he ever hit something with that .300 Weatherby Magnum.

We decided to hunt two legs of a high beech and maple ridge, split by a deep gulch, around the head of which Honey and I had seen plenty of game sign a few days earlier. So Archie's hunter wouldn't suspect we are trying to help him out, we went there separately, worked both sides of the ridge, in hopes of Honey and me being downwind of them.

Archie, being a wise old guide, was also content that I would be handy enough to help drag the critter out should the Duke connect.

Morning showed us another beautiful day. I hadn't bothered to try to explain the grand strategy to my hunter; she was thrilled just to be heading out for one more day in the hills. Not caring whether or not she filled her remaining deer tag, she intended to take some pictures and catch up on her diary. "Be razy, make picnic," she described it.

I have brought along extra lunch, binoculars, and the old .30-30, just in case. We worked our way around the near side of the ridge all morning. Sitting a lot, talking a little, taking some pictures, enjoying ourselves just being in the woods on such a morning. Slight frost overnight, and leaves were falling faster now. Soon Indian summer would fade into early winter.

Honey seemed more subdued today, a bit nostalgic as the trip wound down I suppose. She told me that her husband has changed his mind about continuing on to hunt in the west. He felt he might get rid of his rifle and devote his full attention to business.

Leisurely lunch by the brook, this would be the last time we "make picnic." We lingered over a second kettle of tea. "Two o'clock," I pointed out. "Let's wander up the ridge and see if we run into any game."

We didn't go very far before we jumped a tremendous buck up from his bed, and got a glimpse of him as he went over the crest. Had been right there all morning, watching, listening, smelling smoke from our fire. Headed in the right direction at least. We picked our way on up. Peeking over the top, I spotted him. I eased Honey up beside me, passed her the rifle. She saw him walking slowly, broadside, easy shot. She turned, smiled, handed the .30-30 back to me.

"Too much pletty day, no shoot now." We watched him walk away, twelve-pointer at least, I think, massive rack, probably make the Book. "Oh, well, what the hell," I agreed with her. Maybe he would stumble into the Duke.

Just over the crest, we found a place to wait, where we could scan the narrow valley and the other slope which I knew Archie would be working along, into the wind. We were partially in the shade, sun at our backs. I dug out our rain gear to lie back on, and went to glassing.

Have you ever lain out on a ridge on an Indian summer day in the Northland? Frost has long since taken care of the bugs. It's warm enough to peel off some clothing, warm enough to remove boots and socks, feel the breeze on your sweaty toes. Reclining on a blanket of red, yellow and golden leaves, watching the last few trickle down from above against a cloudless blue sky. You can smell the woods, the sun-warmed leaves, the forest floor underneath. You want to store it all up, to get you through the approaching storms of winter. At such times, even now, I wouldn't trade an hour of it for a million dollars, wouldn't change a minute to call the King my uncle.

Between glassings, I lay back and dreamed into the blue sky, listening to the various woodland sounds, sensing rather than seeing the closeness of my companion. We were part of the scene, hunters in a drama as old as the earth, equally at home here as the squirrel scampering around storing beechnuts, as the doe that comes tiptoeing up the ridge before us to stamp, stare, and finally bound off with a snort as she gets our wind.

I continued to glass the opposite ridge, my knapsack and boots under my head, as comfortable as being in bed. A rustle in the leaves, a sigh, a warm little bare foot on top of mine, a hand on my arm. I was glassing the ridge, totally the hunter, senses tuned to the breaking point. A shifting, rustle of clothing, "Ah, Fled, so sad going away." Sweet warm breath on cheek. I glassed the ridge.

A snuggle, another sigh. "Ah Fled, husband nice man but too much old, no get election."

Insanely I blurted, "Jesus, Honey, I don't know nothing about politics in your country."

Frantically I continued glassing, lenses fogging up. What's that? Across the gulch I spotted a flash. Sun glancing off metal. Maybe glass? I strained to see into the trees.

"Ah Fled," she breathed, hand slipping under my shirt, "wanting stay in Canada with you, husband no good bed time."

Trembling binoculars focus at last, two figures beneath the trees.

"Oh shit!," I croaked, "hope no good shooting either, I'm looking right down the barrel of that goddam .300 Weatherby Magnum."

CRACK! Overhead a branch big as your thumb started to fall in slow motion, *KA-BLOOM*, the delayed sound of the shot reached my ears. I whirled around to flee, and there, outlined on top of the hill above us, was a bear, caught in the act of raking beechnuts. All the noises were not squirrels after all. Instinct threw up the .30-30. *BANG! KA-BLOOM!, KA-BLOOM!, KA-BLOOM!* the valley echoed.

Panic stricken, mad scramble for gear and clothing, bare footing it across the ridge, we tumbled over the crest together. Holy sweet Jesus! Heart pounding, gasping for breath, trying to get boots on, feeling one another over for bullet holes. We collapsed in hysterical laughter. Not the time to hang around here, let's just get the hell off this hill and figure it all out later.

It was the last night in camp and traditionally the guides are invited to dine with guests. Fine social occasion, drinks were passed, conversation was lively. Only a couple of us being quiet as a mouse. The duke is holding forth on how he slew the trophy bear. "From one mountain to another, fine shot, fine guide Archie, fine, fine rifle, .300 Weatherby Magnum, kill everything.

Shy little smile, pressure on knee under the table from Honey. Shifty-eyed glance from old Archie.

Next morning our guests departed extremely happy, the Duke with his trophy bear, Honey with her diary full of memories. Archie took me aside, held up two brand-new fifty dollar bills. Lot of money in those days.

"One of these the Duke left for you." I'm surprised. Archie went on, "I don't know what in hell he saw through that telescope, but after he emptied the gun, he got over there faster than he's moved for the last two weeks. Once we got there, though, all he had eyes for was the dead bear. He never even noticed that deer bed in the leaves, not these either." He handed me a little white sock and an empty .30-30 shell.

"Funny thing about that great big rifle," he adds, "Only made one hole through the ribs, about the size of a .30-30. Makes a guy wonder. Got us a nice tip, thought." He clapped me on the back and said, "Come on partner, let's go down and meet the new party, and see if anyone's got a .300 Weatherby Magnum.

HARD LUCK BEAR

(Appeared May 1972 in Fur-Fish-Game)

Darkness comes late in the Tobique country of New Brunswick the last week of May, so it was nearly eleven o'clock as my guiding partner, Tom Everett, and I drove up the Riordan Gulch road to pick up our last bear hunter for the day.

"What do you bet he'll say the same thing tonight?" I wondered aloud as we skirted a couple of rocks and plunged through another mudhole.

"Well, I wouldn't want to bet, but he can't say 'Nothin!' forever, and I've got a kind of hunch that tonight is it." Tom went on, "After all, Ray is one of the best hunters we've run across. You and I have been breaking our necks for a month trying to put him in the right place, and we've just got to break the jinx sooner or later."

The hunter we were discussing was Ray Petersen from New Jersey. Normally one of the guides would have accompanied the hunter on the stand, but Ray, having been with us so long and being competent in the woods, had obtained special permission to go on the stands alone.

Pulling up at the pick-up point, the familiar figure stepped out of the woods and, as always, checked to make sure his rifle was empty by the lights of the truck. But this time when he came to the window, his greeting was different. "Boys, he was a long time coming, but he's a nice one and I'm sure the shot was good."

Ray went on to explain how the bear had come in very slowly and cautiously and had stopped at last for about ten minutes behind a blowdown, searching and testing the wind. In the gathering dusk, waiting for a better shot, but knowing the bear might disappear any second, Ray had weighed the odds and from 150 yards had finally shot at the only portion visible, about two inches of his back showing above the log. At the crack of the .30-06, the bear had dropped, then with a mighty roar had risen partly up, only to vanish from sight again down into a ravine.

It didn't take long to decide that this was a job for daylight. Following up on a wounded bear in the dark, while never any picnic, would in this case be foolhardy. Naturally we hated to leave game unaccounted for, but in this instance had no choice. At this particular stand, on the sharp end of a ridge, just about any direction was down, real down, into gulches up to six hundred feet deep. Just the year before, we had tracked a wounded bear from this same spot in daylight and had ended up with a few exciting moments and a hard climb back. We wouldn't gain much sleep but would have a much better chance of success in the morning, so we pulled out for camp.

Later, lying in bed, my mind went back over Ray's story and all that had led up to this moment. Any guide can tell you of times when game is down but not yet in the bag. Your mind covers all the facts; you know the ground, you know the game, you know the hunter is a good shot. But you also remember all the times when a twig was in the way, the scope was blurred, or when the hunter had been just a little too excited.

Finally I settled my mind with the thought of all the game that Ray and I had killed since I first started guiding him, of the bucks he had flattened cleanly with one shot, and I went to sleep thinking that surely, at long last, we had broken the bear jinx.

I operated a small outfitting business at Nictau in northern New Brunswick at the time. We handled a limited number of sportsmen, hunting spring and fall, fishing in summer, and running cats with hounds and trapping in the winter. When I decided to take spring bear hunting parties, Ray Petersen was one of my first clients. For years I had guided Ray on the fall deer hunt. He had always hunted from stands and had always been successful. A real pro, Ray could stay on stand from daylight till dark, never discouraged, never disgusted, and always ready for that one second that spells success. As our bear hunting would be done from stands, I felt that the results were assured; we'd get a bear for Ray, no trouble at all.

He had told me stories of having hunted for over thirty years in all the eastern states and in Canada, always successful on deer but never on bear. Dozens of times he had been close. Others in his party might get shots at bear and he would see bear the day after the season closed, but never once did he get a chance at a trophy bear himself. Now it was our chance to prove to him that there wasn't any bear jinx on him, just a little hard luck.

Starting in May 1969, we weren't very long finding out that apparently Ray's bear luck wasn't going to be easy to change. No matter what we tried, no matter how hard we worked or how long we stayed on stands, the result was the same. There are times, as any guide or hunter knows, when it doesn't matter how good you think you are or how hard you try, if you can't get two seconds of luck, you may as well stay out of the woods. This was the case.

The second week of Ray's vigil, another party arrived from Lancaster, Pennsylvania, and two of the hunters bagged two lovely bears the first evening. This improved my spirits a lot but didn't do a thing for Ray. The next week, three were killed but still none for Ray. We decided at last to let it lie until fall hunting time arrived, and I assured him that our chances, while not as good as on the spring hunt, should still be pretty good in October. I should have saved my breath.

During the fall of '69, the bear in that area, due mostly to the failure of the beechnut crop, apparently went into den weeks before they normally would. For two weeks we scoured the country, killed a ten-point buck deer and a large doe, had a good time, but never once crossed the path of a bear. As a true sportsman, Ray took the view that "that's the way she goes." By this time, I didn't have many theories left myself. I could only tell him to return in the spring prepared to stay until we beat the bear jinx or the season ended.

Beginning around February, the preparations used to start for the spring hunt. Most hunters never saw or realized the amount of labor and money spent before they arrived. If the rates quoted sometimes seem steep to some people, they should have some insight into the effort involved. For instance, Tom and I trucked bait a round trip of two hundred miles. It was then transferred to a four-wheel-drive for the next step and then delivered by snow-mobile sled to the stands a distance of anything up to fifty miles. As can be imagined, if our time and gasoline were ever figured up, the rate for bear hunting would be far in excess of what was actually charged.

Coming up to the spring hunt in 1970, Tom and I were confident that we were about to end Ray's search for a bear. Our careful preparations and our excellent record of success with other hunters, along with Ray's ability as a hunter, convinced us that the quest was nearly over.

Being understandably anxious, Ray arrived before the bear did. The first week didn't discourage us too much, as they were just not out of hibernation and moving about. However, by the end of the second week, with bear being killed elsewhere in the area, it began to be apparent that we were jinxed again. No matter what we tried, the results were, as Ray said, "Nothin!" On three different occasions either Tom or myself saw bear while traveling to or from the stands, while Ray, supposedly in the right place, saw nothing. At a time like this, every angle is tried, every wind shift and bit of cover is analyzed. It all came down to the same thing. We just couldn't find anything wrong except our luck.

Another party of three hunters arrived in camp and promptly killed a couple of bear. Nothing for Ray. Two more hunters arrived the next week and killed two bear. Again, nothing for Ray.

By this time the bear jinx was on the way to becoming a legend. Having hunted this area for a number of years, Ray had a lot of friends among the guides and other residents and was fast becoming known among visiting hunters as well. Every time I went to the settlement I was bound to meet someone who would inquire as to how Ray was making out with the bear. Most agreed that patience and persistence just had to pay off, but some were beginning to wonder if there wasn't something to the jinx theory after all.

Now at last, in the fifth week of steady hunting, the bear had appeared, Ray had shot, and it now remained for us to do the rest. Arriving on the scene shortly after daybreak we went to work. Tom and I always started in the same manner, first checking the position occupied by the hunter, angle and distance to the game, and then carefully checking where the bear was standing. Careful study of the tracks, amount and type of hair, blood and any sign that the bullet may have struck elsewhere, would give indication of whether or how hard the game was wounded.

In this case the sign found coupled with Ray's description led us to believe that a hit had been made high on the shoulders and possibly the spine was broken. For the first few yards the bear had dragged himself, then regained his feet to dive over the side of the gulch. Tracking on bare ground isn't always easy, although some experience and a system helps a lot. One of us always took the track and stayed with it. The other would stick with the hunter, generally staying above and working around the tracker, carefully scanning the terrain and alert for the game to break out. This allows the tracker to devote all his attention to working out the track without having to worry about the game itself. Everyone will hasten to assure you that bear aren't particularly dangerous. However, it has always been my view that even if you are tracking a rabbit, if he weighs anything over two hundred pounds, you don't want to be in his way when he starts out. Someone in the bunch should have his head up and be alert for any possibility.

After working at it for over an hour, it began to look as if the old jinx was going to beat us again; however, we were prepared to spend the week if necessary. Sign at last was next to non-existent, and Tom was making steady but slow progress. I decided that Ray and I would split up and start making circles, thus doubling our chances. An hour later, from way down in the next gulch, I heard a happy shout from Ray. It was fitting that after such a long struggle that he had been the one to find his bear.

It would be hard to find a happier hunter or two more pleased guides. As with any real sportsman, the end is anticlimax. The hunt and the challenge are the thing, you are happy with the trophy but sad to realize that the hunt is over. Ray's bear, although not the largest we had ever taken, was exceptional by reason of the white markings on his chest. The markings formed a perfect "V," signifying, we hoped, our victory over any further bear jinx that might arise to trouble us.

ELVIS

(Appeared in *Victoria County Record, 1976*)

T *he coming to our area of the various types of eastern coyote or brush wolf, and the harassment of wildlife by supposedly domesticated canines, reminds me of how closely we are all still linked with our less civilized past.*

Twenty years ago an Outport Newfoundlander named Jim, a north coast Quebecer named Emil, and myself, were winding up a winter spent on the head of the watershed in central Labrador. Besides hunting, fishing, and running traplines, we were supposed to be manning a weather station and carrying out scientific observations related to defense. Although Emil couldn't speak English and I couldn't speak much French and neither of us could talk Newfie, we all worked our share and it was a pretty happy camp.

The fourth member of the expedition was a no-account runty dog named Elvis, in honor of the way he wagged his whole body instead of just his tail. Somewhat in the same style as that currently becoming the trademark of his namesake. Elvis had been a reject from a Nascaupee trapper's dog team, which put him fairly low on the social scale, but he was a welcome addition to the crew nonetheless. What he lacked in brains, he made up for in eagerness and besides, he was someone all three of us could talk to without using sign language.

Jim kept camp and looked after most of the official duties, while Emil and I ran the traplines. Accompanied by Elvis, we traveled constantly, practically living on snowshoes, towing our gear on a toboggan.

In that particular area, winter travel was relatively good for the same reason that summer travel is nearly impossible. On this inland plateau there are innumerable lakes, joined by short streams, with areas of higher ground lightly covered with black spruce, none of it bigger than a stovepipe. On most lakes you could remove the snowshoes and fairly skim along.

Running four roughly circular lines, with four small overnight camps or tilts, as they are called, we were covering a big area with the main camp as center. It was a good setup.

Around early April, the caribou started moving through the country, and with them came the wolves. It was as dramatic as the change from day to night; there was not a caribou or wolf track in the country and then suddenly they were there. The night we heard the first wolf howl, Elvis disappeared.

Next day, tracking him, expecting to find his remains to bait a wolf trap, we met him coming back. Did you ever see a dog grin? Where he ordinarily wagged, he now fairly vibrated, and the look in his eye said, "Boys, it's been a nice winter, but spring is just around the corner." We figured that Elvis had found himself a temporary lady friend among the wolves.

Figuring we knew what was best for him, and not wanting to haul the toboggan without his help, we took him back to camp and locked him inside.

For two weeks the caribou straggled through and the wolves were everywhere. They could be seen skirting the edge of the lake just about any time and in the morning their tracks were all around the yard. Their songs, especially at night, just about drove old Elvis crazy.

Then came an evening when we realized that we hadn't seen a caribou or heard a wolf for two or three days. It was a beautiful, clear, cold night. The crust would be hard enough in the morning to strike out on the southern section of the line. Stepping out to once again check the weather, I let Elvis slip out as well.

Suddenly, from across the lake, came the howl of a wolf and without so much as a "See you later," away went man's best friend. I whistled, I hollered, I begged and I even threatened to get the .30-30, but to no avail. Across the lake, straight as an arrow, and into the woods, this was the last we ever laid eyes on old Elvis.

Toward morning the weather changed and dumped down snow for two days. Although we later watched for sign throughout our wanderings, when break-up came six weeks later, he still hadn't returned. I guess he probably ran for miles on the crust, with that female, and when the new deep snow came he couldn't make his way back and perished of starvation. Or most likely they fell in with other wolves and he was torn to shreds by the pack.

But I sometimes still wonder, if just maybe, up there between the headwaters of the Natashquan and the Hamilton River drainage, there's a brand-new breed of wolves that can't wag their tails without swiveling in the middle.

N ineteen sixty-eight is known in our part of the country as "The Winter of the Big Snow." Ab Higgins and I were trapping the headwaters of Mamozekel. Heading for home one day we encountered a strange vehicle with a Maine license plate. This was when we first met Ash Peasley.

Twenty miles up a woods road, kept plowed only for the logging operation, one rarely met a stranger, so I pulled over to the side of the road to introduce ourselves and see what the intruder was up to. After a few minute's conversation to establish credentials all around, it appeared our new-found friend was a game warden from over the border in southern Maine, and the box in the back of the Chevy Blazer housed a pair of bobcat hounds.

"Boys," he said, "I've been driving along the road here, watching for tracks and it appears to me that you have a good bobcat population in this area. Has anyone ever hunted them with dogs around here?"

I informed him that a few years back I had purchased a redbone hound through a magazine advertisement, had seen that it would indeed follow tracks, but that I didn't have the knowledge to train it properly, so the project was a failure.

"Well," he said, "down at the general store in Riley Brook, I asked the same question and they just laughed at me and said that you would have to put snowshoes on a dog to catch a bobcat in this country. What do you think of giving it a try?"

Sounded fine to me. I realized that he had received the standard treatment reserved for "outsiders" by the local village idiots, who never got more than a few hundred yards from the Coke cooler in Phoebe's Store. That, of course, made them experts on everything connected to the woods.

My partner Ab agreed. "Sure," he remarked, "I know by reading the magazines that they catch bobcats in Maine with dogs, and I don't see why that Boundary Line would make it any different, and we're only fifty miles away."

Thus started a friendship and the introduction to about the finest sport we had ever engaged in. The friendship endures over all these years. The hunting, alas, lasted only about a decade, before the declining rabbit cycle and massive clear-cutting of the forest brought this chapter of our life to a much regretted end.

Ash not being a braggart, it took many hunts over a couple of winters before we came to know the full story of his bobcat hunting record. By accident and from other sources, we learned of the life-sized painting of Ash and his best old dog, Blue Boy, which hung in Abercrombie & Fitch in New York City. Eventually, we obtained a copy of the ad by Marlin Firearms, which was done for the Big Three outdoor magazines utilizing this painting.

At the time of our meeting, Ash was the chief ranger at Wesley, down near the coast. He had for years hunted on predator control for the state; all of his cats were bountied, recorded, and studied by the game department. His records, including the weight of the cats, were authentic and they surely stand to this day, as bobcats, along with wilderness, have long been gone at least to the extent that we knew at that time.

It was only after he retired and moved with the offspring of his famous dogs to somewhere out West, that all of a sudden there sprung into the magazine ads, the various and numerous "World Champion Bobcat Hunters," across the state of Maine. One of these would-be imitators even changed his first name to "Bobcat." We older hands referred to him as "Pussy."

The first of many lessons that we learned was a simple one. Most members of any hound breed are born with the ability and the desire to follow scent trails. Most of them are born to hunt, the problem is to teach them to hunt with *YOU!* Like firearms, automobiles, or anything else, different people like different breeds, but a few have been outstanding. Some breeds have developed as crosses, some have retained the bloodlines that first came from Europe. Ash's dogs had pedigrees a mile long, but, as he often remarked, "Those papers don't kill cats, the dogs kill them."

Blue Boy, his oldest dog, came from a line of purebred English hounds that Ash had brought up from Sandy Creek, Georgia right after the war. It took one full generation for them to acclimatize to the harsh Maine winters, to be able to handle deep snow, and hardest of all, to tolerate the extreme low temperatures.

Blue Boy, at the time we started hunting, had over 260 cats to his credit. Blue Warrior, the rangy, rowdy son of Blue Boy, had in the neighborhood of 140. The totals achieved before old age phased them into retirement went well beyond anything remotely possible in later years as wilderness and cat populations decreased. It is hard to believe that in the late Sixties and up until about '73, we still collected fifteen dollars for every cat tail turned in. The fur value was so low they were not worth skinning, and their numbers were so high that game managers wanted them cut down. I hasten to assure anyone interested that hunting by hounds and the few taken by trappers, did not even make a dent in the annual increase—as long as the woods existed, roads were few, rabbit populations were high, and the Eastern brush wolf had not as yet appeared on the scene to compete on the food chain.

Changes over which we had no control spelled the end of this era, and in most places today in the Northeast, seasons and limits are very strictly controlled to keep the cats from extinction. The forestry practices of the big multinational companies have meant that even if there were bobcats, there wouldn't be a tree big enough for them to climb in most areas we used to hunt.

Education, for Ab and me, began that very first afternoon. While the main money on the trapline was provided by beaver, otter, and sable, we also kept a line of dummy sets for bobcat and fisher at known crossings. Going back over the road, we stopped to check one of these. Sure enough a big cat track led right into the cubby, but as often happened, a Canada jay had been in the trap, so Mister Cat had a free morsel courtesy of a poorly made set.

"Boys, that track looks awful fresh to me and it's early in the afternoon, let's just see what old Blue Boy thinks of it."

The dog wasn't long letting us know his opinion. By the time we had snowshoes out of the vehicles and strapped on, he was heading up the side of the ridge, and soon we were treated to our first hound music.

We had taken off from One Mile Landing on Mamozekel. In one hour's hard mushing we were over the top of the ridge and pausing to roll a smoke. Way down in the valley of the Right Hand Branch, we heard him barking "Treed." Within twenty minutes of downhill loping we came into an area crisscrossed with cat and dog tracks and just ahead was Blue Boy at the foot of a four-log spruce. Scratch marks on the tree and bits of bark on the snow told us we had a cat, just as soon as we could locate him among the top branches.

Before long, our bobcat was stretched out on the snow, a big mature male, larger than any we had ever taken in traps. Ab and I were hooked. We were hound dog converts all the way.

Looking back later, I realize that Ab and I probably thought there was nothing to this game. Just grab a cat track, turn loose the dog and load the shotgun. Naturally, starting out with the best cat dog and the best cat hunter in the world, on a nice day with excellent snow conditions, surely made it look easy. We had a lot to learn.

I soon lost Ab as a trapline partner when the lumber company offered him a steady job. He was replaced by Tommy Everett. Whereas Ab was considerably older than me, Tom was a bit younger. Tough and determined, lean and hungry as I was, he soon proved to be the right guy to share the trail. Feeding and clothing a family on the income from trapping and hunting, even in those days, soon sorted out the men from the boys.

While we still depended on Ash Peasley to visit two or three times a winter with his championship dogs, we also endeavored to train and hunt our own hounds. Acquired through our contact with Ash, we worked with a number of them, all related to his Blue Boy and Warrior dogs. One of the meanest was Blue Streak, a litter mate of Warrior, who had been hunting with another game warden in the Rangely Lake area. Later, I found out why the man was so kind as to give us a real deal.

91

Streak was big and rough. He was mean, which is uncommon in the hound breed. A real killer, he would fight with any other dog who came near. It turned out that his former owner had had a really prized and expensive hound which had gone missing. He drove the roads, placed ads in the papers around the country, all to no avail. A couple of months later, when cleaning out Streak's winter house, he found a well-chewed skull and a collar bearing the name of the missing young favorite.

With a good nose and fearing nothing, that Streak was a real heller on cats. Anything running ahead of him had the choice of getting up a tree or being tackled on the ground. We had many an epic chase, most of which resulted in another dead bobcat.

Come the spring hunt we found out he was equally good on bear. On one occasion we had put him down to follow a bear that one of the clients had wounded the night before. Old Streak ran that one out quick, a very large and very dead male bear. Then before we could collar him, he struck off on the fresh track of one that had visited during the night, and we had a day-long chase on our hands.

Within the first half-mile, we realized that the out-of-shape client was never going to make it, so we sent him back to the truck before he got far enough away to get lost. Tom and I lit out with the .30-30, down off the ridge in the direction of the hound noise. Every time we would top a ridge we would stop to get our breath and listen. At one time he was out of range for a couple of hours. Running on bare ground certainly is a lot easier than snowshoeing, but of course has the disadvantage of being next to impossible to track the dog in a hurry. You just have to keep on, hoping that if he doubles back you will hear him.

Finally, late in the afternoon we heard him across a deep valley, out on the point of a hardwood ridge. An hour later, toiling up what we figured was the last hill either of us could manage, we could tell he had the bear treed. As we got up there—it was a fairly open ridge—we could see ahead where Streak was running back and forth and jumping up against a big smooth beech, with not a limb for about the first thirty feet.

Finally we saw the bear, about a three-year-old boar, a real athlete fit to give us such a chase. As the dog would turn toward us approaching, the bear would start to back down the tree. We have seen this before, and have seen them bail out and jump clear. This one made the bad mistake of backing down too far before jumping. In a flash, Streak leaped and got a mouthful of bear testicles, and hung on for about the first twenty feet of a most panicky ascent.

Tom and I rolled on the ground laughing, while old Streak, his teeth full of bear hair, strutted at the foot of the tree and the bear looked down over his shoulder with a very hurt expression on his face. You couldn't have coaxed him down with a hind-quarter of mutton after that experience.

Although I had the rifle, we couldn't think of any possible use a dead bear would be to us. Fortunately, Tom had the choke chain and leash in his pocket, as it took a lot of convincing to get Blue Streak away from that tree.

A year later, his courage, or meanness, whichever you would term it, brought an end to his career. A client had made an unfortunate shot, breaking the hip of a fairly large bear so he was unable to get up a tree. Before I could arrive, Streak caught him in a blowdown and this time the bear came out the winner.

We were very fortunate in replacing him with a smallish young dog, another offspring of Ash's Blue Boy, named Blue Ben. Right from the start Benny taught us more than we could ever teach him, and this continued right up to his retirement, which coincided with the downturn in the cat population a few years later.

Bobcat hunting, as a supplement to our wide-ranging traplines, was proving to be a worthwhile venture. Never satisfied to stick with a good thing, I got the bright idea of offering winter bobcat hunts to southern clients. Thus began another era, another course of education that probably would be best forgotten. We did, however, learn a lot more about bobcats, and about humans, enough to fill at least a couple of books.

Bobcats being as elusive as they are, we came to realize that most of what was thought to be "local knowledge" was a combination of misunderstanding and pure fabrication. Prior to our switching over to hounds, very few bobcats were being taken and none of them weighed. The total of cats trapped in that area, in the best season we ever heard of, would be less than a couple dozen. These were invariably taken in what were referred to as "dummy sets," reflecting more the ability of the trapper than the animal. These were all-purpose brush cubby sets. When visited by anything worthwhile, they were almost always frozen down, covered in snow, or more likely, full of flying squirrels or birds.

In two weeks in February 1970, we caught more cats than the entire local take all winter by trappers. On our best morning we treed three, on our best day we accounted for five. Naturally, such a short-term record is based on having great dogs, absolute snowshoeing fools as hunters, lots of bobcats, and most important, ongoing excellent snow conditions.

A word on size and weight of cats. In all of Ash Peasley's literally hundreds of cats, he weighed four over 40 pounds, and the largest went 44 on the official scales of the game department. In one week that record year we took 13 cats, the smallest of which was 28 pounds, four over 40, and the largest a few ounces over 45. One hears of 50-pound bobcats, and I feel confident that probably such existed at that time. We just didn't run across his track. These are tremendously big bobcats, that is, if one actually shakes out all the exaggeration and puts them on an accurate set of scales.

One incident proved to me the worth of local knowledge. We had always heard around the village of Riley Brook about good old Pete or someone trapping a bobcat of a hundred pounds. Into the dooryard one day came Dave, one of the local experts. "Boys, you should see the big bobcat they have down at Bernice's store. Tipped the scales at 87 pounds."

Out in one of our camps hung a good big cat, one that weighed 33 pounds. "Come on out, Dave, and look at the one we picked up on Little Tobique yesterday," I invited.

His eyes bugged right out of his head. "What did that one weigh?"

"Well, Sir," I lied through my teeth, "that one topped out at 117.

"By Jesus," exclaimed Dave, "wait till I tell them down at the store, why that one down there wouldn't make gut for this one."

Thus started another local bobcat legend, which since has been expanded even further.

Many also were the myths about bobcat behavior and what they lived upon. If you asked the game biologists in the Capital they would tell you that cats lived entirely on rabbits and very rarely, if ever, killed deer. The local country gentry held the opposing view, that every deer went around with at least two bobcats on its back. Like most of these cases, both are wrong, and the truth is somewhere in the middle.

Granted, when the snowshoe hare population is high, a very large proportion of most bobcats' needs are filled, supplemented

Tom Hennessey —

95

by targets of opportunity. We found they killed squirrels, mice, and birds of any description when they could catch them.

They also kill deer, many more of course when rabbit cycles are lower. Don't for one second believe the "conservationists" who tell you that large predators only cull out the weak and the old in the prey population. That is, to put it politely, absolute bullshit. Any predator has an eye for the very best prime specimens, and when possible, that is what they will prefer. Naturally, if they are really hungry, weak or diseased themselves, or terribly inept killers, they will take small, weak victims.

Having followed on the snow, many, many bobcats, I believe I am more qualified as to their behavior than most game biologists, who learn out of books written by equally inexperienced educators. I can tell you for certain that I know more about bobcats than some hippie dreamer who believes all animals are sweet and cuddly and only the human predator is mean and evil.

The truth is that some bobcats, like all predators (including my sport hunting clients) are swift, strong, and expert. Some are weak and slow and would starve to death, like our antihunter friends, if someone else didn't do their harvesting for them.

With bobcats it is simple. A good killer will stalk to close range, leap upon the front quarters of a deer, and with one bite behind the head, death is almost instantaneous. We saw one such kill, a big mature ten-point buck, with antlers still intact in early December, killed on snow with about as much struggle sign as if he had been shot with a .300 magnum. This was done by a large male bobcat.

We also saw a case where eight deer, of varying sizes, were killed along the ice of Little Cedar Brook, after being harassed out of their yard and unable to get off the ice due to the deep snow on the banks. We ran that cat and killed it after a hell of a chase, and it was a 24-pound female.

We also came across many, many cases, where dumber cats had tried unsuccessfully to kill deer. They chased them, then jumped all over them, they got blood and enough hair to stuff a mattress out of them, but the deer eventually got away. Some got away badly mauled and died, some escaped relatively unscathed, and some injured the cats severely.

There are without a doubt some cats that never know the taste of deer meat, and some that live on little else even during high cycles of other prey species.

When you live in the wilderness as we have done, you get to know the other guy's side of the story, whether the other guy happens to be a bear, a bobcat or the human critter. The truth is that it is a cruel old world out there and some of us are grazers, some are predators, and some are prey.

At risk of further unhinging our bunny-hugger friends, there is more than ample evidence that the typical "family unit" is somewhat similar to what the human population is becoming. That is female single parents, with males that come around to gobble up or otherwise abuse the kiddies. Probably the answer is more Day Care Centers.

Some of the things we learned and practiced would apply to all cat hunting with dogs, in any area. Some methods and items of equipment, of course, would vary as to terrain and conditions.

In general a hunt would go as follows: The night before we might go out and drive a section of road. In those days there would be tracks everywhere. We would discount all the deer, fox, rabbit, fisher, and other tracks, but would simply scratch out with our boot any recent-looking bobcat tracks. The next morning, often before daylight in the short winter days, we would drive the road again. This time we would be able to select only tracks that had crossed in the night. What we looked for was, of course, big cats, preferably headed into flat country. This was always an illusion, because you inevitably ended up in mountains and gulches anyway, regardless of the initial direction. Aside from desiring the biggest male cats, they were the easiest to run. One only has to contemplate a race between myself, fat, lazy and sixty; and some gung-ho high school athlete, to see the good sense in this approach. Big old tomcats also tended to be a bit arrogant, and after a short chase would stroll up the side of a tree, hang over a limb with their elbows hooked like a drunk in the bar, and owlishly contemplate this noisy thing jumping at the foot of the tree. Poor tactics when Tom and I were coming along the trail with the shotgun.

Young cats and females were much more apt to run forever, then jump from tree to tree, or bail out and run again for another ten miles. Once we got to hunting with visiting clients, we avoided these at all costs.

On a typical good track, in good snow conditions, Ben or Blue or Streak or Warrior would light out with a few sharp howls to let you know they were happy with the track. Invariably after the first few yards, they would pause to empty their bowels, and look back, as if to say, "Let's get this over with, because there won't be any time for fooling around later." Just as invariably, any client tagging along would step in it and have it frozen in a lump on his snowshoes.

The rest was simple, or at least it is simple to tell. Once the dog was out of hearing, you follow the track, like reeling in the string that represents the last twelve hours of his life. In some lucky cases the cat had stopped to hunt, or to eat from a previous kill, or had laid down in the snow and slept. These ones you had in short order. In other circumstances that old cat might just be walking around his ten-mile territory and had never paused since crossing the road the evening before.

Most of the time, the end result would be a cat up a tree, somewhere, a dog at the bottom, and if the hunter is physically able would come along later. Sounds simple for sure, but things rarely followed the script.

I can brag somewhat, and tell you that when Tom and I were on the track alone, there were extremely few unsuccessful runs. Equally sincerely, I can tell you that once we started doing it with clients, the exact opposite was true.

A typical hunt with a client would go as follows: First, in the booking process I would answer every question, give every bit of advice the English language is capable of expressing. I would tell them it was *HARD*, that they had to be in good shape, that they had to bring appropriate clothing, and most importantly, boots that would fit snowshoe harness. I would tell them to leave their firearms at home, that we would kill the cat with my old full-choke, single-shot, 12-gauge shotgun with No. 4 shot. With this gun, one can fall down in the snow all day, use it to bang ice off your snowshoes if you fall in the brook, use it for a cane going uphill, then when you get there open it up, blow out the snow and kill the cat.

Naturally, none of this advice was heeded in even the slightest way. They would arrive in the Cadillac, fat, out of shape, great big down parkas and boots that you couldn't even begin to get into harness. When asked to at least attempt to fit their gear to the harness, and to walk around the field in the evening getting used to the snowshoes, the answer was: "Don't worry about us. We will get there even if we have to crawl."

Tom and I would go out in the evening, usually with at least two of them jammed onto our laps in the truck, smoking, drinking and bellering. Every time you stopped to look at a track, instead of taking ten seconds, it took ten minutes to all get out, tramp around, take a leak, open another bottle of beer, and climb back in.

In the morning, stuffed too full of breakfast, suffering the pangs of a satanic hangover, we hit the trail. First good cat track we stop, everyone gets out and mills around offering their expert opinions. The dog is put out, he sneezes the cigar smoke out of his lungs, adds his own yellow spots to the snow bank, goes over the snowplow rim, and is gone on the track.

Next follows a completely maddening scenario. Tom puts his snowshoes on. I put my snowshoes on. Our clients now find out a day too late that they have to adjust every strap on two five-strap harnesses before they get their jumbo-sized bulldozer operator boots attached. They then waddle over, put the nose of one snowshoe up on the bank, pick up the other foot, and fall flat on their ass in the road. More to this than meets the eye, they now admit.

About this time, I would motion to Tom. He would take the shotgun, jump over the bank and take off into the woods on the track, the dog already a mile out of hearing. In the meantime, being as diplomatic as only I am capable of, I would work on adjusting harnesses, telling the clients that *NO*, I did not want to carry their thousand-dollar automatic Browning shotguns or high-scoped varmint rifles.

Sometimes I would even get them up over the snowplowed rim before they foundered in a brushpile and broke my snowshoes, but most times it was back to the truck and the coffee thermos. Then it was hours driving around the road, listening to and telling outlandish lies, trying to figure out where Tom would surface after catching and killing the cat. As the day went on, most of them would tell me that they would never even consider taking a cat home unless they killed it themselves. One hundred percent of them, in fact, did just exactly that. Thankfully, I was not around to listen to the stories back in New York.

In case any one wonders, that is why when I hear about bobcat hunts in the East and lion hunts in the West, and see record book entries under the names of people that I know personally are not physically able to sit on a deer stand in Texas, I do not take them too seriously. One famous line is that old favorite, "I have a great outfitter, he calls me when things are absolutely perfect."

This translates to one of the following: The cat is still in the cage, the cat is up the tree with the rancher's wife and kids and all the village dogs keeping it there for seventy-two hours, or in most cases, the cat is safe in the Deep Freeze.

Not to be unkind, and to let the few good ones off the hook, and let the others pretend, I will add here that once in a while the client actually saw the cat when it was still breathing.

When I was young and tough as rawhide, when I was hungry enough to need the money, when I enjoyed the chase and the pride of owning the dogs, bobcat hunting with hounds was the greatest sport I ever attempted. As a hunt with clients, it was a nightmare, and as a commercial outfitting venture, it was a total failure.

About the time we began to wear it all out, clear-cutting and the crash of the rabbit population brought the cat numbers down to unacceptable lows. We entered a period when the Eastern brush wolf became established in the country, to further deplete the food supply. Just when cats were starting a slow increase again, the price of hides went to unheard-of highs and every part-time woods-man and welfare case lined the woods with snares and killer traps. We were forced into retirement.

Looking back, the economic history of the Webb family is once more apparent. The year we could not give bobcats away and were forced to try taking clients to attempt to make money, we killed nearly fifty cats. Three years later when they were pay-ing up to four hundred dollars for mediocre cats, we managed to snare six. Our bobcat days ended on this sad note.

Blue Boy, Warrior, Blue Streak, and Bennie remain in our memories as cherished comrades, reminders of the days in which we were young, lean and hungry, when every turn in the road held the promise of a hot track in eight inches of new snow.

LONG RANGER CAT

The last week of March is too late for good bobcat hunting, but things were slow, and I wanted to get in one more hunt before laying up the snowshoes and the dogs for the season.

Heading out alone, on such a strenuous hunt, with always the chance of some mishap, is normally not too smart. However, the weather was warm, overcast and threatening rain or snow, and I figured I could luck out and grab an easy track. As it turned out, I was not that lucky.

There had been a lot of splash and splatter along the road caused by the big logging trucks, but I spotted a track just below Riley Brook. It looked like an average-sized cat, perhaps a female, had come up from the river and crossed in the night, heading west. At about ten in the morning, stripped down for traveling and not carrying any lunch, I loosed my young dog, Benny, and took the track.

The first couple of miles were easy going, through open soft-wood timber—this was before everything was cut down in that part of the country. About noon we started to get into the tangle of Haley Brook branches and gulches, and things became more interesting. When you get into finger ravines when on a cat track, the only option is to simply stick to it and work them all out. It is strenuous work.

Finally getting onto the high ground, there were mazes of thickets, caused by regenerating softwood growth, following a fire that went through the country about thirty years previous. Here the cat, as usual, had worked and circled while hunting rabbits. Again there is nothing to do but try your best to force through on the track. If you get smart and circle around, you might walk for miles and come back to find the cat had emerged again nearly, but not exactly, where it had entered.

I was soaking wet with sweat and dislodged snow, but further discomfort was on the way as it started to drizzle, a cold spring rain. Rain doesn't help the tracking either, but I knew that Ben had a superb nose and would stick to it as long as he thought I was still coming.

Miles and hours later, I heard him open up, way over on another ridge. By the sound of things he was in sight of the cat, picking hot scent from the air or maybe even running by sight alone. It was his "get up a tree or fight" music. I had heard it dozens of times; not many cats heard it more than once.

I looked at my watch, standing there steaming and dripping and totally miserable. Just about three o'clock, less than three hours of daylight left, at this time of year. Taking stock, I had had nothing to eat for about ten hours, was soaking, wringing wet and situated somewhere between the main road, which I could never get to before dark, and the Burma Road, which went in to a lumber camp on Sisson Lake. Traveling alone, I had carried the shotgun but no ax. I had four dry matches left and a belt knife.

"Oh well, what the hell," I said. "I'm not going to perish in a country full of wood, even if it does keep raining." But I was under no illusions about how comfortable the night would be if I was forced to stop because of darkness. The only thing to do was keep on the track, at least it is straightened out and headed for the Burma Road.

After another hour's slogging. I was headed uphill and within hearing of the dog. However, it had me puzzled; instead of baying "treed" he seemed to be still in hot pursuit but mostly in the same spot. I came at last to a vast area of absolutely horrible spruce thicket. The cat was on the ground and Ben was valiantly trying to force it to tree or bay, but he was just too exhausted to put on enough pressure.

I circled, frantically trying to get a glimpse of the cat, making sure the gun barrel was clear and pushing in a load of high-brass magnum 4. If I could just get one pellet into the cat, it would worry him enough to tip the scales in Ben's favor. There, at last, up with the gun. The dog was right on top of it, wait for another chance. Off they go, straight back east.

Floundering back around the thicket, I could see the story in the tracks. The wily cat had struck my snowshoe path and took back down it as fast as he could run. Boy, this might turn into a night's work yet.

Half-an-hour later, the rain was letting up and it was getting colder. I hear Ben way off in the distance, this time yodeling in triumph at the foot of some tree. Now if I could just get over there before it was too late to shoot.

After twenty minutes of hard mushing, I came up onto a small wooded knob in the middle of an old burned-over acre. There at the foot of the tree, looking to me, then going back and jumping up on the trunk, was my valiant little Blue Benny. It took a lot of looking in the gathering dusk, but at last the cat moved, perhaps to launch out of its high perch to run again. This time the luck was all mine, and at the report of the 12-gauge, down tumbled the quarry.

Stretched out on the snow, it was not a big cat, a female, as I had thought, weighing in the low twenty-pound range. She has sure taken us for a trip, much harder to bring to bay than most big old lazy tomcats.

Now for the map and compass. Never lost, as the saying goes, but sometimes turned around for half a day. No time for that, this time of night; hit the straightest course for the Burma Road and hope to find the easy route.

A couple of hours later, burdened with the cat and my dog at heel on the leash, I stumbled out on top of the Big Hill on the Burma Road.

I had worn a pair of snowmobile boots which fit my snow-shoe binding. The boots themselves and the felt liners had just about disintegrated; they are like two big wet pillows weighing ten pounds apiece. My feet had been wet, like the rest of me, for the entire day. As I slogged along down the road, buried now in six inches of slush, it occurred to me that the boots were just not adding much to my comfort. I stopped long enough to take them off and toss them over the bank into the woods and went on down the road. I had about ten miles to get back to my truck, unless I should get lucky and someone comes along.

My prayers were answered. I heard the clatter of bunks and chains, then the motor. The trees lit up, and around the turn comes one of the company's big tractor-trailers with a load of tree-length lumber. I waved the shotgun and hoped he would stop.

Thankfully, it was a driver who knew me. In we crowded, dog, cat and all, and soon we were all three steaming up the cab with the heater turned up on high. Gratefully, I heard that he would turn upriver to deliver us at my truck, before reversing his course downriver to the mill in Plaster Rock. I can only guess at what he would tell the next driver he met about picking up a bobcat, a hound dog, and a bushwhacking idiot walking down the road in his sock feet in the middle of the night in half-a-foot of freezing snow.

It wasn't the biggest cat or the most brilliant chase, but it was still one to remember.

BREAKING THE ICE

I t was the summer of '76, and we were expecting a new party to arrive in camp for some salmon fishing. The season, up to that point, had been terrible, but as they say, hope springs eternal.

When one is angling for Atlantic salmon, it seems as if you are always plagued by water that is too high, too low, too hot, or too cold. Those are the excuses we guides quote to the sports. One of the few outdoor pursuits that the devotees will return to year after year—with so little encouragement—it can be compared only to woodcock gunning, another diversion evoking the same level of fanaticism as the Quest for the Holy Grail.

Fortunately for us, at that time in history, northern New Brunswick, if not actually "Abounding in Fish and Game," as the government brochures stated, at least had enough so that a good guide could bluff his way through the week. Nowadays it would take a much more accomplished liar than I am to carry it off.

On this particular trip, our guests were to be Mr. and Mrs. Gene Hill. I had long been an admirer, along with millions of others, of Mr. Hill's skillful and sensitive treatment of all outdoor subjects. Through reading his articles, I knew he was a most avid salmon angler and was very pleased when he contacted me about coming up to try some Tobique River fishing.

The Tobique at that time, while not to be compared to Iceland or the Ungava Rivers, offered salmon fishing as good as any in the East, open to the public. Gene, being an old hand at the game, asked only that there be water and that there be some fish in it. He knew that this was about the only guarantee a salmon guide can make in this most uncertain of sports.

We were working that summer out of a bunch of old log camps, up at Waters Brook on the Mamozekel. While good brook trout fishing was possible almost from the camp veranda, we would drive out each day to fish the main Tobique by canoe, or one of the other prominent streams, the Serpentine. The other guide was my longtime friend and chief helper, Coleman McDougall. Coleman was then about sixty, a teetotaler, born-again Christian and one of the finest guides in that—or any other—country.

I knew that I could trust Coleman's gentlemanly demeanor to balance out some of the more pagan instincts inherent in my own nature. We agreed that if we were to make a good impression for our outfit, I would just have to curb my tongue and hold back on some of my more colorful ravings.

Upon the guests' arrival, it was immediately apparent that all the stories Gene had written detailing the tons of gear he considers essential to a successful expedition, were no exaggeration. We did, however, manage to get everything stored in a cabin that usually held eight men and luggage. Immediately charmed, we were introduced to Mrs. Hill, whom at her insistence, we were to address as Marcia. She further endeared herself to Coleman and me by declaring that she would take over the cooking and, in fact, had looked forward to doing so. This was great. Coleman, who would be the lady's guide when on the water, would be her assistant in the cook shack. I was thus at leisure to get better acquainted with Gene and to plan our next day's assault on the salmon.

After a most enjoyable dinner we sat around the stone fireplace in their cabin as Gene entertained us with tales of fishing on some of the most famous waters in the world, places that we had only read about. Puffing away on his pipe, with a glass of scotch and Mamozekel water (in absence of any ice being available), he was the complete sporting gentleman.

I tried to add to the entertainment with tales of our own country but found myself nearly tongue-tied with a lack of suitable descriptive phrases that wouldn't offend the ears of our guests. Besides envying Mr. Hill's command of genteel language, I was also suffering the pangs of jealousy, as he savored the aromatic smoke and the amber liquid. Having only recently reformed from being a drunk of Boone & Crockett proportions and quitting a nicotine habit of twenty-plus years, I was in a cold sweat most of the evening.

After we blew out the lantern in the guide shack, Coleman spoke up in the dark: "My, we are going to have a fine week's fishing. These are really nice people, and you are doing just fine . . . haven't said a bad word since they got here."

"That's great for you, being religious and all, but before we go in to breakfast, I'm going out back in the woods to have a goddam good swearing session so I won't blow up or something."

Next morning at daylight, it was calm and overcast. It was going to be a bad day for black flies but probably a pretty decent time to go fish some of those shallow pools up on Serpentine. After breakfast and with lunch all packed, we loaded all of Gene's equipment and Marcia's one rod case into the truck and headed off to the river.

We were going to leave the truck and walk about three miles through the woods, down to McArty Falls—a great chance to pick up a fish or two before it warmed up too much.

Coleman and Marcia were soon packed up with their gear, the lunch stowed in Coleman's pack basket. Gene meantime decided that he couldn't really choose which rod to use until he saw the layout of the pool. So we took the two Hardys, three different weight masterpieces from Orvis and one of the Leonards. The selection of various reels, with appropriate lines of different type and caliber, filled my packsack. After all, one must never appear on the bank with anything less than the perfect combination.

I am not too adept at mathematics but have always wondered what would be the cumulative total of all possible combinations of rod, reel, backing, casting line, shooting head, leader, and fly. Whatever it is, we had a damn good start on it. Struggling off through the bushes, encumbered with my own packsack, an immense shoulder bag on each side, a tailer hung from my belt, and a long-handled landing net (the mesh of which catches every obstacle in the woods), I must have presented quite a sight. I could only imagine what was going on behind me as Gene, carrying the various rods in tubes that kept swinging crossways in the trail, brought up the procession.

I tried to fend off disaster as dead branches speared at my eyes and the brushpiles plotted to ensnare me. From the permanent holding pattern of moose flies circling my head, the occasional vicious bastard darted in to snatch away a piece of my flesh to devour at his leisure. Denied the solace of throwing a screaming, cursing, foaming-at-the-mouth seizure, I didn't know how much longer I would be able to endure.

About at the end of my tether and boiling to the point where I was about to blurt out some offensive expletive to blister the ears of a saint, I was saved from disgracing myself by our arrival at the river.

We stepped out onto the rocks near the head of the little falls, from which one may cast nicely to the tail of the pool, where—if any salmon are in residence—they may be tempted to take the fly.

Coleman had already climbed the lookout tree, and with his newly acquired Polaroid sunglasses, he was able to see a half-dozen fish holding in their usual lie. In a few moments, he had Marcia rigged up and she then prepared to make the first presentation.

She had unlimbered her rod, mounted the reel, attached a leader, and taking Coleman's advice, selected a "Thunder and Lightning."

Gene, having studied the situation to his satisfaction, had at last selected the Leonard as being appropriate to the occasion. I watched in awe at a master at work. With utmost deliberation, a reel containing the proper backing and a weight-forward line was duly attached. By this time, I was getting buck fever.

Would the fish hold there? The sun was starting to come out from behind the clouds, and they were in awfully shallow water. Should I suggest a certain fly, or was it better not to break his concentration? I was about to bust a gut in anticipation when he, at last, reverently removed a "Blue Charm" from the eighth box he examined. Then it took a little time to get the pipe going, and then there were the little scissors and the special little glasses to aid in performing the absolutely perfect knot.

Marcia, a saint of patience up until now, finally broke point, stepped out on the rock, made one false cast and began a back cast to double haul to the foot of the pool.

I watched in fascination. The back cast line wrapped around Gene's neck about three times, the double-hooked "Thunder and Lightning" snagging his off-side ear. In slow motion he reached up and grasped the line, took out his pipe and in the most gentlemanly of tones, inquired, "Marcia, just *what the fuck* do you think you are doing?"

The ice was broken; we were among friends, and I knew we would go on to many years of shared enjoyment of the wild places and peoples. For the time being however, it was sufficient to know that we would, as Coleman said, "enjoy a great week's fishing with some great people."

SOMETIMES THE MUSKOX WINS

t is 5 April 1990 and I am waiting at the airport in Coppermine, Northwest Territories. Temperature around minus twenty and reduced visibility in blowing snow remind me that, despite the lengthening days, winter still has a grip on this part of the country. As I braced against the wind and watched pilot Rene Laserich drop the King Air onto the strip with precision, I felt anxious to meet one of my clients. A few evenings previously, in a fit of immodesty, I had boasted to friends that in thirty-five years in the guiding business, we had never experienced a fatality or serious injury, despite the rigors of the land we deal with. Now I was waiting to meet the victim and hear his story of a near-fatal confrontation between a southern guest and an Arctic muskox.

Otis Chandler is an internationally known lifelong big-game hunter and sportsman. Veteran of several previous northern hunts, survivor of the hazards of polar bear, grizzly, and brown bear hunts in Alaska, he is no stranger to the Arctic. On many occasions, throughout a quarter-century of safaris to Africa, he had experienced the excitement of stalking potentially dangerous big game and come away unscathed. Now, he had been injured while hunting an animal that most people do not consider dangerous under normal conditions.

As the pilot and I helped him off the plane and into my truck, I could see immediately that, with an arm in a sling and moving stiffly, he was still in considerable pain. "Otis," I asked as soon as I got the door closed, "What in the hell happened?"

"Well, Fred, it's a complicated story," he said, "but basically I'm the sort of guy who runs into burning buildings when I probably shouldn't, and this time it caught up with me."

As the report later unfolded from Otis, another guest involved, and the two Inuit (Eskimo) guides on hand, it became apparent that like most accidents, it had elements of both bad timing and bad luck. Had anyone done anything differently, at any point in the episode, this near-fatality would have been avoided, and I would not be writing this account of it.

Our company, Webb Qaivvik Ltd., with our Inuit partners of the Kugluktuk Hunters and Trappers Association, operates muskox hunts out of Coppermine in the central Arctic. Five years of handling hunters for muskox and grizzly in this region, and years of guiding caribou hunters in our Barren Land camps, has developed a crew of well-experienced guides. Starting with a traditional hunting lifestyle, coupled with on-the-job experience, these men have the special skills needed to take care of the southern guest in this northern setting.

After three decades of guiding hunters around the wild places of Canada, I no longer accompany every trip personally. We develop the hunts, book the hunts, and are present to oversee the operation.

This spring we had started late in March, hosting six clients on the first trip, including one bow hunter and two lady hunters, to a 100 percent successful conclusion. We were now into our second hunt. Muskox hunting can be described as a genuine "Arctic adventure." You leave the community on a big sled called a *komatik,* hauled by your Inuit guide on a snow machine. You may travel fifty to one hundred miles out to the hunt areas and live with what you carry on the sled. Every precaution is taken and the best equipment available is employed, but you are still on an Arctic expedition, an experience that can contain hazards. Potential guests are advised of the conditions, required to submit a statement as to their physical ability, and indicate their acceptance of our services with this in mind.

At this time of year the weather is still cold by southern standards, but dry and with long spring days offering good travel. The first herds of muskox are usually encountered one day out. Hunting is successful within a couple of days, and you return to the comforts of the Coppermine Inn, well within the week's schedule.

At any time though, you can be reminded very abruptly that you are indeed traveling in a country untouched by time, at the mercy of both the elements and the animal inhabitants. You realize just how fragile is life in this Arctic environment.

On this occasion, five experienced hunters from "down south" were going out to Victoria Island, with five of the best guides in the central Arctic. Jack Atatahak, George Annablak, and Charlie Bolt are not only acquainted with handling sport hunters, but spend most of their lives trapping and hunting from outpost camps on Victoria Island. John Akana and Patsy Avakana, youngest of the crew at about age thirty, are veterans of years of guiding for me. With a gas cache previously set up on the island, good equipment, and fairly good weather forecast, they took off from town for the eight-hour trip across Coronation Gulf to Victoria.

Back in town, we are able to maintain radio contact with the groups. By midnight that night, word was received that they had made landfall on the coast, set up a snug camp, and were ready to hunt the next day.

Early the following morning, the parties split up somewhat and within a few hours, guests Bob Rolfe, Pete Studwell, and Perry Harwell had all collected their trophies. Otis Chandler and Jim Foral from Nebraska had teamed up with guides Charlie Bolt and Patsy Avakana to travel out several miles farther to an adjacent area. Otis shortly succeeded in tagging an extremely good bull, and the party went on to look for another for Jim. Late in the afternoon they encountered two big mature bulls together, and it was decided that Jim would take the better of the two, After an hour's stalk, the trophy was down, but then a complication arose.

Muskox are not normally considered a particularly dangerous game animal, and should present no problem to the modern rifleman under ordinary circumstances. However, it must be remembered that this prehistoric animal, living in its Arctic environment, has no experience and no fear of humans. The herd bulls constantly guard themselves and their kin against wolves and bears. They are extremely defensive, and have both the weapons and the temperament to put at peril anyone approaching too closely.

In this case, with one bull down, the other steadfastly refused to back off, determined to defend its herd mate. Not being on the scene myself, I must rely upon accounts of the people who were there. Fortunately, these differ only slightly, depending upon one's point of view. Hindsight and "what I would have done," of course, have no relevance either.

The easy options, such as simply abandoning the trophy and coming back later, were put in doubt by the lateness of the day, the remoteness from their tents, lowering skies, and rising wind, all of which put pressure on everyone to complete the job and move out.

Several attempts were made to drive the defending bull away by rushing it with the snow machines, waving, shooting, etc., all to no avail. The animal simply would not move away. Guides are trained and warned not to hunt while guiding, and the shooting of an extra animal would have been unacceptable and probably unexplainable to the game department. Inuit guides, in accordance with their culture, tend to consider the guest to be a hunting partner who is capable of sharing the responsibility of handling any potentially dangerous situation. While they might "baby-sit" clients that I have specifically indicated to them, they admire those who can hold up their own end. Therefore, they did not insist upon the withdrawal of the clients while the situation at hand was being taken care of.

With no success at driving the defender away, it was decided that perhaps one of the sleds could be hauled into such a position as to screen the dead animal so that it could be dragged away some distance. In the course of this attempt, the muskox charged Patsy on his snowmobile, striking and upsetting it with considerable damage—and scattering some of his cargo.

Nimble on his feet, Patsy avoided being hit himself and managed to recover possession of his machine, but only after throwing some of his tools at the enraged animal. Finally, a rope was secured to the downed bull, and with two snowmobiles it was possible to drag it some distance away from the live one. Instead of leaving, the bull hung around, making a nuisance of itself.

At last, the trophy animal was caped and quartered and the party was ready to leave the remaining one on the field of battle.

Again, hindsight would indicate that this was the time to go. By all accounts a joint decision was now made that the guide's tools and binoculars, which the bull was standing guard over, were essential to the operation, and an attempt must be made to recover them. The plan they made was a simple one; Otis volunteered to dash in behind and grab up the tools while the guides would divert the animal's attention. As Otis told me, "I leaned down and picked up the binoculars. Had I jumped up at this point, nothing would have happened, but I spotted some of the other tools, diverted my attention from the muskox, and reached for them. At this time, the freight train hit me."

Otis was struck a tremendous blow side-on. He remembered rolling along the ground, trying to get clear of the animal as it tried to inflict further injury upon him. Others recalled it attempting to hook him with its horns and rearing up to stamp him into the ice. The recollection of the guides and Jim Foral is that Charlie Bolt rushed in and was successful in diverting the ox's attention, so that Otis was able to roll clear.

It was immediately apparent that a serious and painful injury now had to be dealt with, late in the day, and far from help, but fortunately with a group of people prepared to deal with emergencies. Rudimentary first aid was given on the spot, the injured man was loaded gingerly into the sled box, and the group headed as fast as they could to camp, where the others already were. Here a radio call went out to us in Coppermine, the casualty was given hot tea and painkillers, and made as comfortable as possible under the circumstances.

Naturally, we all hope that accidents will never happen, but when they do, the individual's chances are a lot better with people with experience and on-the-spot presence of mind to handle it, rather than having simply been sent up North by some travel agent. Back in Coppermine, I was hurriedly called to the radio and advised of what had happened. We immediately knew that the injury required more than simple first aid and that evacuation was urgent before the weather deteriorated further. In a case like this, I am thankful to have the help of people who know their way around in the North. The party was stranded on the south shore of Victoria Island, much too far to reach help at Coppermine across the rough ice a day away. There was, however, a DEW (Distant Early Warning) line radar site within their reach, about thirty miles away. Keith Hickling, the local game officer, who helps in coordinating our hunts, was able to contact this site at Lady Franklin Point. Ordinarily it is impossible, for security reasons, to communicate with these stations, but Keith not only knew how to do it, but also knew the man in charge. We were given immediate permission to use the airstrip and assured of any further help we might require. Kerry Horn, who runs the Coppermine Inn, being an ex-radio operator, knew who to contact in a hurry to secure an aircraft for the evacuation. Here some luck came into play as there was already a plane en route from Coppermine to Cambridge Bay which could be contacted to land at Lady Franklin.

As can be imagined, it was a terribly painful trip for an injured man, being transported over rough ice and snow in a box behind a snowmobile, Everything possible was done to make him comfortable, foam mattresses in the box, painkillers administered, etc., but it was surely no pleasure trip. Within a short time of arriving at the radar site, he was loaded into the aircraft and flown to the nursing station in Cambridge Bay, the major community on the east end of Victoria Island. By midnight, I was advised by head nurse Kathy Fitzgerald that his immediate problem, a dislocated shoulder, had been taken care of, but that further injuries were suspected and that X-rays had been taken to see if he could be safely moved south at the first opportunity. Next day, courtesy of Adlair Aviation of Cambridge, Otis was transported back to Coppermine and consequently returned to home and medical attention in California.

Through ongoing concern and contacts we have learned that his injuries were even more serious than first discovered. I am

116

again reminded that despite the best of preparations and experience, trophy hunting expeditions to the wild corners of the world can still be hazardous.

Mr. Chandler is determined to return to the North, and we are looking forward to hunting with him again.

CAMPFIRE PHILOSOPHY

OR WHAT'S IN A NAME?

I was reading the other day where a prominent figure in U.S. political circles has declared his intention of renaming a significant portion of the population.

Under his designation, members of a particular ethnic background would be instantly categorized by a point of geographical origin, regardless of how ancient and tenuous the connection. One has to wonder just where in the order of priorities this matter appears for the people involved, and how many of them would be happy to be known as just plain old "Americans."

As a Canadian, a member of a very mixed society, and with an ancestry composed of some people who came over on the *Mayflower* and others who were there to meet it, I have been called a lot of things by a lot of different people in my travels through life. Being part English, part French, and with a hefty dash of native North American thrown in, has exposed me to a wide variety of so-called racial slurs, but none of them have had any horrifyingly traumatic effect on my soul, nor any measurable impact on my bank account. It has been my experience that people of every background have at least some degree of natural prejudice against those outside their immediate clan, and that this is certainly not restricted to only one segment of the world's population.

In a discussion around a fire with some of my American friends and clients, it came up that we downtrodden residents of eastern Canada are referred to by our more affluent cousins of Ontario as "Bluenoses" and "Herring Chokers." This mystified my friends who made the mistake of saying that they had always considered me a "Canuck."

"Hell no," I said. "A G.D. 'Canuck' is a *French* Canadian and does not apply to us English-speaking, mostly white, other Canadians."

"But," they pointed out, "we have never heard you use the term 'Canuck,' but rather names like 'Swamp Singers,' "Lily Pad Hoppers' and 'Bogan Yodelers."

"Well, yes," I said. "Those terms all refer to the original designation of 'Frog' which comes from the fact that in the far distant past, people of French extraction were known as 'Frog Eaters.' Everyone knows that."

"But," they wondered, "as you are part French yourself, how can you use such derogatory terms?"

"Oh, but you don't understand," I said. "My friends who are *REALLY* French term me a 'Square Head,' a 'Limey,' or if they are of the *Seperatiste* type, they call me a *Maudit Anglais* and worse."

"But, what is this term *Seperatiste,*" they asked. "Are they French as well?"

"Yes," I explained. "But they are *Quebecois* of a particularly virulent political strain, not to be confused with our more tolerant friends of the 'Cajun' persuasion in New Brunswick, or the 'Jackietars' of Newfoundland."

"Oh, ho," the breakthrough came. "Now it becomes clear. It all depends upon where you come from as well as simply the ethnic background of the person concerned."

"Well hell yes," I said. "Geographical designation is even more important as a way of insulting your neighbors. When working with the 'Goofy Newfies' on moose hunts, friends of thirty years still call me a 'Come From Away,' while government officials and other enemies heap the direst insult upon my head by calling me a 'Mainlander.'"

Figuring I had the boys hooked, and seeing as there was some of their rum left, I continued their education. Besides, they were intrigued with how thick a skin one must have to live in such a mixed society as we have in Canada.

"How do you manage to get along with the native peoples of Canada, being of mixed ancestry yourself?" they asked.

"Well, simple," I pointed out. "While admitting to a lot of redneck instincts, I take people as they come and only ask that they give me the same consideration. My Eskimo friends, for example, want to be called 'Inuit,' so I do so. As to myself, in the eastern Arctic they call me a *Haloona*, in the western Arctic it is *Kabloonuk*, both meaning the equivalent of 'Crazy White Man,' and the ones who suspect I am part Indian don't speak to me at all. My native Indian friends in one area insist upon being termed 'Dene,' while dozens of other dialects across Canada offer other terminology. What they all agree upon is that they don't want to be called 'Indian.' If they are particularly charitable, they might call me *Metis*, meaning one of mixed blood, but mostly they lump me in with all the other 'white guys,' which has a meaning all its own when used by certain more politically minded native peoples."

"Oh," my friend wondered. "Do you mean there are no real 'Indians' in Canada?"

"Please," I begged. "Don't get me started on that subject at this time of night. Let's just say they are not native to the part of Canada I work in. They are numerous in Vancouver, Toronto, and certain sections of Montreal, and they have their own terminology, I suspect, for various sects, religions, and other people differing from themselves, including you and me."

"Gee, you would think that the whole population would be at odds with someone or other all the time and there wouldn't be time to think or make a living," one of my friends put in.

"Well, fortunately," I said, "we don't spend a whole hell of a lot of time worrying about it. As my mother used to say 'Sticks and stones can break my bones, but names can never hurt me.' I guess I pretty much get along all over the world with that philosophy. Being called a 'Round Eye' by my Asian friends, a 'Durty Prod' in Belfast one time, a 'Colonial Oppressor' and a 'Tool of Yankee Imperialism' during one part of my career, a 'Gross Murderer' by the antihunting element and a host of other endearments by my wife over the years hasn't really stunted my growth or destroyed my faith in human kindness. Most ethnic nicknames have basis in past racial or geographical origins, and as such we should be proud of them.

"However, I have wondered since 1963 what they meant when they called me a 'Honky Mother' in the Zu Zu Club in Philadelphia."

NATALIE

CRACK, *I'm jolted awake.* CRACK, *again. What the hell? Something hitting the outside of the aircraft.*
Looking out, I see the cause. Chunks of ice being flung from the nose cone of the port side propeller. More ice is building on the leading edge of the wing and strut and I can only imagine what's happening elsewhere on the plane.

Glancing into the cockpit of the Twin Otter, I sense controlled tension as pilots Kevin and Dan adjust the throttles, check and re-check instruments. Two of the finest "off-strip" pilots in the North; if anyone can get us to Yellowknife, these guys will.

Flying is a science balanced upon speed, altitude, weight, and fuel. Now the equation is made more interesting by one additional factor: icing. Two questions now arise. Will the weight of fuel burned off compensate for the ice we are making, so that altitude can be maintained? Will the remaining fuel get us to our destination?

I sneak yet another look at my watch. Oh well, what the hell, in another ninety minutes we will either be drinking coffee in the terminal in Yellowknife or parked in a snow bank in the Barrens.

As I try to doze off, I am comforted by the thought that it is out of my hands. Like most of what we do Up North, all we can do now is wait. If we have to go camping, at least I am in good company. Mixed in with the cargo of snow machines, bags of Arctic char, caribou and muskox meat and trophies, are some of the finest companions one could wish for.

Jorgan Bolt and McCauley Niptanatiak are two of our most experienced Inuit guides from Coppermine. The clients are Hugh and Sara Beavers from Virginia, and Natalie.

Natalie Eckel, comes from Encino, California. Complete with long manicured nails and her trademark gold jewelry, she's at home in the world of international jet set society. With well-worn hunting gear and Weatherby rifle, she is equally at home in the world's wild places, one of our most traveled and experienced big-game hunting clients.

Still in her Arctic gear, catching up on her sleep after an exhausting hunt, nothing much bothers Natalie.

It has been a long hard trail since Natalie first approached me for aid in her quest for North American trophies. One gets to know everyone around the annual convention circuit, and we had talked hunting occasionally. We finally got serious about it during the show season of 1990.

She had hunted in most countries and taken an extremely impressive list of animals. Now it was time to see what Canada had to offer in the way of adventure.

While everyone has read the articles about "how to pick an outfitter," it is my policy to reverse the process a bit and check into the reputation and abilities of prospective clients. Everyone I talked to, mutual friends and professional hunters alike, assured me that despite the fancy fingernails and jewelry, Natalie was a real hunter.

I like to get all the bad news on record right up front, so I explained that we would start with one of our toughest hunts, sled travel for Greenland muskox. I laid it all on the line. "Natalie, this is cold, rough and tough. Can you live with the fact that there is no camp, no bathroom, and you will be sleeping in a tent at thirty below zero with your Inuit guide?"

"Well," she replied, "if it isn't any worse than sleeping in a damp cave on a mountain with eight Mongolians and a yak, I think I can handle it."

That settled it to my satisfaction. We sat down to figure out the schedule and how to fit it around her trips to other areas of the globe. Under our direction, she would see the three most interesting sides of Canada; east coast, west coast and the Arctic coast. The trophies would eventually include muskox, Quebec-Labrador caribou, woodland caribou, central barren ground caribou, mountain caribou, Arctic Islands caribou, eastern moose, and western Canada moose.

With a considerable amount of juggling hunting seasons, areas, and airline connections, we finally came up with a plan of action. With good luck everywhere and tight connections, we would be able to accomplish all of these hunts during 1991. The first, and one of the hardest, would be the Greenland muskox hunt, out of Coppermine in late March.

Although we are frequently asked this question; there is no *easy* way to go on a *good* muskox hunt. Some of our competitors keep trying time periods and methods that we discarded years ago, but the fact of the matter is that muskox hunting is not for the faint-hearted or those looking for any easy vacation.

The time of year when the hide is best, the days long, and traveling the easiest, is during March and April. With the proper clothing and equipment, you travel with your Inuit guide, camping out in the hunting area. This is real hunting, not a harvest situation, and while people will tell you it is cold and rough, they also describe it as one of the finest hunts, if not *the* finest they have experienced anywhere.

Arriving in the central Arctic community of Coppermine, guests are met by my son Martin. After briefing, obtaining licenses, and being fitted out with traditional Inuit caribou-skin clothing, the guests are introduced to their guides. In very short order they are on the trail, heading out on the tundra, or in some cases across the frozen ocean. For someone having left Los Angeles less than a day ago, it is both a climate and a culture shock, for certain.

Natalie was being guided by Gerry Atatahak, one of our most skilled Inuit guides. They would travel with George Anablak, and his guest, Leo Neules, who was hunting with a bow. George is one of the "old-timers" who spends most of the year hunting and trapping from his outpost camp on Victoria Island. On this trip they were headed for the Island, to an area approximately 125 miles out from Coppermine. Of the two types of muskox recognized by the record book, we hunt the Greenland on Victoria and the barren ground in four separate areas on the continent.

Like all the hunters, Natalie was being hauled on a large sled called a *komatik*, behind the guide's snow machine. Properly dressed and in a padded and shielded box, one might describe the experience as "survivable." We have tried every option, but we have never been able to make it actually "comfortable." The guides stop frequently to make sure the guest is not freezing and to offer a hot drink. Then it's back into the box and on the trail again.

Traveling alone in good conditions, the guides might average thirty miles an hour or more; traveling with guests, ten miles per hour is considered fair time. It depends upon how rough the trail may be, the weather, the stamina of the guests and the number of breakdowns. This type of travel and the loads being hauled guarantee that there will be equipment failures. The wonder is that they are not more frequent. The skill of the guides in overcoming problems as a matter of course and carrying on with the hunt never ceases to impress the visitor to our country.

Everything required for safe and relatively comfortable camping, is carried on the *komatik*, along with the necessary fuel, food, and the guest's personal equipment. When stopping for the night, the tent goes up, tarps and caribou skins go down, sleeping bags on top, the stove is pumped up, and soon the guest is enjoying a hot meal prior to turning in. One is encouraged not to drink ten cups of tea before bedtime. It is a long way to the bathroom.

While amazing to the visitor, camping in all kinds of Arctic conditions is taken for granted by the guides. This is how they spend a major portion of their lives, guiding, hunting, fishing, and trapping. Their knowledge of the land, age-old traditional skill and a mixture of old and high-tech modern equipment make it all possible.

Muskox hunts are estimated at a week's duration; in Natalie's case it was a bit shorter. Evening of the third day, Gerry was on the radio. Both Natalie and Leo had been successful, and weather permitting, they would be back in town in another day. We were off to a good start with a record-book class Greenland muskox Natalie's first northern trophy.

Our schedule called for Natalie to be back up north in August of '91, to start on the hunts for caribou. Unfortunately, due to a poisonous bite of some kind acquired on a trip to the South Pacific, Natalie had to cancel one section of the plan. This would throw our schedule out of gear and make it impossible to accomplish all the hunts during the 1991 season. She would, however, be able to make the eastern hunts for the Quebec and Newfoundland species. The rest would have to carry over to 1992.

Late in September, accompanied by Pat Ackerman, our western representative, and a group of other clients, Natalie flew to northern Quebec for the Quebec-Labrador caribou.

Back in the early 1980s we had helped the Inuit of George River establish caribou camps on the shores of Ungava Bay. Although nothing will ever equal those early years, when less than one hundred sport hunters annually hunted the Torngat Mountain herd compared to the rest of Quebec, this area still offers good hunting.

Flying east from Kuujjuaq, clear up nearly to the tip of Labrador, the group would hunt with my friends, the family of Sandy Annanack. Dead at a tragically early age, Sandy was an outstanding individual. When in his teens, during the years when the area was still remote and relatively unknown to southern people, Sandy gained his first experience in guiding while working for Bob May and Bill Littleford, who established the very first sporting camps in Ungava. A true Inuit entrepreneur of the late twentieth century, working in partnership with southern friends, Sandy acquired and developed Helen Falls, one of the finest Atlantic salmon fishing camps in Canada.

My son Martin and I, working with the Federation of Cooperatives of Northern Quebec, had helped establish the highly successful caribou camp at Akuliak, and worked with Sandy at Helen Falls. As Akuliak was constantly booked to 100 percent capacity, it was decided to open another limited access camp even farther up the coast at a location locally known as Eetjwootuk. When completed, the camp became known by the more prosaic name of Weymouth Inlet. From this camp, Natalie and the group would hunt the legendary bulls of the Torngat Mountains.

At Weymouth, the hunting is by boat travel around the islands and inlets of Ungava Bay, with two Inuit guides taking care of two hunters in large freighter canoes. As at any location on this coast, tides range to an unbelievable forty feet and more, so travel must be timed accordingly. The scenery is magnificent, and hunting usually the same. Natalie was successful in taking two bulls, one of them a great representative of the Quebec-Labrador species.

With a half-day layover in Montreal, our adventurer was off to the wilds of Newfoundland in pursuit of the woodland caribou and eastern Canada moose. Here she would be hunting in a fly-in camp, with people I had been working with for many years. My brother Gary, nearly a lifelong resident of the Island, would accompany her, not because Natalie needed any baby-sitting, but as a translator of the fact that, although a lady, she was one of the most highly experienced hunters to ever land in Newfoundland.

I had warned her that this would be the most difficult hunt in the series, for a number of reasons, including weather and terrain. With the luck one sometimes encounters while hunting, the day after she settled for just a fair representative caribou, they encountered one which would have stretched the top of the book. Never a whiner, Natalie went on and collected her moose, and when I questioned her about just how hard the hunt had been, her only comment was, "Fred, when someone books a series of hunts with you, don't ever send them to Newfoundland first."

This concluded the 1991 season; we would meet again at the winter conventions in the States, and schedule the remainder of her hunts for her other North American species.

On the second week of September, 1992, Natalie was back with us once more, this time at our caribou camp on Courageous Lake, 150 miles north of Yellowknife. She would be hunting the central Canadian barren ground caribou. Courageous hosts ten guests at a time, on an immense lake system situated at right angles to the migration route of the Bathurst caribou herd. Hunting here is by boat travel, with one Inuit guide looking after two hunters. In this case, Natalie would be teamed up with Bill McClure from Pittsburgh, and guided by her old friend, Gerry Atatahak from Coppermine.

Lining up at the sighting in bench on the day of arrival, I am always an amused observer of the gentlemen sportsmen when a lady comes up to the table. Most of the time their expressions of

127

skepticism change to respect when the results come back from the target tenders. This time was no exception. With her one and only companion .300 Weatherby, Natalie put any skeptic's mind to rest as to whether or not she would hit the caribou.

Courageous Lake is the camp in which my wife, Irene, and I spend the season. With permanent buildings and most of the civilized amenities, except of course TV or telephones, it is a relatively comfortable place to spend a week in the middle of the barren lands. While one rarely encounters those mass migration herds of thousands so dear to the movie industry, there are usually plenty of caribou to make outstanding hunting. This week was no exception. With beautiful autumn weather, the land in full color and a great group of guests, it was the kind of week everyone enjoys. Natalie, holding off for "just the one I wanted," took an extremely good trophy herself, and enjoyed Bill's success in bagging a good caribou and a wolverine.

Leaving Courageous Lake on 12 September, Natalie would fly to Yellowknife, then to Norman Wells, where she would meet Stan Simpson and fly into the MacKenzie Mountains for her mountain caribou. Winter was coming to the mountains early this year and Stan was near the end of his long season. Hunting by horseback, and making an impossibly long shot, Natalie filled her tag, thus leaving only one of the six species of caribou to be hunted later in the fall.

The next leg of the journey was from Norman Wells to Yellowknife, to Edmonton, to Vancouver, to Smithers, B.C. Again, with winter closing in fast and making hunting tough, my friend Dennis Yost was able to lead her to a decent western Canada moose, just before closing down for the season.

Heading home to California for a well-deserved rest, Natalie could now repack her gear and winterize her Weatherby for one last swing into the Arctic.

It had been a busy fall season for Martin and me as well. Since closing the caribou camps, Courageous and Lac de Gras, we had cleaned up the bookwork in Yellowknife and driven a truck down the road to Vancouver. Within two days I was back in Cambridge Bay, a week later back to Vancouver. Never one to hang around anywhere too long, I was back and forth across Canada, then back to Yellowknife in late October gearing up for the Victoria Island hunts for muskox and Arctic Islands, or Peary's caribou.

The Peary's caribou, so scarce as to be endangered on some of the High Arctic Islands, reside in great numbers in areas of the Central Arctic where good game management and quotas are in place. There are various areas and methods of travel, all of which we have tried over the years. Most have had serious drawbacks. One can hunt in early autumn, when the animals are in velvet, by boat and ATV and hiking. Considering that winter comes *early*, that high winds and ice are always considerations in August and September, plus the difficulty of any overland travel, this is one of the options we discontinued as results were less than outstanding.

There is a relatively short period, late October and early November, after the ice in the lakes becomes strong enough to permit safe snowmobile travel, before the shortening days and bad weather make it impossible, and before the bulls shed their antlers. As I tell people, there is *no* easy time to hunt Peary's Caribou, but when all is considered, this is the *best*.

Working out of our permanent base in Coppermine, we fly small parties into two outpost camps on Victoria Island. At Richardson Island, about 125 miles northeast, Charlie Bolt and his family live nearly year-round, trapping and guiding and fishing commercially for Arctic char. About the same distance from Coppermine, to the northwest, Jack Atatahak and his wife, Naomi, live in their camp at Read Island. Both places have cabins to accommodate the hunters and airstrips that can be used by Twin Otters on wheels or wheel-skis. Nothing is easy at this time of year and no one can control the weather, but this beats anything that we know of for fall hunts for Greenland muskox, or Arctic Islands caribou.

On a wintry 30 October, Martin and I were back in Coppermine getting ready. Charlie and Jack were with their families on Victoria. Fishing had been good, and each had a load ready to come back to town. They had marked out their strips and were geared up to await the hunters. From Coppermine, Gerry would be going over to help Jack at Read Island; McCauley and Jorgen would be working with Charlie at Richardson.

November 2nd, the Twin Otter arrived from Yellowknife, in the middle of a very short day, at about minus thirty degrees but clear. Gear, food and fuel were loaded, along with the extra snowmobiles. Mr. and Mrs. Hugh Beavers, Natalie, and the guides, were soon on their way across the gulf. Darkness comes early in November this far north of the Circle; the Twin Otter arrived back at Coppermine in the dark, in plenty of time for supper.

November 3rd, we had light enough to fly by 10 A.M., another clear, cold day. Gerry Atatahak, with guests Frank and Audrey Murtland and all their assorted gear, were landed safely on a frozen lake near Jack's outpost, at Read Island.

A check of my radio log shows contact with Richardson Island late that evening. Natalie had taken a good Arctic Islands caribou the very first day of her hunt. At the other camp, muskox had been encountered, but they would have to travel farther afield for caribou.

Over the next three days, despite steadily deteriorating weather and some long trips tenting out, both camps report that all tags have been filled, for both caribou and muskox. The parties are ready to be brought in, if we can just get the weather to work with us.

On 7 November, we awake to very unsettled weather after heavy blowing snow all night. By the time the plane is dug out, cleaned off and fueled up, it is approaching noon. Initially intending to grab the first party from Richardson, bring them back to Coppermine, then refuel and go pick up the party at the other camp, we could see that in a short day and with the weather coming down again, it would be better to fill all the fuel tanks on the plane, to save time later. Leaving Martin to close our base in town, I decide to jump on the plane to help speed up the loading at the other end.

Crossing Coronation Gulf at low altitude, we could see that while nearly all frozen over, it would be a few weeks yet before it would be safe to travel by snow machine. Probably everyone would be back to town in time for Christmas. As we approached the coast, abruptly we were into the first stages of a real blizzard. I once again marvel at the cool professionalism of northern pilots, setting down through the blowing snow.

Bouncing along to a stop, in wheel-deep snow, for the millionth time I wonder as well at the versatility of the De Havilland Twin Otter aircraft. Despite the increasing blizzard, I am relieved to see that everyone is here and ready to go. Hugh and Sara are huddled together leaning into the storm; Natalie, relaxed as usual, cigarillo in hand, is stuffed into a box on one of the sleds. In the Arctic, warm friendships are made that will be long remembered and fond are the farewells as Charlie's wife, Marion, parts with her guests of the past week.

As we clear the coast and gradually climb out of the driving snow, it begins to look as if we will enjoy a break in the storm system. We'll need a couple of hours of decent weather and a bit of luck besides. With daylight hours so short, by the time we drop this load in Coppermine, fly to Read and bring that party over, then load everything up again, it will be dark. If this all works out, the final leg of the journey to Yellowknife, where the airport is equipped with all navigational aids, will be no problem, dark or not.

All plans in the Arctic are subject to change. Approaching the mainland coast, the lead-colored, thousand-foot ceiling begins to squeeze down on our heads, until once again we are engulfed in blinding snow. This, I can see, is going to get interesting. I learned long ago that the people behind the bulkhead do not drive the airplane, so one may as well relax. I'm sure the pilots know that in Coppermine, an off-center or short touchdown will put us in either the town dump or the sewage disposal station.

Three missed approaches later, rewarded by only one fleeting broken glimpse of the runway at forty feet, and we have to climb out. Visibility limited by snow is one thing, but now with mixed freezing precipitation covering the cockpit windows, it has become impossible. Time for decisions and the options are limited. Leveling out on top, the pilot gestures me up to the front end. "We've checked with Air Services by radio; Cambridge and Hollman are closed, Lupin is socked in solid as well. If anyone gets curious, you can tell them we are going on to Yellowknife."

Sounds fine to me, considering the alternatives. I settle back for the two-hour-plus journey, thankful that Martin is back in Coppermine to take care of the other group at Read Island. I am extremely thankful as well for the fact that we had topped up every fuel tank on the plane when we had the chance. I'm hopeful as well that we encounter a layer of warmer air and clear sky to reduce the load of ice that persists in growing on the wing surfaces.

The lights of Yellowknife have never looked better as we descend straight in through scattered light snow, touchdown smoothly and taxi over to the Ptarmigan Airways terminal. It will take another couple of days and a break in the weather before I see Martin and his group, but for Natalie the trip is over.

A few hours later I see Natalie, still in her Arctic gear, aboard a late-night southbound jet, the first step on her way back to sunny California.

It is difficult to express, in a hug and a handshake, one's total feelings at the end of a two-year adventure. Sufficient, I guess, that we both knew that we had enjoyed the association.

I am sure there are many other guides around the world who will join me in a toast to Natalie Eckel, a remarkable lady and one hell of a hunter.

HEADED NORTH

If you believe in predestination, I guess I was always bound for the North. Being born in the middle of the Great Depression, on a "stump ranch" in the eastern Canadian province of New Brunswick provided the proper background for a career in the out-of-doors.

My paternal grandfather, with three of his brothers, had come out from England around the turn of the century. There are pictures of him working in the lumber woods and on stream drives on the Tobique River. Members of my mother's family had been in Canada for many generations, including one branch which had been here literally forever. On both sides of the family, our people had been woodsmen, hunters and guides, on the Saint John and Tobique River watersheds.

Some, on the English side, had migrated to the far western plains of Saskatchewan and to what later became the Northwest Territories. As a young man, my father journeyed halfway across Canada to work for two of his uncles who were homesteading farms on the prairie. He came back with stories of another uncle, who had become a trapper, farther north on the edge of the Barren Lands.

By the time I was born, Dad had settled down and was working at mixed farming, in what could only be compared to a Mississippi sharecropper arrangement. He was determined that if back-breaking labor could ensure success, we would never starve to death, worldwide depression or not.

During the first year of my life, times not being hard enough, the house burned to the ground and we had to move into a small windowless building, which had previously been used to store grain. While others in the county may have been even less fortunate, we literally "didn't have a pot to piss in nor a window to throw it out of."

Surviving the Great Depression was of course easier for people living in the country than it must have been for the poor unfortunates on the bread lines in the cities. However, although we were almost self-sufficient, cash money was still needed occasionally. I can remember Dad saying years later that raising chickens to lay eggs, which had to be sold for eight cents a dozen, after walking four miles to town, was not really showing a profit. It barely covered the depreciation on the old hen's anatomy.

Like all country boys, my earliest memories revolve around working with animal critters. I can hardly forget the occasion when the Old Man, attempting to shoe a half-broken stud horse, was kicked in the groin with such effect that, after crawling into the house, he could only roll in agony on the kitchen floor. It was so seldom that he had the time to play around at my level. I rolled around with him, deciding for some reason that it was hilariously funny. Probably unappreciated, come to think of it.

Every bush farm in those days had a dog, mostly of indeterminate breed, the greatest boast not being pedigree but the elusive virtue of being "good with cows." The first of a long line of such dogs, as I recall, was named "Tippy," some sort of spotted dog. He managed to get himself run over by the mail man. He probably wasn't too swift of foot, or intellect either. Mail at that time was delivered by horse and wagon.

Living in the country certainly meant that my younger brother, Gary, and I enjoyed more freedom than can ever be found in urban surroundings. When our father, along with the other adult males of the family, enlisted in 1939 to go fight the Germans, in the second "War To End All Wars" I became temporarily the "man of the house," to my mind at least.

Besides the badly needed few dollars a month involved, Dad always said it was the first chance he ever had to own a suit of which the pants and jacket were the same color.

As for my brother and I, hunting, fishing, and running traplines took most of our attention. Rifles and axes became tools of the trade. Activities like keeping the wood box filled and feeding the chickens weren't resented too much as I remember; in those days everyone expected to work.

Going to school was another matter. All the grownups used to say, "You will look back on it as the best years of your life." To which I can say with no hesitation whatsoever, "Bullshit!" I hated every minute of it then and still do fifty years later.

Thankfully, someone, somewhere along the line, instilled in me a desire to read everything I could get my hands on, especially anything dealing with bush skills and northern expeditions. Beyond that, I could have gladly skipped any further exposure to the educational system of the day.

Our involvement with town and the "townies" was for the most part, far from a pleasant experience. Coming from "the country," we were viewed as being totally alien. If we went to a cowboy movie on a Saturday night, we soon learned to ally ourselves with the Maliseet Indians from the nearby Reserve, or end up having the hell beaten out of us by the little darlings of the urban intelligentsia. In some respects, it set the pattern for the rest of my life.

With the end of the war, Dad was back home again. Both he and his brother Charlie suffered wounds which left them partially disabled for years to come, but at least they came home alive as many others from our area did not.

I struggled on through the school system, resigned to it as an inescapable evil. While the teacher tried to choke the history of ancient English kings down our throats, I found escape in the county library, where much more interesting fare was available. Although up to that time apparently nothing had ever been written regarding our own Canadian history, I was able to devour tales of various Arctic expeditions as related by American or British sources.

Aside from the library, the out-of-doors supplied the major portion of my education. Seasonal work on neighboring farms, in the lumber woods, on the trapline, and guiding brought in sufficient spending money to support a modest social life. Guiding fishermen and deer hunters was of necessity "unofficial" at this time, as I was a few years short of the legal age for registration.

Partway through high school, with no interest in anything except the woods and a young lady who would later become my wife, I decided that having already learned how to work, it was time to quit wasting everyone's time and get on with life.

In those happy post-war years, there were jobs for anyone who wanted one. Driving truck, working in the woods, and guiding—all of which I was adept at—paid more than the wages of the school teachers who were attempting to convince me that higher education should be my goal. With a pretty girl, enough money to run a truck, over-the-border trips for Yankee beer and the drive-in theater, what more could anyone ask for? Unfortunately all good times come to an end.

Somewhere on the other side of the world, in a place called Korea, a new war was in progress. Canadians were fighting and dying in the frozen hills of that faraway land, for reasons that no one has ever been able to explain to me to this day. On a trip to town one Saturday night I saw a poster on a telephone pole. "Join the Special Korean Force," it said. "Veterans and recruits, seventeen to forty-five, your Country needs you." Powerful stuff when you're just past seventeen and looking for what we now cynically call "adventure."

Great career move, as it turned out. In a burst of misplaced patriotism, helped along with a heavy ration of Moosehead beer, a bunch of us, including my soon-to-be brother-in-law George, were off to the provincial capital to volunteer. Things from then on happened swiftly. While still hungover, I found myself standing in front of a picture of the Queen, with my hand on the Bible and no turning back.

My friends were posted to a rifle regiment, but I, the loner as usual, not being content with just any old soldier job, felt compelled to volunteer for the Airborne Infantry. About that time, a movie starring Alan Ladd as "The Paratrooper," made it look like fun and games, just the sort of thing I always wanted to do.

This dream was soon shattered by six weeks of intensive and brutal basic infantry training, combat training and parade square bashing. As a reward, the survivors then proceeded to jump school, for a month of even more concentrated torture.

Till this day I am amazed by the fact that people actually enjoy throwing themselves out of airplanes, and even pay for the privilege. For myself, I can only admit to being scared absolutely shitless. However, at the time, we were all convinced that going out the door was infinitely preferable to the alternatives.

Finally, about the time we were fully trained and pumped full of "gung-ho," came the word that all overseas drafts were on hold as it looked likely that a cease fire would be signed.

For those involved at the front it naturally came as a welcome relief. Just as natural, I suppose, was the feeling of letdown experienced by the ones all geared up to go, but now standing down until next time.

Quite some time later I graduated with a degree in shining boots, jumping out of airplanes, and cleaning weapons. Although I didn't figure to run a shoeshine stand, and would never again be stupid enough to jump without being pushed, learning fifty different ways to clean a rifle has occasionally come in handy.

Military service did have one benefit. After a year of civilian life guiding and driving a truck, I was recruited into a scheme whereby the Canadian government would send me to school to expand my military skill in communications. The contract stipulated that one was bound to accept employment anywhere in the world upon successful completion.

The financial incentive that went with it gave me 150 dollars a month to at least partially support my wife, Irene, and our two daughters, Cindy and Janice.

The training was abbreviated and intensive; the end result was to qualify for a Radio Certificate, which would allow me to act as Radio Officer on foreign-going ships, as well as mobile equipment of every sort.

This generous program, like everything else connected with government, had a purpose behind it. We were not long in finding out that while the opportunity might someday arise to sail to exotic south seas destinations, the immediate aim was to meet the demand for manpower in the Canadian Arctic.

Up until this time in history, although Canada had long claimed ownership of the Arctic, it was far from being recognized officially by a number of other nations. Everything on the maps north of Toronto, was colored in red, denoting the fact that it was supposedly part of the British Empire. However, various people, from the American and Russian military to the Greenlanders who crossed over to Ellesmere Island and hunted the island's muskox to near extinction, were not too impressed by Ottawa's claim to this immense area.

Aside from widely scattered tiny settlements, mainly gathered around a trading post, mission, or sometimes an R.C.M.P. station, there wasn't too much Canadian presence. The annual summer re-supply ship, along with the hospital ship *C.D. Howe* and the icebreakers that opened the navigational routes across Hudson Bay to allow the grain ships to reach Churchill, provided most of the "official" Canadian involvement.

No wonder everyone, except the Inuit who had lived there for ages and knew better, thought the country was open and up for grabs.

The majority of Inuit at this time still lived as traditional Arctic hunters, although a few found employment around the trading posts and as guides and interpreters for the Mounties who fulfilled just about every official function. In order to emphasize Canadian sovereignty, contribute to the defense of the hemisphere, and carry out scientific exploration, Canada was about to greatly expand activities in the North.

While many of my fellow students on the communications course were plotting ways in which to avoid going to the Arctic, there's no way I could have been kept from it.

Upon graduation from an additional course, this one in meteorology, the first northern assignment was not long coming.

Canada was preparing for participation in what would come to be known as the International Geophysical Year. This would mean the establishment of programs covering a wide range of scientific observations, most of which would be based out of existing radio and weather stations across the North.

My first posting, to a station right in the middle of the wilderness of Labrador, began a series of jobs that, over the next few years, covered most of the Arctic, and led to even more interesting assignments in various parts of the world.

NEVER THE SAME AGAIN!

We were drinking tea and poking sticks into the fire one fall day a couple of years ago, as we waited for the last of the deer hunters to come in off the ridge for lunch. One of the guests made the mistake of saying, "My, what a wonderful area you have here." It was sufficient to set Coleman, the other guide, and me off. "Man you should have seen this country years ago. Now it's all cut down. There are roads everywhere, and it's harder every year to find a little corner where we can hunt by ourselves."

I have been guiding over thirty-five years, and Coleman McDougall, senior guide and longtime friend, has been at it since about the time I was born. Having seen the country as it used to be, he could only agree. "Yes, this country is sure getting used up. It will never be the same again."

Lying in bed that night, thinking of how our Tobique River area, in northwestern New Brunswick, is in some ways a microcosm of what had happened to hunting elsewhere, I came at last to some conclusions.

If one could look back a million years, to the days of the saber-toothed tiger, I have no doubt you would see a bunch of cavemen, sitting around the fire, swapping lies about their hunting trips of days gone by. And I am equally sure that at least one of them would toss the bone he had been gnawing on into the fire, wipe his hands in his armpits, and sigh, "Boys, she's all gone to hell. We've seen the last of it. This country will never be the same again."

The history of guiding visitors to the interior highlands of New Brunswick is as long as the history of European settlement on the continent. First the French and then the British, military officers and explorers, pushed up the watershed to explore, map, and wonder at the endless bounty of the forest resources.

The original inhabitants had roamed the country from time immemorial, so they aided the visitors on their journeys. This, in time, of course led to changes. Agents of the king surveyed the seemingly infinite expanse of timber available, and soon the lofty pines, destined as masts for the Royal Navy, went floating down the river. One can easily imagine the Indians watching in awe as great rafts of lumber cleared the mouth of the Tobique for the long trip down to the head of tide and the shipyards of Saint John. While I don't speak the Malecite language, I am sure they said something like, "What are these crazy white men up to? This country will never be the same again."

The first written mention of my own family becoming involved with the area, was around the turn of the century, although some rumors would predate this by a few thousand years. A faded photo exists of my father's father as a young man, working for one of the lumber barons of the day, when logs were cut all winter and floated down to the mills in the spring. The logging camp and stream driving songs of the day are all reminiscent of the fact that things will "never be the same again."

My mother's mother, brought up along the river, had an uncle who for years searched the wilderness for a locally famous lost gold mine. Some say he found it, but if he did, he evidently managed to lose it again. At least none of it came down to my generation. I am sure that as lumbering continued and farming gained a foothold, the old guys sat around spitting into the fire, and one of them was bound to have said, "Boys, she's over with. This country will never be the same again."

My father, born in a settlement at the mouth of the river, worked as a young man on the first telephone line to come into the area. He later fished and hunted to the headwaters of the river. Many times, as we looked at pictures of bygone days, he would tell us, "You should have seen the Tobique country when I was young. It will probably never be the same again."

From my grandfather's time to my own, the area's involvement in the "sporting business" went through many changes. Modern transportation made for easier access, and social and economic changes in the rest of the world had their impact as well.

Throughout a period of fifty years, an outfitting business evolved that catered mostly to the wealthy visiting sportsmen from the United States. Guides, cooks, packers, and wardens were inhabitants of the area, and they also worked in the logging camps and stream drives during parts of the year. The country was to a great degree still untouched; travel was still primarily by river and by tote teams on primitive trails. The big game pursued included woodland caribou, moose, and bear. Only later did the whitetail work its way north to become the main trophy animal.

Large fishing clubs, made up of wealthy nonresidents, controlled the angling rights for Atlantic salmon, their members enjoying the autumn hunting as well. This could probably be termed the "Golden Age of Outfitting" in New Brunswick from everyone's standpoint. For the guest it was the joy of hunting and fishing in a virtually untouched wilderness, and for the people of the area there were jobs. Nearly everyone of that era held loyalty to one or the other of the big outfitters or the clubs. Although some of these operations lasted right up until my personal involvement began in the late 1950s, most of them had declined with World War II. I have always considered it an honor to have worked with many of the guides of that era. Sadly, many of them are gone now. With their passing, times on the Tobique will indeed "never be the same again."

Although born fifty miles from the mouth of the river, my early interest was always in the woods and streams. For about a decade I worked away from home as a radio operator and sometimes guide, on scientific expeditions to parts of the world as diverse as the High Arctic and the Caribbean, returning to guide and trap on the Tobique between trips. Around the mid '60s, with a young family, my wife and I decided to forsake a steady paycheck and return to what I really loved, working for myself in the guiding business.

At that time, while the wilderness certainly wasn't the same as in the past, it still had plenty to offer. Outfitting had shifted to a more community-based operation, but there were still many areas inaccessible except by river or by walking the ridges. With lots of hard work, worry, and the help of a few steadfast friends, we built up a business second to none in the East. We catered to the rich, the famous, and many just plain good people. Relying heavily upon bear and deer hunting, we extended our season with the more glamorous sports of salmon angling and bird shooting.

The following fifteen years or so I look back upon as the "good old days" of my own generation. Changes due to lumbering, increasing pressure from resident hunters and various government policies, brought this era to an end around the early 1980s.

Where once we roamed with relative freedom, people living locally have been forced by the hunting practices of residents from other parts of the province to put up the dreaded "No Hunting" signs. Woodcock hunting, in anything resembling quality, is a thing of the past, and deer hunting isn't very far behind it. There remains some bear hunting, in ever smaller and more remote areas, mainly because New Brunswick residents have not shown much interest as yet. The famous Atlantic salmon fishing has declined to a shadow of what it used to be. One can almost imagine the ghosts of an old-time guide and a club member, sitting out in the Forks Pool, and see the dismay on their faces when they are confronted with the situation as it exists today. What would they think of a river that is dammed from the headwaters to the tidewater, where fish are trucked up and dumped in, to be then fought over by the native food fishery, the resident angling association, and the occasional visiting sport? What a pale comparison to the years of freedom and plenty.

Some of our old parties, from all parts of the continent, still contact me occasionally. Remembering their enjoyment of the fishing, the hunting, the comradeship with the guides, and the beauty of the country, some of them ask if we could host a "return to Tobique" for old times' sake. I can only point out the obvious, that the woods are gone, the game is gone, the guides they knew and admired are gone, and the country for damn sure will never be the same again.

As I lay there that night, thinking all of this over and feeling sorry for myself, a few other more hopeful thoughts began to intrude. I remember that in order to make a living as an outfitting family, we have had to move into new and exciting places in the north and west. "New?" I wondered. "Unspoiled?" Then it began to dawn on me that "wilderness" is in the eye of the beholder. The most remote corners of the world have been the home of someone or other for a million years. Everyone from the caveman to Coleman and I have seen a lot of changes and probably said the same thing about these changes.

And again I thought, even in New Brunswick with its dammed up rivers, its cut-over forest, its mistaken government policy that has confused "outfitting" with "tourism;" maybe we can still salvage something. Perhaps even here, our guests coming from places that have long been buried in concrete and pollution, will see it with bright new eyes and think it is a "wilderness."

Although this time, irreversible damage to the environment and to the guiding industry guarantees that we have seen the last of the good old days, there may be a chance for at least some semblance of the sporting business to exist. Perhaps, to some degree, our sons and their sons may carry on the Tobique tradition of guiding visitors to the wilderness.

I pray that someday, guides may sit around the fire and recall with fondness that Coleman and I, way back in 1989, figured that it was "all gone to hell and would never be the same again."

THE WHISKEY EXPERT

W e meet a lot of interesting people in the hunting business. One of them we remember as the "Whiskey Expert from California."

Most hunters that I know appreciate the occasional toddy. Certainly, a drink around the campfire at the end of a pleasant day afield adds to the enjoyment and camaraderie, for which many of us journey to the far places. However, in hunting camps, where safety is a prime consideration, the use of spirits must of necessity be governed by some rules. When one is a couple of hundred miles out in the Barren Lands, in case of an accident dialing 911 is definitely *not* an option. Perhaps in this regard I have a reputation for being a bit "hard assed," but will live with that image, rather than go down in history as the Genial Drunk who let the idiots kill themselves.

Having been a student of human nature as it applies to hunting camps, for a good many years, I have also noticed that the guest who plies the guides with booze, so as to be entertained by the antics of the simple rustics or the colorful natives, is usually the first to complain when things go amok. They are quite outraged when some fun-loving soul fires a couple of shots through the tent, or fails to show up at the crack of dawn, bright-eyed and bushy-tailed. We therefore have a few simple rules regarding social intercourse between guests and staff when booze is involved.

As with all rules, of course, there are bound to be some people who insist on stretching them. Such was the gentleman from California, who professed to be the world's foremost authority on whiskey, bourbon whiskey in particular. A guest at one of our Arctic caribou camps, he arrived with a very pleasant group of people, and along with everyone else had received a copy of the camp information, including our policy on giving liquor to the staff.

In this particular camp, all of the guides are Inuit from the Central Arctic. They are excellent guides, combining the skills of a people who live on the land, with years of experience in our employ guiding southern guests on trophy-hunting expeditions. Like guides everywhere, myself included, they do enjoy a drink, and indeed a beer ration is supplied when space on the aircraft allows. Beyond that, all understand that the "hard stuff" is off limits until we are clear of the camps. Like people of any culture, however, they are susceptible to persuasion.

We were only into the hunt a couple of days when it became apparent to myself and Dan, the camp taxidermist, that the Whiskey Expert not only left his booze lying around prominently, but didn't appear to believe in our camp policy of not treating the help. Dan had already quietly advised him that we would be happier if he didn't insist upon taking his guide into the tent before supper every evening to "treat" him.

Evidently being a Whiskey Expert, to the point that he said he could identify fifty brands, by taste alone, blindfolded, he assumed that everyone else had his practice in handling it. He was also, I suspected, one of the type who would work the guide to death, bribe him with booze, and leave him with no gratuities beyond the empty bottle and a hangover.

Needless to say, I was not too happy with the situation, but thinking that perhaps a friendly chat would remedy the matter, I attempted to keep a happy face on things. One should, I suppose, give the guest the benefit of the doubt, before calling in an airplane to get rid of him. I tried to convince him that the guides were all family men, they needed the job and their end of the season bonus, and thus if any rewards were in order, a cash tip at the end of the trip would do them more good than a smash of bourbon before supper. All to no avail.

One must realize here that the guide involved was one of my best employees, a good friend, one who ordinarily was no problem whatever. Now he was sort of stuck in the middle. To the best of his ability, he was trying to please the guest, while at the same time not letting me down. Though technically stretching the camp rules, he was responsible enough to have just one, say, "Thanks, I'll see you in the morning" and let it go at that. He certainly didn't want to get himself in a mess, let us down and lose his season's bonus.

Dan the Taxidermist was probably even more upset about the situation than I was. As a special friend of the guide, he felt that the Whiskey Expert was taking advantage of him, attempting to bribe him with booze to increase an already outstanding effort.

Finally came the last day of the hunt. Everyone had been successful in taking great caribou trophies, and were now out fishing and taking photographs. After the boat crews are all away from the beach, one of the duties of the taxidermist is to shut off the oil stoves in the guest cabins and sweep them out. In the middle of cleaning, Dan came up to the cook shack and when he left took a water glass with him, a fact which puzzled the cook enough to ask me what he was up to. I promptly forgot all about it, with plenty on my mind getting the next day's airplane charters organized by radio.

By late in the afternoon all of the parties were back in, everyone happy as clams at high tide. It had been an extremely successful week; many of the trophies taken would make the record books. Up at the taxidermist shack, as they all gathered around taking pictures of the caribou racks and comparing scores, I noticed the Whiskey Expert, with his usual glass of amber liquid in hand. I also noticed that Dan and the guides were throwing glances his way as they worked at padding the racks for shipping out the next day. One of the guests remarked, "Boys, it has been a wonderful trip, but I am glad we are heading out of here. It was really chilly out there today. Winter is on the way."

"Yup," says the Whiskey Expert, "I came in chilled right to the bone, but after a couple of damn good belts of this bourbon, I'm starting to thaw out pretty good."

For some reason, the guides drop what they are doing and sneak around behind the shack, where I find them doubled up with laughter. "Come on down to the cook shack," Dan blurts out, "I've got to tell you something, and I want the cook to hear. She will appreciate it."

Mystified, we gather in the kitchen. "OK Dan," I demanded, "what in hell is going on?"

"Well," he said, "you know how many times I told that old bastard to keep the booze to himself?"

"Yes, and so did I."

"Well, last night I asked him once again very politely if he would just simply take that jug of whiskey off the table and put it under his sleeping bag, where it wouldn't be tempting any of us."

"Yes," I said, "and I asked him to do the same thing, but I guess he isn't the kind who will listen."

"Well, sir, this morning," says Dan, "I took that water glass down to his cabin."

"Jesus, Dan, drinking the guests' booze is something I have never known you to do."

"No, no," says Dan, "I didn't drink a drop of it. I simply poured out a whole water glass, took it outside and poured it down that squirrel hole behind the tent."

"Weren't you afraid he would miss it was gone from the bottle?"

"Hell no," he says, "I just pissed the glass clear full and poured it back into the bottle, so it was right back up at the same level."

The cook and I can't believe what we are hearing.

"Yep," he goes on, "when the guide came in I told him about it, so he turned down the supper drink this time. Now I guess we've got a couple of things settled. The guides will be damn leery about accepting drinks from now on, and we know that that old son of a bitch isn't such a great Whiskey Expert after all."

148

THE HONORABLE MR. O'KING

We had a "sport" one time, a judge from upstate New York, whose letterhead named him as the "Honorable Francis O'King." He was booked to us by an agent in Pennsylvania. In his first letter he set himself out to be quite an expert on bear hunting, laid down his terms of reference and even warned us that if we didn't meet them, he would be terribly dissatisfied and raise all kinds of hell. I should have known at the time not to accept a guest with an attitude such as his, but I always want to give my fellow man the benefit of the doubt. I thought that maybe he was just a poor misled pilgrim and that a few words to the wise would set him straight. So I talked to him personally on the phone.

He was coming bear hunting in October and wished to bring his wife. I told him, "Mr. O'King, fall bear hunting is very uncertain; it can be good this year and bad the next. Many factors enter into it, few of which we can control. That is why our fall hunts are considered primarily deer hunts, but with a chance of bear if the conditions are right. However, should you want to try it, we'll do our best, we guarantee nothing, but we will hunt for you to the best of our ability. About bringing women to a hunting camp, I want you to know there is nothing for her to do here for entertainment. If the lady can hunt, that's fine. If she can sit in the camp and read a book that's fine, but if she expects to be entertained she's coming to the wrong place and that's that. Take it or leave it, I want no misunderstandings."

Mr. O'King straightened himself around, professed full understanding and seemed very happy with the arrangements as stated. So we booked him for mid-October, first week of the deer season with the understanding that we would try for a bear as well.

Throughout the spring and the summer we fed the bears on the ridges up in the Shanks Brook country. They were coming in good shape through June, July, August, through September. They were eating bait as fast as we could haul it right into October.

At last, on the appointed day, the guests started arriving. We had Mr. O'King and his wife, plus four other guests from Virginia. That evening I gave the welcoming pep talk. I told them bears have been baiting all summer long, but as this is a year with no beechnuts, they may go to den early. It was a grand fall for deer; as for bears, we may see some, we may not.

"We've made the preparations," I told them, "you've got good guides, you go on up there and hunt and we will see what happens." The boys from Virginia were happy with it all. Judge O'King took me aside out of earshot. "I want a key for my room in the lodge," he said, "I'm afraid my fellow sportsmen may steal us blind or come in and rape the wife." I told him in all honesty that in twenty-five years of operation we've never had to lock a room. To myself, I had doubts as to who would be attracted to his wife, but if he wanted a key we'd give him one.

He added, "By the way, my wife has nothing to do."

"I told you she would have nothing to do," I reminded him, "however, we have a vast library of sporting books and magazines and I'll give her the television from the house, and that's all we can do. We are not in the entertainment business, we are in the hunting business."

"One more thing," he went on, "I want you to know that I am a very serious hunter. I want to sit on a stand that no one has ever hunted on before."

I said, "All right, that can be done."

"Now another thing, I have boiled all my clothing in cedar boughs and hung them outside all summer. I don't want them contaminated. I will have to ride in a truck in which no one else is riding, I can't be anywhere that someone may have been smoking."

I said "Fine, we can do that. We'll send the other party in a different vehicle. I'll send you up on a truck all by yourself, but you'll have to put up with the driver. He doesn't smoke anyway.

We'll put you on a stand that no one has ever hunted, we'll give you one guide all to yourself, although you have paid for a two-on-one hunt."

Seeing as how I'd turned the entire operation upside down to suit him, apparently he was at last satisfied. That evening I heard him telling all the other people that he had researched my outfit very carefully, and he wanted them to know that they were in the best camp in New Brunswick, the best camp in the East, perhaps the best camp in the world.

So they went out on Monday. My son Martin, who grew up guiding bear hunters, was his guide. He hauled him up in splendid seclusion and put him on a totally virgin stand. Leaves had been falling on the ridge, they were a foot deep. His Honor said, "Where are the bear tracks?"

Martin explained, "They have made bear tracks through June, July, August, September, and the first two weeks of October. This is the third week of October. The leaves are on the ground, and the bear tracks are covered up. The bears have eaten three truckloads of bait here in the last six months, they are still coming here very regularly. Please just sit up there in the stand and hunt."

So Martin put him in the tree, set him up properly, wished him good luck, and departed. One hour later, Martin and the other guide, Coleman, were working down the ridge opposite, checking other stands. They could see ravens flying up over on the ridge where Mr. O'King was supposedly sitting still as a mouse. The ravens were carrying on, making a racket a mile from the bait, so the boys knew Mr. O'King was out of the stand and walking around. Can't hunt bears that way.

He came in that evening, very disgruntled. No one had seen a bear, but we'd seen enough bear sign to know that they were still active. We knew that when you don't see bears the first day, you simply go back out and hunt the next. The Virginia hunters were happy. They understand that, after all, as one of them said, "It's called hunting. Not shooting, but *hunting*."

The next morning after breakfast, Mr. O'King said he guessed they would go home. His wife had cabin fever after spending one day in camp, there was no entertainment, and the television had only one snowy channel. So they left.

We managed to finish the week without them. The other four hunters took two bear—one a nice one—and two deer. Not terrific, but far from a total disaster.

A month later I got a letter from the tourism department down in the capital. They said that Mr. O'King has filed a very nasty report about our hunting outfit. He said that we have stolen his money, we are very unfriendly people, we abused his wife, and he thinks we are just terrible, and something should be done.

A few days later, a guy in a suit drove into camp. Snivel Servant from the tourist department, wondered if the dog would bite, wondered if we have indoor washroom facilities. He had driven a couple hundred miles to interview me on the matter of the honorable Mr. O'King. Asked me very solemnly, "How will the minister of tourism reply to this gentleman and what are we prepared to do about this very serious complaint?"

I told him that he was free to say whatever he liked on behalf of the government, but if he was quoting me, I suggested he inform the gentleman as follows: "You have paid for a hunt. We have given you the opportunity to hunt. You chose not to hunt. If you are now looking for 'Sympathy,' you may find it in the dictionary, it is just between 'Shit' and 'Syphilis.' Amen."

He probably could have saved a long drive if he'd had brains enough to use the telephone.

CULTURE

(A GUIDE STORY)

*I*t seems like nowadays there are always government people sniffing around our part of the country, asking crazy questions and writing stuff down. Usually some ugly white woman who couldn't get laid down south, or some beard with a clipboard. I guess they figure that if they can't get rid of us country people any other way they are going to study us all to death. One of them the other day was telling me about how we should be keeping our quaint traditions and culture and stuff. Made me think about a guy from the States we met a few years ago.

Beatle Joe Coon and I were running fishing parties down the Right Hand Branch that summer. This was before they cut the woods all down, dried up the rivers and made the country all full of bulldozed roads.

Beatle Joe is a sort of faraway cousin of ours, on the Indian side of the family. Young guy then, about twenty or so, learning how to guide the tourists. I'd been at it quite awhile. My wife and I kind of adopted old Beatle there for a few years.

Beatle's mother, Martha, was a really nice lady. Big lady, not fat, just everything big. Big nose, big ass, biggest heart in all the world. Martha went up to Labrador to work on the air base at Goose Bay and married a Cree guy from Quebec, name of Joe Coon. Goose was a great place in those days—lots of jobs, lots of beer and excitement—but I guess Joe liked the bush better. He got drowned one summer, guiding Yankee salmon fishermen, and Martha came back to our part of the country. She brought along a kid named after his father. After a while she got to like rock-and-roll music, and she made his first name Beatle.

A couple years later, Martha's sister-in-law came down here to live after her mother died. Her name is Harriett. Really good worker, camp cook, runs a canoe like a man. Pretty, lots of boy-friends, but she won't marry any of the local guys; says she wants to travel. Both she and Beatle Joe were working for me that summer, good crew.

I'd been getting letters all winter from a guy named Jones, in Indiana, USA. He said he and his son wanted to come on a trip. Said his son was shy, needed to go places and meet people from other cultures. He didn't tell me that the kid was twenty years old, weighed two hundred, and ate like a wolverine. Anyway, we set up a trip for the middle of August.

Getting close to the time for the Jones party, I figure maybe we'll run from where the truck road crosses the head of the watershed, down into Trousers Lake and into the Right Hand Branch. Should be an easy enough trip, even with summer water, done it one time in two days with high spring water.

On the proper day the party arrives, one large older gentleman, one really big kid who hangs back when we shake hands,

and a whole truckload of gear. I look at Beatle, he kind of squirmed his shoulders, looked at the sky. Hell of a lot of weight for two canoes in August water. Beatle and I are good boat runners, and we've got big twenty-two footers, but we can't handle all this stuff. I had figured it out to charge Jones for two guides, now I see I'm losing money already. I'm going to need another canoe. Guess we better take Harriett; she can run one load and cook too.

My wife always puts on a good supper the night before we leave on trips. Beatle spears into the first pork chop when Jones says, "Hold it. I wish to say Grace." We all freeze while he talks to the Man in the Sky. Lots of stuff about traveling the sinful pathway and things, nothing much about pork chops and mashed potatoes. I sneak a look at Beatle, he sort of shivers and looks at his plate.

The old guy talks some more after supper, says how happy he is to share dinner with people of another culture. Tells us that the letters after his name mean that he is a Doctor of Divinity. I say, "Fine, always glad to have a doctor along on a trip in case someone gets cut with the ax or stuck with a fishhook."

He laughs, sort of like a fox barking, "No," he says, "I am a servant of the Lord. You may call me Reverend Jones. My son there is Junior." Junior wiggles his ears, looks at his plate and says nothing.

"Oh, yes," I'm beginning to catch on. "A priest. Me and B. J. are quite religious sometimes."

Beatle Joe speaks up for the first time. "Got a new priest down home, nice guy, gives away lots of cigarettes. The Mounties took away the old one for bothering small boys."

My wife looks really mad, Junior makes a strangling noise, the Reverend gets all red and swells up some. I can see this is going to be a really great trip.

In bed later on, I tell the wife, "Don't worry, everything will go okay. Just try and stall off the bill at the grocery store until I see if this Reverend Jones is going to pay us." Later on, I'm still lying awake, thinking about loads for three canoes, hoping it rains and raises the water. Don't know if the fish will bite, but maybe we can at least show Junior some culture.

Next morning we get away. In the really old days, people paddled and poled and lugged canoes for a couple weeks to get up to the headwaters. That summer we were doing it the easy way, bumming a ride on a flatbed logging truck, up to where the road crossed the head of Trousers Lake. Nowadays, you can drive anywhere all over that country in a Cadillac car, if you don't mind the dust from the logging trucks.

Riding out on top of the load of canoes and gear, Beatle and I are making plans. "I better take the Reverend," I tell him, "you take Junior in your canoe and the cook can run the extra gear." Nice day riding along, bit rough but not bad, not too dusty. Reverend Jones is really having a great time. The truck is noisy but he keeps hollering about being in God's great outdoors and jabbing the kid with his elbow, pointing out everything we pass along the way.

After a while, I'm sort of dozing along. Harriett is on her knees sorting out groceries in the grub boxes. Junior is paying less attention to his father than he is to sneaking peeks down her shirt when she bends over.

In the hottest part of the afternoon, in a great screeching of brakes and rattling of chains, we haul up at the lake. A few minutes of frantic effort unloading canoes and gear, then the driver waves and with a couple of hoots of the horn, he is off again, headed for a logging operation farther on.

Standing there in the middle of our scattered gear, a feeling of loneliness descends, along with clouds of black flies, as the lingering strings of dust drift away on a breeze. We are on our own now, for better or worse, with no way out except down the brook, water or not.

There's a funny thing about canoe running. The old guys are always telling about how they used to run all the small branches, how they used to pole from Riley Brook to Serpentine Lake in two days. I guess you could, in the days before the forest was all cut and the feeder streams dried up. I've never yet met anyone who could pole a canoe over dry land the way we have to nowadays.

I always figure the first night out is to shake down, make the right loads for the canoes, then the rest of the trip goes smooth as butter. Harriett is soon busy getting supper ready, while the rest of us make camp, putting up only one tent for the guests. It's going to be a nice night, the guides can sleep under the canoes, no problem. Reverend Jones is kind of worn out, the bugs and the heat have been hard on him, not much energy left for talking.

Junior is trying to help, mostly getting in the way. Tries to chop wood and drives my good sharp ax into the rocks. Jesus, time to show Junior some culture. I take him over where the old man can't hear and tell him what part of his anatomy I'm going to cut off if he touches my ax again. He sort of scrapes a hole in the ground with his boot, new cowboy hat down over his face, big tear rolls out from under the hat. "Oh, shit," I relent, "come on over here, and I'll show you how to cut wood without cutting off your feet and spoiling the only ax in the outfit."

Pretty soon he's piling up the wood as if we're staying all winter, trying out all the new words he heard me and Beatle saying. And making enough noise so the old man doesn't hear him.

After supper, while B. J. and I have a smoke, Junior tries helping Harriett wash the dishes. Upsets the dishwater into the fire. Funny thing, she doesn't swear and holler at him but gives him a big smile when he brings up another pail from the lake. Not so much as a "pick up your goddam feet," which is what she landed on Beatle the last time he did something awkward.

Sitting around the fire later, the old man perks up a bit and starts telling us stories about his life as a boy. About how hard he had to work on the farm in Indiana, half the time hungry, all the time with his old man hollering at him. Sounds like a pretty normal life to me and Beatle. I get up and shove the fire together a bit under the kettle to make a last cup of tea as he goes on with his story. Seems he got resigned to doing as his family wanted, got through school and afterward to another school to learn to be a preacher. Got married to the girl on the next farm over, only had one kid for some reason or other. Pretty well settled in, never saw much of the world except for the *National Geographic* magazine but always hungered for the chance to get away to far places and see people from other cultures. Now he's beginning to think that he has been too strict and demanding of his own son. He feels that exposure to people from other, freer cultures, will bring Junior out of his shell. Maybe.

We take it all in, but don't know what to say about all this, don't understand a whole hell of a lot about this culture stuff, but always have a rule that if the tourist wants to talk, we got lots of time to listen.

When everyone's turned in, I check to make sure the fire is safe, and sit down by the shore having a last smoke. Nice night, North Star sitting right up there where it should be, chilly enough to keep the midgets down, trout rising out on the water. Guess the Reverend is right, we might not have a hell of a lot of money, but we've sure got some great culture.

Next morning we're on our way down the long lake. Beautiful day, bit of a breeze in our face, just enough to keep us honest. Never in my life paddled down one of these lakes with the breeze behind me. Reverend Jones seems to be back in good voice again, keeps throwing himself around to face me while he tells me something or other every two minutes. Finally have to tell him to sit still or he'll be in swimming with me and all the gear. Behind me a little way I can hear "ker-chunk, ker-chunk, ker-chunk." Junior's trying to help paddle, beating on the gunwales every stroke, making Beatle fight to keep the canoe on course. He finally quits when old B. J. treats him to a burst of culture. We slide along, whisper of water along the canoe, few drops from a raised paddle, loons tuning up across the silence. These are the days that make memories for guides now gone or grown old. Now it's all gone to progress, to clear-cuts and roads, gone with the water, the fish and the game. No sense crying about it, I guess.

After noontime tea and biscuits, we slip through the small chute at the outlet of the lake, into the head of the River Dee. It's all downhill water from here to Nictau, the forks of our home river, Tobique. We'll take it easy, the water is still quite shallow, and our guests are enjoying themselves catching and releasing trout after trout. I have to remind them to keep a dozen for our dinner later. Although termed a "river," we are in a small rocky stream, alder banks close in, enough water to let us get in the canoes and snub along occasionally, but mostly wading and picking our way along.

Camping tonight at Shingle Gulch, it's another nice evening around the fire. I can't believe how the weather is holding up. By now things have sorted themselves out, everyone knows what they are doing, or supposed to be doing anyway.

Beatle has a couple of the canoes out and dried off to make a few patches. He always carries a bit of canvas, copper tacks, Ambroid cement, and part of an old silk stocking for small cuts. It's hard to get those silk stockings anymore, but they work the best. Some of the guides nowadays are going to fiberglass canoes. Some things are better about them, I guess. They stand a lot of wear all right but when it comes to hitting a sharp rock, the old canvas has a lot more give to it and doesn't cut so easily. Guess we'll stick with the canvas. We always seem to like the old stuff best, probably had a hell of a time to get the grandfathers out of the bark canoes and into the cedar and canvas ones. Those old bark canoes were really something, and all made from things right in the forest, just cedar wood and birch bark, spruce roots and pitch for the seams. Nowadays of course there isn't a birch tree left in the country big enough to get canoe bark from. No long, straight cedar either. No going back to that part of our culture, whether we wanted to or not.

I'm drying my boots and pants from wading half the day, talking to the Reverend about all these things. Doesn't take me too long to figure out that although he wants to see some country culture, he really thinks that we are lucky the white people got here in time with fiberglass and aluminum canoes, or we'd all be walking. He's also keeping a sharp eye on Junior and Harriett, giggling and rubbing elbows over the dishpan. They seem to be enjoying themselves anyway.

Next day is pretty much the same, the river still narrow and rocky. Alders right to the bank, hardly enough breeze to notice, the flies today are really getting at us. Around midmorning, I'm out of the canoe, sliding it down between some rocks, when all of a sudden, right in front of me, a calf moose bursts out of the bushes, clattering and slipping in panic across the brook.

I haven't had time to take this in when the cow steps partway out, halfway down the side of my canoe. I cringe under her blazing stare, not daring to move, nowhere to go anyway. Is she going to charge me or jump into and destroy the canoe? All of this goes through my mind in a split second. A grunting whine from the calf, "*naar*" breaks the spell. One last glare in my direction, the cow circles my canoe and rushes across the stream, disappearing into the alders. "Good-bye to you, old girl, I'd rather face an angry husband or the biggest grizzly bear in Alaska than an upset cow moose in the alders."

It's a long day, still half-poling and half-wading along. Harriett is having the hardest going in this stuff. Beatle and I are running twenty-two footers with only baggage when the guests are out wading. The cook is stuck with all the camping gear, food, etc., in the big twenty-four. Great canoe for running, but pretty tough when out dragging over the rocks. I notice, though, that today Junior has put away his fishing pole and is helping out in the hard places. The Reverend seems to be a bit out of steam today. Even the most eager fisherman has to give up catching and releasing trout eventually. I try not to worry about people when you are in the bush or you'd soon drive yourself crazy. Sometimes people from down south tire out easily, being out of their natural element. Slippery rocks, hot weather, and fly dope can all combine to get you down. Harriett is always really clean around the cooking, and always rinses the dishes in hot water. We don't want anybody coming down with the worst bush disease there is, what the old guides used to call the "dishwater shits." Good day to quit early anyway, no hurry. We'll camp where the River Don puts in, tomorrow will be a little easier with more water to help us along.

Just before bedtime, I'm down putting a stick at the edge of the brook, as a mark to see how much the water changes in the night. The Reverend follows me down and sits on a rock. Wip-

160

ing my hands off, I roll a smoke and join him, I can see he wants to talk about something away from the crew. "Look," he begins, "we are having a wonderful time and this is everything I wanted for Junior, but there's something I think I better tell you." I sort of grunt to nudge him along, whatever in hell it is, he's got me wondering now. "About two months ago, I got took to the hospital and they told me it was a warning kind of heart attack. Everyone wanted me to stay home, but we already had this trip planned and I didn't want to disappoint the boy. Also thought it might be the last time we get to do something like this together."

Oh, Jesus, I'm thinking, here we are halfway down the river, low water, heavy loads, and no way in hell to get out of here except for about four more days of hard picking. He goes on to tell me that one time this morning he took a bad pain but had slipped a couple of the little white pills he carried under his tongue and now felt pretty good altogether. Probably we shouldn't worry, everything would be okay, "the Lord willing and the creek don't rise." First time I ever heard that saying, but I told him, "Reverend, I don't know about the Lord, but me and B. J. are willing, and you better pray that the creek does rise. We'll get out of here a hell of a lot easier."

Talking it over with Beatle Joe and Harriett later, we decide that if we can we will push along a bit faster tomorrow. The stream from here on down is a bit bigger, and we'll only have to get out once in a while for a sweeper or a shallow bar. Maybe if we push it we can get down to the mouth of the Serpentine before camping and then we'll only have a couple of days out to the Forks and a telephone, in case the old guy takes a spell on us.

Harriett doesn't butt in too much on how to run things, but now she speaks up. "Maybe we soon get lots of water, see that ring around the moon?"

"Come to think if it," I say, "guess my mind has been on other things, but the wind has shifted a lot to the south all day and that cow and calf moose were out traveling in the middle of the day. Maybe we are in for some weather."

"Notice how the birds are still singing and making noise this late at night?" Harriett goes on. "See how smoke from the fire is hanging right on the ground and going clear around in circle? Think we better tie down tent ropes and make sure the canoes are hauled up really good."

I learned a long time ago that stories from nature handed down by the Old People are always better than the White Man's weather forecast. Just to prove it, far off in the northeast, we see heat lightning flash across the sky. Time to roll in. Might be the last dry chance we get to sleep.

Sure enough. Wind wakes us up in the night, definitely stronger from the south now, bringing warm and heavy air, thunder in the distance. We hurry through breakfast, break camp, and get into rain gear while loading the boats. First drops hit, big as oranges, no worry about putting out the fire this time. Coming down in buckets, as Beatle says, "Like cow pissin' on flat rock." I guess he learns all this kind of talk from the clients. Nothing for it but to swing out and start downriver. At least the wind isn't in our face, sort of side on and gusty, though, making it hard to handle in the narrow runs. Water is coming up fast, must have been some hell of a rain all night back up in the headwaters. We're glad to get it now. If we're going to be wet, we may as well have good, fast going.

Running canoes the way we do, standing up with a pole in the stern, has been called an art by some people. To us every move comes natural. It's just a job, and we never think any more about it. One of the most important things is to have your load right, heavy in the bow running downstream, light in the bow when poling upstream. Funny how simple that sounds, but some people never seem to learn how to do it. They are always surprised when the heavy end wants to go downhill and they spend a lot of their energy fighting it. When running free you mostly let the bow follow the current, kind of sculling with the pole to keep the rest of the boat following, and giving her a shove once in a while. When you have to do a lot of turning and picking around rocks, you snub up with the pole, shove the lighter stern over where you want it, and hold until the bow swings into line. It's a lot easier for any of us to do it than it is to try to tell someone about it. You need good flat-bottom canoes, with no keels, and they will ride like a school mam when loaded right. You need a good strong-but-springy spruce pole with an iron socket on it so it holds on the rocks a little without getting all broomed up and slippery. As an old guide neighbor of mine tells it, "Don't let anyone talk you into running shallow, fast rivers with keels on your boat, or any of them aluminum piss pots, or you'll spend all your time on your ass out in the river."

When we are hauling passengers, we sit them ahead of the front crossbar, with their duffel tarped down in the middle, paddle and spare pole slid under the center crossbar where we can grab it if necessary. Sometimes snubbing in a hard rapids, your pole might get hung up between the rocks, you have about a half-second to make up your mind whether to break it, leave it, or leave the canoe. That's when the spare comes in handy.

Harriett, running the longer cook boat, is balanced out bow-heavy with the gear all tarped and lashed in case of an upset. She had to snub up and hang back in the fast water, as the bigger canoe always wants to run over the leader.

Miserable as it is, water beating in your face and down your neck, fighting the gusts of wind, it's almost fun when you've got lots of water to run on. The Reverend is enjoying it, seems to be in good shape again this morning, hollering back at me every time we take a splash over the bow. Quick glance behind shows Beatle right on my heels, Junior in the bow enjoying the hell out of it all. He reaches back for the paddle to help, and Beatle raps him over the knuckles with the pole. He doesn't need any help. I must remember to tell B. J. to keep that paddle farther back in the boat and to tell Junior to just keep his hands in his lap.

I wave them and Harriett to back off a bit. If I have to make a swift turn in the middle of a rocky run, I don't want someone running their boat through the middle of us. It strikes me funny how the Reverend and I use the same words a lot, but the back of his neck gets all red when I use them. Probably Junior is picking up a bit of culture from Beatle back there also.

I'm thinking that the way this river is coming up, maybe by tonight we can get down to the millionaires' fishing lodge at Seven Mile and spend a comfortable night in the guide shack. Run out easy the next day. The rain hasn't let up a bit, if anything, coming down even harder. You can see trees blowing down ashore, but can't hear them over the noise of the wind and water. We're coming down toward the mouth of Jimmy Brook when a giant spruce uproots and lands its top right out into the middle of the stream. In normal water, this is just a little downhill run, where you hug the right-hand bank and slide out into the salmon pool. Now it's something else altogether.

I snub furiously, dodge past the end of the tree where it is lodged on a big rock and shoot out into the pool. Sculling around, bow upstream, I think maybe we'll get ashore and try to make a fire for tea.

The Reverend steps out to hold the bow as I look up to see Beatle coming around the bend above the sweeper. Okay so far, I think. Suddenly, as he snubs on the left side to set over from the rock, the bow for an instant swings close by the end of the hungup tree. Junior, always helpful, reaches out, grabs it and pulls the bow behind the rock. Instant disaster. "Jesus," I'm screaming against the wind, "let go, let go, push out for Christ sake." Like a nightmare in slow motion, I see old Beatle, every muscle straining, trying to hold it against the current, roaring who knows what at Junior, who pulls the bow in farther behind the rock. The pole breaks, stern out in the torrent, bow hung behind a tree, canoe wraps around the rock, swamps upside down, cuts in two. Junior disappears under the sweeper, Beatle under the stern half of the canoe, rolling down through the rapids into the pool. Junior, in spite of his heavy rain gear, flounders ashore across from us, Beatle, like a madman, is struggling to capture some of the luggage floating away. I am wading out, too, trying to grab a packsack, when Harriett pulls in just in time to help us.

Beatle is so infuriated he is white, and we are all soaked to the skin and shivering. I'm looking at half of one of my best canoes, the summer's profit lost in a second. Old Beatle Joe, last of a line of proud canoemen, who has never in his life been dumped into the river, turns to me and says, "Well, boss, by Jesus, that's Lesson Number One." That strikes me and Harriett so funny we're sitting on our ass in the river, up to our armpits, laughing our heads off, when we look up and see Junior on the far bank pointing frantically across at his father.

We struggle out of the river, slipping over the wet rocks to the old man. He's down on his knees by the canoe fumbling with his rain jacket, teeth clenched, paralyzed with pain. Finally I locate the bottle, nearly dump the little pills into the river, but manage to get two or three of them poked into his mouth with my fingers.

Pretty soon he's dragging in some big raspy breaths, sweat running down his face along with the rain, but at least his color is coming back and he's trying to crawl up onto the bank. First thing is to get him up out of the rising water, under some cover, until I figure out what in hell we are going to do now. On the south shore of the pool we are under some good big trees, with a high knoll behind that breaks the wind somewhat, lots of firewood, one of those places where guides have been camping forever.

We manage to get a tent up, flapping in the wind. A Coleman stove started to warm it up a bit, and from there work at getting him into a sleeping bag. It's half-wet but a lot better than lying out in the river; at least this would give me a chance to think while we make some tea. Beatle and Harriett try to cheer up poor old Junior and get him involved in salvaging the rest of the gear. As Beatle said later, "Poor bastard looking like a muskrat that drowned in the trap, didn't know whether to piss or wind his watch."

This is the kind of situation that every guide lives in dread of. Due to the economic facts of life, we end up taking the people who can afford our services into the wilderness, and they are more likely to be of more advanced age than they are to be teenage athletes. Aside from rudimentary first-aid training and common sense, there really isn't much a guide can do except hope that medical emergencies will not arise. When they do, you just have to keep your head on straight and do what seems best under the circumstances.

I'm in the tent with the old man trying to make him more comfortable when another seizure convulses him. Again the little pills under the tongue, in a moment his eyes seem to focus, he starts to get his breath and tries to roll onto his side to be sick outside of the sleeping bag. Jesus, I think, this is a much more serious deal than we can handle with aspirin tablets and tea. Somehow or other we've got to at least try to get him out to the settlement and a doctor.

He's still looking pretty green, sweat pouring off his face, when he motions me down so he can whisper, "I'm terribly sorry to cause you all this trouble, and spoil this wonderful trip we've been enjoying."

I tell him, "Oh, hell, Reverend, don't worry about it a bit, we have enjoyed the pleasure of your company too. I'm sure you will soon be feeling better, but just to be on the safe side I am going to get you out of here as quick as we can. In order to do that we are going to use Harriett's big twenty-four foot canoe. It'll ride like a Cadillac. I'm going to leave Harriett and Junior camped out here with the extra gear and come back for them after we get you to a doctor."

He seems to accept the good sense in this and asks to speak with his son while the rest of us get things ready.

The crew has managed to salvage most of the luggage from the busted boat, a good big fire is holding back some of the driving rain and the old black boiling kettle is about ready for the handful of tea. "Okay," I tell them, "here's the plan. B.J. and I are going to take the old guy out. The water is still coming, and probably this rain will last awhile yet although you can see it's starting to lighten up a bit in the south. We'll lay him in the twenty-four, take just his gear, an ax and a tarp so we're running light and we'll hit her for the Strathcona Lodge at Seven Mile. At least we'll get him under cover in a camp with a stove, then go on out tomorrow."

We get the canoe ready to go, chopping off some short poles to go in the bottom to try and keep him up out of the worst of the water. In a couple sleeping bags and a tarp, he'll probably still be half-soaked but this is about the best we can do. I take Harriett aside, "I know you can look after the kid, you've got enough food and gear to stay the rest of the summer. If it clears up by tomorrow morning, while you've still got lots of water, you run as big a load of this gear as you can down to the mouth of Serpentine, come back up for the rest of it if you have time, then camp and wait till Beatle and I come back in with another boat so we'll get all this stuff out of here."

"No problem Boss, we'll be okay. Don't worry about Junior, he isn't half as much a kid as you and his old man seem to think he is. After all, he's only two years younger than I am." She elbows me in the ribs, "Cheer up. All he needs is a little more culture."

Loaded up, the patient laid out, wrapped up, and lashed like a Christmas turkey under the center crossbar, we are ready to hit the river. Beatle is in the bow, poised to push her out when Junior bends in to say good bye to his father and wish us luck. "Okay, B. J.," I holler, "turn her loose, we're off to the races." Just before we round the first bend, I grab a look back to see Harriett put her arm around the kid, while he watches us disappear in the rain.

Must be about three o'clock in the afternoon or so; with all the excitement you lose track of the time. We had a chance to grab a cup of tea before leaving and Harriett packed us a bag of bannock and jam and some cold meat, so we won't starve anytime soon. The rain is definitely easing up, but the water still seems to be rising. The river is well out of its banks, right into the alders on the right-hand side and high up on the side of the cliff as we sweep down upon what, in normal water, is a salmon pool halfway between Jimmy Brook and the mouth of the Serpentine. "She's piled up in the middle like a cock of hay, just keep on top and let her dangle." The bow man is on his knees, with a paddle, alert mainly for the big rocks we usually snub around, now buried in the torrent of brown water. I'm in the stern, mostly using the pole as a sweep, occasionally going down on one knee as we take some of the bigger swells. I've been on this river a long time, from early springtime log driving to the lazy days of summer, but never seen anything like this.

The Reverend seems to be taking it okay. I hope he isn't getting too soaked; we've taken a good bit of water over the bow. Poor old bastard won't have a hope in hell, wrapped up like he is, if we ever swamp. When I bend over and pull the tarp back from his face a bit he winks and tries a smile, then his teeth clench again in pain. Not much I can do on the run. It's just coming dark, and the rain has stopped when we hit the mouth of the Serpentine, flushed out of the branch "like shit from a goose." Serpentine coming in on the right adds its own flood of brown water, bringing down all the old dead wood and whole green trees, roots and all, that have caved into the river. It's almost like running among logs on the stream drive, only this stuff is more apt to catch the bottom and jam or roll up on you. In what seems like just a few minutes we round the bend above Strathcona Lodge and look down the long stretch, no lights on that I can see. I had been hoping that there might be guests, maybe even a medical doctor among them, but as we pull ashore in front of the guide shack, it's clear that we have the place all to ourselves.

"Beatle, you go on inside and get a fire going, while I try to get the Reverend unwrapped and ashore." His breath is coming in short little pants and his face looks like marble, he beckons me down so he can whisper, "I hate to be such a bother, but I don't think I can move. If anything should happen to me, will you do your best to look after Junior?"

"Don't go talking that kind of stuff," I tell him, "try a couple more of these dynamite pills and we'll see if we can get a cup of hot tea into you." I tie the boat good and scramble up the bank to the guide shack. B. J. has already got a fire on in the big cast-iron stove. "Before you get too cozy in here," I tell him, "I guess you better just grab enough water to make a quick cup of tea, if there's a snowball's chance in hell of getting him out alive, it's got to be tonight."

We're ready to hit the watery road. We managed to dribble a bit of tea into the old man, along with the last of our aspirin tablets. B. J. and I wash down some bannock and meat with a scalding cup, and cast off. At least the rain has quit, the moon has started to peek through the swift-moving clouds. We're getting a bit chilly, but our clothes are rapidly drying on our backs, as we get to work again. Down through the little rapids below the lodge, now only a big standing wave with all this high water, around the turn and through the rapids above Rocky Pool. Enough light is filtering through the clouds, now that our eyes are used to it. The white water looms up like a skunk in the fog. Biggest dangers now are the deadheads and sweepers. Old Beatle is hanging over the bow, paddle poised like a harpoon to fend off danger.

Now above the roar of the river we can hear an even more ominous rumble, the Right Hand Branch Falls around the next bend. In ordinary water, and even in fairly high water, you sweep down through the first section, then take the Corkscrew Chute, just to the right of center, snub right, then hard left and you drop over about a five-foot drop into the tail of the rapids. Now in the dark, riding this torrent, guess we'll just take her as she comes. No sense in even thinking about portaging around. On the right-hand side the water is right in the woods, behind the big boulders. On the left it's right up against the cliff. No way in hell to get this old man down through that stuff in the dark. Beatle hollers back, "Well, Boss, I guess it's shit or get off the pot."

"Set back to the crossbar when we tip over or we'll fill her for sure," I have time to yell, when we're into it. I'm headed dead for the Corkscrew when a three-log spruce running with us catches the bottom and starts to swing out in front. Jesus, I frantically snub, damn near fall out, but get around it. With a "Yahoo" from Beatle we shoot over, taking a few drops of water aboard but nothing serious. Now we're into the hard downhill water of Rocky Bend. A mile-long sweeping turn studded with rocks as big as Volkswagens, this is normally hard picking. On this flood it is a series of chutes and big waves. Making one dodge, I catch the pole between the rocks and it's broken before I can let it go.

Grabbing the spare before we have time to get in trouble, I'm able to make the turns as Beatle plies the paddle madly. The roar of the rapids recedes astern, the valley widens out, and we're clear of all the dangerous going now, just a fast run to the Forks.

Finally got a chance to sit down for a minute, try and dry my hands enough to roll a smoke. Hell of a job, holding the pole jammed under my armpit, three torn papers and a half-dozen matches later, I'm sucking in the nicotine. Funny how much trouble we'll go through to poison ourselves. With Beatle keeping us straight ahead, I'm able to unwrap the patient to see if he's still breathing. Not a whimper, face is cold as a dead lamb's tongue. I finally find a pulse under his jaw, so faint I'm not sure if it's the real thing or just wishful thinking.

"Beatle, I don't know whether this old guy's alive or not," I said. "I guess we better just push hell out it and hope for the best." Coming down now to the high bank across from the mouth of Rocky Brook, Grassy Island is coming up next. Probably on this flood, old Grassy and the flats above Tom Pole Brook will be just part of the river.

Sure enough, with the river widened out, it's hard to tell exactly where we are, but we sure know where we are headed. Half Mile is usually a deep and placid salmon pool. Now the water dashes against the face of the cliff and bounces off in a big swirl. I can't see but sense the cross current, as Mamozekel comes in on the right. We shoot out into the Forks Pool, where the current of Little Tobique nearly swamps us before spitting us out on our new course.

In a few minutes, with what I figure is about the last ounce of effort left in my carcass, we bow her upstream and land against the bank in front of the Nictau Gate. Thank God, there's still light on, not as late as I felt it was. LeRoy Johnson, the gatekeeper, lives here on the end of the road, the end of the telephone line. I told Beatle, "I'll hold on here while you get up there and see if LeRoy can raise the doctor or the Mounties."

Within an hour, we have the patient on the way to the hospital, alive it seems, but barely. God knows what will happen now, but at least it's out of our hands. Around the stove we hear from LeRoy that the phone lines have just been restored, trees down across them, water over the main road in a dozen places. It seems that we've been swamped by the tail end of a hurricane. "My God, men," he tells us, "you two look like something that's been dunked in the river and drug through a knothole. How in hell did you ever get the old feller down here without drowning the lot of you."

"Well, sir," I had to admit, "if it wasn't the nicest moonlight sail we've ever been on, it was for damn sure the fastest. Now let's have one more cup of that hot tea and get a few hours sleep, we've still got a lot of work to do in the next couple days or so."

Heading down the river to the hospital next morning, I tell the wife that I've got things pretty well figured out. Beatle and I have to go back up and gather the rest of the crew. Harriett's got plenty of food, so no hurry, but it will take another canoe to bring out all the gear we were forced to leave behind.

At the hospital, we get a look at the patient. Funny how shrunk up he looks. Tube in his arm, tube up his nose, a sign says "Oxygen, No Smoking" in big red letters. He's resting comfortably for now," the nurse tells us, but even with good luck it will be many days before he can travel home.

On the way back upriver I tell the wife, "Guess there is no hurry getting Junior down here to see his old man in that shape. "I tell her we'll haul up to Four Mile on Serpentine and spend the night in the camp there. She will have to go along and bring the truck back out.

Good thing we took the power saw along. In those days the tote road going up to the Salmon Hole camps was a pretty narrow trail. After the big wind and rain, there were long stretches full of tangled blowdown. Nowadays there are damn few places where anything bigger than a raspberry bush is left to blow across the road.

Next morning we're on the water just after daylight. The sky looks good, great day to be on the river. The water is still well up, although dropping fast. The big twenty-four-footer, loaded with nothing but the ax and boiling kettle, takes McArty Falls in one straight plunge, just a cupful of water over the bow to wake up old Beatle. Down past Clyde Brook, through the Narrows, past the camps at the County Line. Figure we'll be drinking Harriett's coffee in a few minutes.

There they are, camped on the north shore on the high bank across from the Right Hand Branch.

"Looks pretty quiet," I note. "Hope they brought down all the gear, they've only got one of the tents up."

"Yup," observes my bowman, "guess they only got one sleeping bag too. There's Junior's, hanging out over the bushes there. Maybe they been getting some of that culture we heard so much about."

As we swing in to tie up alongside their boat, a head sticks out of the tent, disappears again. By the time we get up the bank and start knocking a fire together for coffee, our cook crawls out, with Junior close behind. Anxious I figure, to hear about his father. "Good news," I tell them, "they say that he will be able to go home in a couple weeks."

"Oh, that's wonderful," says Junior, "and we've got some good news too." He glances over at Harriett standing there with a grin like the cat that ate the canary. "I guess we are engaged to get married."

"Well sir, I guess your father will be just charmed all to hell to hear that," is all I can think of to say.

Turned out that he was, too. That's been a few years ago now. The old man has been dead five or six years anyway. Junior and Harriett and their three kids come back for a visit about once a year. They just can't seem to get enough of that culture.

CAMP COOKS, INDIVIDUALS ALL

O *f all the ingredients that go into a successful and trouble-free hunting outfit, one of the most overlooked is a good camp cook. One hears more about the guides, the pilots, the taxidermist, and the manager, but without a hardworking and capable cook, it all falls apart.*

I consider myself somewhat of an authority on camp cooks, having been involved with hiring several dozen, and living with the results, for over forty years. Fortunately I have one, at least, that I have always been able to count on. Without my wife, Irene, in the kitchen, helping to make our outfit a success, I would still be back guiding and trapping . . . and probably living on welfare.

Having said that, in praise of *one* particular cook, I must go on and explain that just as the cook is indispensable, in what I have found to be the great majority of cases, the cook will also present more problems than all the guides, wranglers, pilots, skinners, and other camp personnel put together.

In all the years of our operations, aside from my wife and partner, I can think immediately of a few great cooks who came and did their job, did not try to run the outfit, did not get drunk, sleep with the clients, or create havoc in general.

Most of these friends for life helped us in New Brunswick, at the main camp, or with Martin up on the mobile camp. Two other super-good ladies cooked for Martin at Lac de Gras. To this elite list I add a fine lady from Yellowknife, and the one and *only* good, trouble-free male cook who we were fortunate enough to find to help Irene at Courageous Lake.

The list of the more troublesome is a mile long. Many of them were all right in the kitchen, but wanted to manage the camp, boss the guides, or socialize with the guests, instead of doing their job. In general, ladies have been far superior to men, despite the difficult logistics of living in a remote camp.

To keep your sanity in the hunting business, it is necessary to retain your sense of humor. I can thus look back upon what, at the time, were disasters, with a certain amount of fondness, despite the contribution these people made to my heart problems.

I can remember spending a fall in a hunting camp up in the Serpentine country with a cook we called "Old Pig Lips." Great cook but you had to watch him in the corners.

Another who fed us on the log drive took good care of us drivers, but robbed his employers blind. There was a legend that he could put a bag of flour and a quarter of beef in his knapsack and walk home with it.

Another who is still alive, at last report, back on Tobique. Great cook but marginally insane, he would quit over some imagined slight and walk forty miles out of the woods to go home and sulk.

Yet another Tobique legend would toss a pie on the table in front of the guests and say, "There, eat that you hungry sonsawhores!"

At least twenty-five "cooks" in Newfoundland started every recipe, from moose stew to lemon meringue pie, with "You puts a bit of salt pork in the pot."

A young lady who appeared in Fort Chimo, back in the hippie days, in sandals and carrying an artist's easel. She said she had come north in search of the "Arctic experience." Ended up giving herpes to half the guide crew, and, I suspect, a couple of the guests.

Another lady whom I took to the shores of Ungava Bay made many friends among the young Inuit staff, sent them Christmas cards with marijuana seeds and instructions enclosed.

A whole series of male, or mostly male, cooks hired for the barren ground caribou camps included one who was a half-decent camp cook until he went to college and learned to be a chef. Another hated hunting, hated Americans and hated Indians and did not last long at Courageous Lake. Three lasted a week, and wasted an airplane ride.

One who was seven feet tall came up from B.C. His former employer mentioned that he was a homosexual. I hired him to retain my image as being politically correct. The first week he ordered fifty loaves of baker's bread from town, plus a case of Kraft Dinners and another of Rice-a-roni. Funny, it said "cook" on his lengthy résumé. He quit the second week, said he was "not comfortable in such a macho atmosphere," and went back to Vancouver where he fit in better.

Reiner, whom we actually picked up on the road hitchhiking in northern Alberta was a good cook, but crazy. Then Pascal from France came up the road the same way, went back east with us and lasted a couple of years. Pascal was an okay cook. We were starting to get him acquainted with North American standards in cleanliness when he disappeared again.

The above are all remembered with fondness. However, the others, predominantly male, who were drunks, thieves, dopers, sexual predators, and racists, I do not recall with such tolerance.

When interviewing cooks for bush jobs, I now have a list of essential criteria. Loyalty tops the list, and whether or not the applicant can cook is at the bottom. We can put up with burned porridge, if it is served by someone with a smile.

TRAPLINES

When I grew up, every country kid had a trapline. Some were able to make a few bucks and keep it for treats, but most of us simply took it for granted that the money we earned went into the family "kitty" to help pay our way.

Fur prices in those days, through the 1940s, were high compared to wages. While our main catch was the simple stuff like squirrels, weasels, and what we called "mush rats," even these brought a fair-sized check when the fur buyer came through the country.

I remember an older trapper saying that during the Dirty Thirties, when wages, for those fortunate enough to have a job, were a dollar a day, pine marten, or sable as we called them, were fetching up to twelve dollars apiece.

Trapping and the fur trade to a great extent opened up North America, for better or worse, depending upon your viewpoint of history. It has for centuries supported, and continues to support, a traditional style of life for northern people.

You will find little tolerance among my friends and family for the mostly white, "southern intellectual urban dweller," who seems totally determined to further the rights of animals, while denying the rights of the aboriginal and other people whose life depends upon use of our natural renewable resources.

For a few years, as life took me in other directions, I was away from the trapline except as a part-time hobby between other jobs. Then came a series of winters when this harvest from the forest became very important indeed in keeping food on the table.

The winter known locally as "the winter of the big snows" found me partnered up with Ab Higgins, a veteran Tobique country trapper. We had two families to support and the trapline was the only option.

While we were still guiding deer hunters in November we had started trapping part-time for beaver, otter, and mink along the streams and rivers. Beaver was the main target, with prices going all the way from about fifteen dollars for kits right up to sixty-five and seventy for blankets and supers. This involved long hours, wet clothes, and cold feet on many occasions, but compared with guiding for six dollars a day, the money was good.

Beaver are certainly the easiest of animals to trap. One must keep in mind that "sport" has nothing to do with it; your aim is to harvest beaver by the most efficient method possible. Despite the uninformed opinions of the animal rights people, the professional trapper makes every effort to assure that pain and hence struggling, is kept to the absolute minimum.

Besides the natural human reluctance to cause unnecessary suffering to the animal, from a profit standpoint alone it is unproductive to have pelts damaged through struggling and lost through escapes.

Long before the animal rights industry had found a fashionable invention of the so-called "humane" killer traps, the northern trapper knew enough to use drowning sets and other methods to ensure the quick demise of the animal being taken.

While we still had open water, sets were made on the spill way of the beaver dam, with a few sticks removed to make sure he came out to adjust his water level. A No. 4 double-spring, or a No. 3 jump trap would be carefully placed at the right depth so that a catch was made, preferably on a front foot. The trap was attached with a one-way sliding device which led down into deep water and was tied to an anchor, usually a rock. Thus was assured a quick drowning, without the wrung-off foot so beloved among the antitrapping cult.

Once the pond was frozen enough to walk out on, sets were made in the feed bed, or on poles under the ice baited with fresh branches. These were extremely efficient.

With the invention of the Conibear 330, the so-called "humane" trap, the life of the trapper became much easier and the harvest of beaver much more concentrated. It takes no skill, and little work, to simply set killer traps in the entrance tunnels of the beaver house. This is poor management practice as everything that comes through is killed, kits included. It is absolutely non-selective.

With our old fashioned, less-than-politically-correct sets, we were able to somewhat manage the resource by making sets designed to take the larger animals and spare the others to grow up and reproduce.

Now to a great extent, skills learned over generations are being replaced by courses in "quick kill" by ever more mechanized and more expensive contraptions.

As a by-product of beaver trapping, the castor glands were collected, dried, and sold to manufacturers as one of the major ingredients of the perfume that goes behind the ears of the lady who contributes to the animal rights industry.

In most cases in the North, the beaver meat is used for both human and dog food, so maximum benefit is derived from this renewable resource. Beaver is also premium bait for trapping any of the carnivores, from weasels to bears. We used it mainly as bait for bobcats, fisher, and marten.

Bobcats and fisher were trapped mainly in baited cubby sets, little houses made of brush, using No. 2 jump traps. With the proper size of trap, the animal is captured and held without undue pain. Most die quickly in the cold climate. In most jurisdictions, traps must be checked daily.

Fox and wolves were usually taken in snares, or in the early season by the use of de-scented and buried traps in what are called dirt hole sets. This is an art in itself, successfully practiced by only the real professionals.

No experienced trapper will use oversized traps that break bones and make it possible for the animal to escape. As in any other endeavor however, accidents occasionally happen. One can certainly sympathize with the poor animal that goes away minus a foot; but looked at another way, have you met many people with one leg who wished they were dead instead?

Life in the forest, like life in the city, is full of risks of one kind or another. I ask myself, "Would I rather be a chicken, 100 percent of whom are destined for the fast food fryer, or a furbearer living free in the forest, with about a 1 percent chance of ever encountering a trapper?"

Putting fur harvesting in another context, I ask another question: "Would I rather utilize a natural renewable resource, or wear fake fur made from petrochemical derivatives that involve degradation of the environment worldwide?"

No contest, as far as I am concerned.

None of these highly technical and philosophical arguments entered the minds of old Ab and me back in the winter of the deep snows. We worried more about feeding our families and keeping the kids in enough clothes to get on the school bus and ride seventy miles a day.

We lived within a mile of the end of the plowed road, and beyond that were many miles of logging company roads and forest trails that could be traveled by snowmobile. I had one of the first Skidoos ever seen in that country, purchased brand new for $650. This machine, rated at 16.5 horses, had a single cylinder, mostly trouble-free engine. Admittedly it was slow by today's standards, although it got along, in good conditions, approximately ten times as fast as Ab and I could snowshoe. That was awe-inspiring in those days.

Leaving from home, with Ab perched behind me on the machine, I would haul a canvas-lashed toboggan containing our camping gear, traps, bait, rifle, shovel, food, and sleeping bags.

Our snowshoes and the ever-present ax went on the machine so we were never parted from them. With those two basic items, a belt knife, and a few matches, no experienced northern woodsman would die, right away at least, in a country full of wood.

Taking advantage of abandoned logging camps and some wigwams built by ourselves, we stayed out anywhere from a couple of days to a week. In a few strategic locations, while the trails were still open in the fall, we had cached gas and oil, extra food, traps, and equipment.

Three "main" camps were utilized with some regularity: Nictau Lake on the head of the Tobique River, Jimmy Brook camp on the trail between the Right Hand Branch and the head of the

Serpentine, and Popple Depot over on the Nipisiquit. To anyone who knows that country, or looks at a map, you can see this covers a lot of territory.

On well-packed trails, this kind of travel is almost a pleasure. However, with the frequent heavy snowstorms that year, we seemed to forever be breaking trail. On most of the hills we would have to snowshoe up first, then return and I would run the Skidoo up, then return for the toboggan and do it again. By this means we got into a lot of new fur-rich areas, but paid for it in back-breaking labor, sweat-drenched and then frozen stiff.

Regardless of whether we spent the night in a comfortable camp, a tent or a brush lean-to with a fire in front, we didn't have any trouble sleeping. One gets used to such living conditions, and most nights one or the other would replenish the fire and not even remember waking in the night to do it.

Just before Christmas, the fur buyer came up to visit us. As we had the reputation of turning out well-handled pelts, he spent an entire day at our place, sorting and grading, sometimes bargaining over the tally. This first sale contained beaver, and a few weasels, which most people neglected to skin because of the low price, but we wasted nothing with fur on it. At last a deal was struck, each side being content that it was a fair one. Two Tobique families would have a good Christmas.

After a few days' holiday, the maps were out again, and new routes plotted out. Again, we would take maximum advantage of camps and caches. Through January, February, and well into March, the legal seasons were still open for all species. Now the catch concentrated on beaver, for which we traveled the frozen streams, and sable, which lived mainly in high country spruce forest.

By late in the winter, some of the land animals, especially the long-haired ones, start to lose their prime, the fur becoming what we called "flat" or "sunburned." Water animals, such as the beaver and muskrats, would continue in prime condition right into May.

We wound up the winter's efforts by taking the wives and all the pelts down to the provincial capital and going direct to the fur company. After the deal was completed, old Dave Glazier, the buyer, sent his helper out for a pint of rye whiskey. We shook hands and gave a toast to an extremely successful season.

My partner, Old Abner, has been long gone to the big trapline in the sky, where every slider is down the wire and every beaver a super blanket. I have trapped in many places, from Labrador to the Northwest Territories, but never again when it was so important to the support of my family.

T hey say that sometimes your fame precedes you. Such was the case of the man we knew as the "Famous Louisiana Suin' Lawyer."

After booking him at one of the Safari Club conventions, and before it came time for the hunting season, I read an article about this gentleman describing in detail how every hunt he had ever been on had been beset with one disaster after another.

This guy had been bucked off horses, crashed in airplanes, sunk in a boat. He had been run over by an elephant, scratched by a leopard, and was currently involved in a dozen lawsuits with outfitters from all over the world.

I was beginning to wonder if I shouldn't simply send back his deposit and get out of it totally, when in the mail I received his signed contract, the contract which says that we are responsible for absolutely *nothing*. Just in case, I double-checked with our company lawyer to make sure the liability disclaimer would hold up in court.

He was coming to hunt woodland caribou in Newfoundland, a hunt that can have an entire set of difficulties of its own, but which people continue to survive very successfully.

Checking over the guest roster, I discovered that he was visiting on the same week as were two of my favorite friends and clients. Weatherby Award winner Butch White, and Craig Boddington of *Petersen's Hunting Magazine*, have hunted with me many times. If anyone could keep things under control, I was confident that these were the guys to do it.

They were going in to the Rock Camp on the inland barrens, right smack in the middle of the LePoile caribou herd migration. With three of our best guides—Tom, Clarence, and Walt—to take care of them, I knew that they would have an excellent hunt. The camp cook, Lockyer Noseworthy, was a longtime friend of mine, well known for pampering the visiting sports, and one of the best storytellers in Newfoundland to boot. I almost wished I was going in with them myself.

On the appointed day, I met our lawyer friend in the airport at Stephenville. He got off the plane in a blue suit and necktie, wearing a pair of fancy cowboy boots. He told me that he had left in a bit of a hurry. He had been in court, rushed home to grab his luggage and rifle, and just barely made his flight.

Needless to say, we stood around for an hour, and of course, his duffel bag, sleeping bag, and rifle case did not appear. Checking with the airlines people elicited the information that it would all follow, in good time . . . . but there might be a delay at customs because the hunter was not accompanying the rifle. At least they promised that when the stuff did appear, they would send it by taxi out to our float base at Mitchel's Pond, about seventy miles away, at their expense.

As things turned out, this was only our first streak of bad luck. When we got out to the float base bad weather had set in, as is quite common on the southwest coast in October. We put the hunter into the Midway Motel, out on the Trans Canada Highway by Crabbes River. Then we turned around and went back to Stephenville for Craig and Butch, who were coming in on an early evening flight.

We had a chance to share a couple of beers and a few stories on our way out to the Midway, and they told me not to worry. They assured me that, what the hell, no one could control the weather. We'd get flying sooner or later and in the meantime they would keep our Suin' Lawyer from becoming too impatient.

Second day, the weather remained the same, overcast, intermittent drizzle and fog. At one point it cleared a little. Gerry, our partner, who was also the pilot, took off and made a circuit, but once he started into the country, climbing up onto the plateau, it was socked in solid clear to the ground. No way in hell anyone was going to get to the Rock Camp in that stuff.

Bad luck again. We were beginning to wonder if our friend from Louisiana had brought some sort of jinx to stay, or if perhaps we were going to appear in his next Bad Luck Hunt article.

The third day, it looked a bit decent at dawn: the skies seem to be clearing out from the west. We took the hunters back out to Mitchel's Pond to sit around the shack, drink tea, and bullshit and see if the weather would lift sufficiently to fly.

Around noon it started to clear out pretty good where we were, so we got the camp on the radio. Lockyer informed us that it was clearing fast. There was a bit of a breeze but nothing Gerry couldn't handle.

That year the helicopter was down with transmission troubles. We still had the 180, but for heavy trips, Gerry had leased a somewhat vintage DeHavilland Beaver from Ashwanapi Air up in northern Quebec.

I had browsed through the log book, and in the column that asked for Gross Weight on Take Off, back in June of 1974, an entry had been penciled in which said, "Not above maximum." For the next ten years there were ditto marks to acclaim that the same still applied: "Gross Weight not above maximum." One had to wonder at the accuracy of the entries in the columns that asked for: Total Time on Engine, Total Time on Prop and Time Since Last Major Overhaul. However, Gerry was an excellent pilot, one of the best I have ever encountered in the bush; he seemed to think it would hang together so I could quit worrying about any lawsuits—over the flying at least.

The plane was fueled up and loaded. At the last minute, just when we had decided to fly Butch and Craig in and hold our lawyer friend for later, a taxi arrived from Stephenville. Here at last were the missing rifle and gear. Gerry was in a hurry to get going before the weather changed again, so our client agreed to fly in to camp in his New Orleans court suit; he could always change when he got to camp.

The Beaver aircraft is a marvelous machine with plenty of power and high-lift wings, it can take a tremendous load out of some pretty tight places. In this case, it was fairly well loaded with three guests and gear plus supplies for the camp, but nothing out of the ordinary for a Beaver. Our Suin' Lawyer requested that, as he had been a pilot in the war, he would like to sit up in the right-hand seat. I couldn't help but wonder that, if things didn't go as he thought they should, perhaps he figured to take over from Gerry.

Gerry taxied quite awhile, down in the end of the pond, warming up, doing his checks and hoping for a bit of a breeze to add some lift on takeoff. It was a dead flat calm.

He described the take off to me later: "I finally gets a bit of a draft and I gives it to her balls to the wall. Halfway down the pond I gets her up on the step and rocks her loose of the water. The trees is comin' up fast but she's climbin' like an angel, the top blows off the Jesus oil fill pipe, down between the seats! Blows hot oil all over Buddy, and his Jesus eight hundred-dollar suit!"

The cap got put back on before too much oil was lost, but there sat our client drenched in engine oil for the thirty-minute flight.

At the Rock Camp there was a bit of a dock made out of rough spruce poles, sometimes covered at that time of year with a skim of ice from the water splashing over it. It was usually possible to get the airplane across the end of it long enough to unload. Butch and Craig got out okay and helped with the unloading, but finally when it came the lawyer's turn to get down from the right-hand seat, he jumped off the float, slipped on the ice, and promptly fell into the lake.

By this time Gerry was pretty much in despair. He could see visions of lawsuits, complaints to the provincial department of tourism, and all the other things that drive most outfitters to drink.

We talked it all over when he got back to base and agreed that Bad Luck Suin' Lawyer or not, we had done everything over which we had any control. The Rock Camp, while pretty snug for three hunters, three guides, and a cook, is nonetheless certainly a lot more comfortable than accommodations featured on most remote big-game hunts. They were in there with good guides, lots of grub, and there were caribou all over the country.

What makes Newfoundland hunting difficult at times is the climate and the terrain. Especially on the southwest coast, the weather is terribly changeable. On a day in late October, you might have fog, drizzle, heavy rain, sleet, and /or wet snow. Consider yourself lucky in the extreme if you see two consecutive days of bright, sunny weather.

On any of the fly-in hunts, once the airplane departs you are going to be walking, so the hunter should be in shape. He should have good waterproof boots that he can walk in, and the strongest rain gear that he can acquire. Terrain consists of rocky ridges, flat, wet tundra, swamps, and bogs. You may be traveling in thick spruce thickets that clutch at your clothing and when unavoidable, you may have to get into the tuckamore.

Tuckamore is a spruce-type tangle, growing flat upon the ground, usually not getting much more than waist high. You get into a tuckamore jungle and you're going to tear your rain gear off, snag your rubber boots, and maybe poke your eyes out. It can be terrifically difficult country, but that is where the game lives, so that's where we hunt.

On our daily radio contacts with the camp it appeared that the hunt was going fairly routinely. They had a couple of days in which the fog was so thick they couldn't get out until noon, but once on the country, the guides were really putting some mileage on the hunters. Game was still plentiful, they were seeing plenty of caribou, just hadn't spotted the big trophy stag that each of them wanted.

According to the cook, who kept the radio schedule while the hunters were absent, our Louisiana friend was having his usual run of bad luck. He twisted an ankle the first day out, but was taped up and hobbling along all right. The next day, crossing a yellow grass floating bog behind the guide, he stepped in the wrong place and plunged hip deep into what the guides call "the loon shit." He had lost the lens cap off his camera in the lake, left his binoculars behind at a lunch stop, and, worst of all, dropped his new SCI cap down the outdoor toilet.

Back at the float base I had the contracts out of my briefcase and was going over them very carefully, trying to figure out just how much of this stuff we might be liable for. However, before the end of the week, they had all taken their trophies, and professed to

187

the cook to be having a good time. After all, that is the aim of the whole operation.

There were no major disasters, but that winter at the convention I heard from the two other participants about a couple of dozen additional minor catastrophes which had befallen our poor hard luck hunter.

The main reward for me was to see the smiles on their faces when they got off the old Beaver back at Mitchel's Pond. I took them all, with their trophies, to the airport in Stephenville, we had a beer in the little airport cafe, all shook hands and parted friends.

Once I was back out in my truck, I couldn't help but heave a great sigh of relief. Apparently we had survived the visit of the Famous Louisiana Suin' Lawyer.

MUSKOX

*T*he muskox is known to the Inuit inhabitants of the far Arctic as oomingmak (various spellings), meaning literally "the bearded one."

Oomingmak, once circumpolar in distribution, roamed the Arctic tundra in the days of the woolly mammoth and the saber-toothed tiger. Thus the muskox provides a link with the past, one of the few opportunities to hunt for a truly prehistoric animal.

In North America, the original range of the muskox included most of the Arctic Islands, and on the mainland of the continent, extended from the Beaufort Sea to Hudson Bay, above the treeline. Contact with Europeans, at first the whalers and fur traders, started the downward slide in population. The hides, highly desired as robes because of their luxuriant long hair and soft under hair, called *quiviat*, became major trade articles.

From the mid-1800s through to World War I, muskoxen were hunted nearly to extinction because of this trade, and by basically unrestricted use by European "exploration" parties, and residents, as food for men and sled dogs.

By 1917 Canada had started to impose restrictions on this harvest and by the mid-1920s, attempts were made to curtail it completely.

Oomingmak has also played a further role in Arctic exploration and the establishment of Canadian sovereignty, in that posts were established in various areas of the Arctic for the dual purpose of protecting the muskox and claiming the land for Canada.

In my own experience, during the late 1950s I was engaged as a communications specialist and guide, on Arctic scientific expeditions. One such trip in 1958 took us up the east coast of Ellesmere Island, Alexandra Fjord to where an RCMP Post had been established at, specifically to advise the natives of Greenland that Canada discouraged the unlimited harvest of muskox on its territory. On other expeditions we worked on Devon, Bathurst and Melville islands, all of which had resident muskox, which, at the time, were protected from hunting except in emergencies.

With harvest restricted, muskox populations flourished in most areas, although some of the historic range remains uninhabited. At the present time, various Arctic hamlets have liberal quotas for the commercial harvest as well as subsistence hunting by aboriginal residents. In some communities, such as Sachs Harbor, Holman Island, and Cambridge Bay, commercial meat harvesting operations supply local processing plants. Thus Oomingmak brings needed dollars to the local economy.

Of much more "economic impact per animal harvested," however, are the sport hunts, conducted by the community Hunters and Trappers Associations. Hunts are conducted in a number of areas in the Western, Central and High Arctic, during various seasons. The principal season is the March-April period, when long days and good traveling make for the most efficient pursuit of good trophies.

Safari Club International Record System has established two basic categories for muskox: Greenland muskox coming primarily from the Arctic Islands, and barren ground muskox from the mainland of the continent. Record books are, of course, under constant revision. At one point most of the entries came from Banks Island and Victoria Island, or the introduced population of Nunivak Island in Alaska. This was because these were the only areas being hunted at the time.

New record books coming out, both SCI and B&C, are going to show the upsurge in high-scoring trophies coming from the mainland areas; east from Coppermine across to the Queen Maude Gulf area. Who knows where they will come from tomorrow, as the more adventuresome keep opening new areas?

Although the majority of hunters carry rifles, muskox have been pursued by men armed with bows and arrows since the dawn of history. Traditional Inuit hunters, armed with short, sturdy bows, backed with laminates of muskox horn, drove wooden arrows deep into the chest of Oomingmak, while sled dogs held him at bay.

Now we outfitters host archers armed with everything from the latest compounds with all the attachments to more traditional long bows, and even some historic replicas.

Although muskox are commonly found in fairly flat and featureless terrain, close stalking has proven successful for experienced bow hunters.

One note of caution: the muskox spends his life defending himself and his mates from wolves and grizzly bears. He becomes very defensive, and is likely to charge anything or anyone who comes within what he perceives as his safe limit, usually about the same range at which you should be stalking for a sportsmanlike and efficient bow shot.

After one of our sport hunters was charged, trampled, and injured a few years ago, posters appeared in game offices across the North, advising people that old Oomingmak was extremely dangerous to monkey around with.

As is the case with many hunts, the actual kill comes as somewhat of an anticlimax, as one is usually hunting in wide open frozen tundra. However, visiting sport hunters are universal in their praise of the experience; of being with true aboriginal hunters pursuing Oomingmak, a throwback to pre-historic times.

POLAR BEAR POLITICS

THE LAST TWENTY YEARS

M*any clients, knowing of our long involvement in the Arctic, ask me when we are going to return to the polar bear hunting business, now that the ban on importation of the trophies into the United States has supposedly been lifted. There are indeed some good reasons why, for the present at least, we remain "on standby" in this matter.*

After the "early" years in the Arctic, for about ten years I had very little to do with polar bear hunting of any kind. Busy striving for a full-time living in the outfitting business in New Brunswick, and still forced to take contract expedition jobs at sea and in foreign countries to keep bread on the table, I made only short and sporadic visits to the Arctic.

I did, however, keep closely in touch with what was going on, especially in regard to the newly permitted sport hunts being developed in the Northwest Territories.

Previously, about the only polar bear sport hunting was being done by a number of aircraft operators out of Kotzebue, Alaska. This kind of hunting entailed long flights over the sea ice, many right up against the coast of Russia, and was highly successful.

There were as well some commercial hunts for marine animals, including polar bear, done from ships sailing from the Scandinavian countries.

This era ended, and sport hunts with American clients became extremely difficult with the passing of the U.S. Marine Mammal Protection Act in the early 1970s.

Demanded by the animal rights industry, and passed by politicians with little knowledge and less regard for impact on the people of the Arctic, this act brought disaster. Not only denying the importation of legally taken polar bear trophies, it also ended the trade in seal and walrus products, the mainstay in the life and economy of native people across the north.

The related social and economic problems continue to this day.

It is ironic to me that many prominent people, especially in the entertainment industry, believe in Hollywood fairy tale "Indian" causes, while at the same time supporting the destruction of the way of life of *real* native people in the North.

By the late 1970s, our family company had reached the point where we were hunting in New Brunswick, Arctic Quebec and Newfoundland. We needed room to expand and new species to offer our growing list of clients, so the Northwest Territories was the obvious choice.

Rather than start from the bottom in yet another far-flung area, we decided to buy into an existing outfit, Qaivvik Ltd. We chose this outfit because it had been the first to take advantage of the newly opened sport hunting opportunities in the NWT.

Almost immediately it became apparent that here, as in other places, the good old days were rapidly coming to a close. For some years Qaivvik Ltd. had enjoyed an almost free rein. Everyone in the hunting world with enough money to participate had lined up to hunt for polar bear, muskox, Peary's caribou, and later the newly listed Central Canadian barren ground caribou.

As can be imagined, this situation did not last for long and soon competition was knocking on the door.

In the Western Arctic, with the settlement of the Inuvialuit land claim, five communities decided to pool their hunts and hire a booking agent. The loss of two of these communities was a real blow to Qaivvik Ltd. The company was better off without the other three

Competition, especially in the Eastern Arctic, became more intense, not only in booking clients, which still wasn't much of a problem, but more importantly, in the selection of suitable areas to hunt.

Qaivvik Ltd. was thus being squeezed from both directions, into the Central Arctic, many areas of which did not offer terrific opportunities for polar bear hunting.

Other attitudes, on my part I must admit, lessened our interest in the polar bear business. I have always believed in being a guide, a hands-on operator of decent-quality hunts, rather than a travel agent sending people around the world to be looked after by others. Our reputation was based upon this premise and every attempt that we had ever made to branch out into the booking agency business ultimately led to unhappy results for someone or other.

Once the "booking agent" method of operation became established, where success is determined by volume, the price structure changed to where there was not sufficient margin available to personally and properly manage the hunts.

Secondly, the ban on importation to the States hampered my enthusiasm for the hunts because I prefer to deal with Americans, people who come from a country where they speak English, where the dollar remains stable and most of the time at a premium to Canadian currency.

The effects of the ban were devastating to our company; the entire balance in the business now depended upon who would aid in breaking the law. I am not revealing anything new; after all these matters are well documented, although many prefer to forget them. We simply refused to become involved in smuggling, or as accessories to smugglers bringing the hides into the United States.

I had long ago determined that if I ever decided to rob a bank, it would be a big one. Likewise if I was going to be a smuggler, there is more portable and much more profitable contraband than a smelly old polar bear skin. Being a crook for such meager rewards just did not appeal that much.

It has since been explained to me by some of the participants (who incidentally got nabbed) that they considered themselves patriots and heroes in defying this undoubtedly bad law. I was not striving to be "noble," and perhaps was only "chicken." But, bad law or not, it was the law of the land from which we draw the vast majority of our clients, and I did not intend to break it.

Believe me, being noble put us at a distinct disadvantage in the business. As a footnote: we did *not* receive any "credit" from either government, or any of the U.S. hunting clubs with all their lofty codes of ethics. Perhaps there is a lesson here.

In retrospect, although I may be guilty of being a coward in not defying the ban, at least I do not have to explain to my grandchildren why Old Gramps has a prison record.

Now I will tell you three stories that illustrate that going on a polar hunt in the Arctic involves just a little bit more than talking to a booking agent and buying an airplane ticket. Keep in mind that having spent a lifetime in this business, I simply abhor the term "adventure," which inevitably can be defined as a "screwed-up deal," as opposed to a safe, simple, and productive experience.

ADVENTURE NUMBER ONE

While busy elsewhere, I was contacted by my partner in Qaivvik with the news that he had booked two overseas hunters into a brand-new hunt to be conducted from a Central Arctic community. I had some misgivings and asked some questions. Why was the tag quota for that community so low? Were any experienced old-time polar bear hunters available to guide? Was it possible to fly out a spike camp to the floe edge?

These were reasonable and prudent questions because I had been on an exploration ship back in the 1960s working to the north and east of this area, and we encountered extremely heavy ice conditions.

The answers I received were not reassuring, but the local Renewable Resources Officer and some younger members of the Hunters and Trappers Association were eager to establish sport hunts in their community. They had heard of others making big bucks in the polar bear hunts.

With very grave misgivings, I sent along Porter Hicks, who had hunted with me twenty times and who does our advertising work in the U.S. I knew Porter could stand just about anything and would come back with an honest evaluation of the hunt. To make a long story at least a bit shorter, my worst fears were realized.

The Game guy forbade them to even think of bringing in an aircraft, available from Cambridge Bay, within easy range, to do a survey of the ice conditions and to fly out a spike camp. He wished to stick with the letter of the regulation requiring dog teams only. This is pure bullshit, because the regulation means that the hunt itself must be done with dogs, and there is no law in the world against aerial ice surveillance or flying in tents and groceries, not even in the NWT.

The result was that they never got more than a few miles out of town, never saw a bear track, and spent more than the time allotted for a successful hunt sitting out in tents, stuck. Fortunately, someone finally had enough brains to send out snowmobiles with dog food and supplies, and they brought the party back to the community.

Fortunately, the two foreigners were content to buy a bear skin from someone in town, and Porter marked it down to experience.

When a meeting was held later to see what went wrong, the young hot-shot guides and the Game guy had no answers. However, an older Inuit gentleman, when asked, spoke for about ten minutes. He said, in effect, that no one but an idiot would try to get out to the floe edge in that direction, and why would anyone want to go way out there with dogs when perfectly good snowmobiles were available?

So much for the agent approach, setting up hunts with long-distance phone calls.

ADVENTURE NUMBER TWO

The second hunt my partner set up in a new area was to take place from a northern Hudson's Bay hamlet. I knew there was a good bear population, at least back in the '60s, because while doing a biological survey, we had come across several abandoned hunting camps strewn with polar bear skulls and bones. Did this, however, indicate the possibility of over-hunting for the fur trade? We would have to find out the hard way.

I had other misgivings. On a visit to the community, I had not been impressed with the fact that a particularly fanatic southern U.S. evangelical group was getting a foothold with the local people. Lest anyone think I am antireligious, please be assured that I am not. However, I might have mentioned that while I have nothing against anyone walking on water, my liability insurance did not cover the clients for such activities.

Once again, I was on the show circuit and unavailable to fly in there myself. My partner assured me that everything was under control and that he had six hunters ready to go. I at least convinced him to break it up, send in two the first time around and the rest later if things turned out to be as good as reported.

The result was that two California hunters flew in. No one was there to greet them at the airstrip. Surprise, surprise, despite the assurance from the people who wanted to be in the polar bear hunting business, nothing was ready.

Food would have to be sent over from Yellowknife, along with our own caribou skin clothing and sleeping bags. The two brothers who had been selected as guides, by the local government guy, did indeed have a six-by-eight tent and a Coleman stove, on which one burner worked.

While they were not really experienced dog drivers, being avid snowmobile fans, they had scraped together an assortment of town mutts, whose previous experience consisted of being staked down with a four-foot chain to freeze all winter and be devoured by flies all summer. Fortunately a somewhat used snowmobile was available to haul camping gear, dog food and the clients.

The results were as one might reasonably predict, even from a distance.

One client told me later, "Starting out of town, people on better snowmobiles kept passing us and laughing. Eight hours later, some of them were coming back, with dead bears and bear parts on their sleds. This was the closest we came to seeing the real thing. We had been told not to expect deluxe accommodation, but that little single wall tent with the roof full of holes and four guys crammed into it, was really uncomfortable."

"Thank God you sent over the skin clothing and the sleeping bags or we would have perished either the first or the second night. The third night we didn't have to worry. Someone came out from town on a snowmobile with some funny smelling tobacco, and the boys bundled us onto the sleds and we returned to town. They said they wanted to watch the hockey play-offs on TV."

One of the hunters purchased a bear, the other guy chased me around for three years until I finally found him another hunt, which I paid for in full, of course.

ADVENTURE NUMBER THREE

The third disastrous episode was my own fault and it came about like this. For years I had been watching all the little old ladies, of one sex or another, happily snapping pictures of the bears in the dump at Churchill, Manitoba. I knew that when the ice in Hudson's Bay started freezing down from the north, the bears migrated up the coast until they could get out onto the ice and start behaving as proper polar bears. It was illegal to assassinate them in Manitoba, but the second they crossed the Sixtieth Parallel into the Northwest Territories, they were fair game.

I knew that weather was stormy and days are short in the fall, but figured that a decent hunt could be arranged out of one of the communities on the coast, which shall remain nameless.

Turned out I was right. My partner, taking no chances, rigged the hunters up in Yellowknife with food, clothing, and sleeping bags, so at least that part was taken care of. I advised them to avoid shooting any bears with big numbers spray-painted on their sides, as about half of them have serial numbers after being studied all summer.

Sledding was difficult, but they began seeing bears just a few miles out of town. One guy shot the first bear he saw, a decent specimen around nine feet square; not a record for sure, but nothing to be ashamed of.

The second guy, who had assured me repeatedly that he would be more than happy with a "representative bear," after seeing a few, decided to become a "trophy hunter." After three days, in which the sport turned down a total of eighteen bears, the guide quit in disgust and took him back to town.

He asked me later, "Whatsamatta *Kabloona*, looking, looking, no shooting?"

This was a valid question from a first-time guide, who thought the aim of the operation was to kill a bear. This is a problem often encountered when asking longtime hunters to be guides, and is only corrected with time spent in training.

Incidentally, the sport still comes up to me at conventions now, ten years later, and whines around the booth because he came home without a bear.

I figured that we had found a decent place to take some hunters. We would go back in, do some badly needed training and make it a good venture for the Hunters and Trappers Association and ourselves. I told my partner to get them under contract.

After a few months and I didn't hear anything, I called to find out that they were not interested in dealing with us. The down south doper who had taken our hunters to the hotel had decided to become a booking agent, and everyone would get rich. They didn't need our help. It took a year of lawyer letters to even get our gear back, and then most of it was destroyed.

These three stories are told, not to elicit sympathy, but simply to point out that there is more to developing Arctic hunting than simply buying an airplane ticket. A decade and more later, it is still subject to uncertainties in many instances. The government of the Northwest Territories has found it necessary to institute a "Deposit Insurance Plan." This was never an issue when a few professionals were involved in northern tourism and hunting; it most certainly is now.

At the end of that particular year, I summarized the economics of sending hunters to places where other people would look after them. Once all the messes had been at least partially cleaned up, and the clients dissuaded from suing us, our company was down approximately twenty-three thousand dollars.

It was time to think it over very carefully and make a decision. We got out of the business.

So now, since the ban has supposedly been lifted, why are we not breaking our necks in the stampede to sell polar bear hunts?

There are several very good reasons . . . beginning with the fact that there isn't enough money in it to interest us. There is no hunt in the world that I am aware of where your exposure to liability claims is as extreme and your profit margin so slim.

The "booking agent syndrome" has prevailed for long enough now, and the people in the northern communities, including the civil servants who should know better, have been filled so full of lies about what to expect in the hosting of visiting hunters, that demands have risen far beyond what the service warrants.

As an example, an issue of our weekly paper last winter quoted an employee of the Department of Renewable Resources, saying that "for rich American sport hunters, the price is no object, $25,000 up to $40,000, no problem." People prefer to believe this sort of fiction, just as they believe that all outfitters are making a fortune.

No one even wrote the paper to inquire as to the source of this remarkable revelation, or what they were smoking when the vision appeared. I would be glad to trade all we made in the last three years we were involved in bear hunts, for one year of that civil servant's salary.

With the lifting of the ban, there has of course been a great stampede of booking agents, and would-be agents, invading the polar bear business and grabbing up deposits from the backlog of U.S. hunters.

Probably viewed from the comfort of the south, the matter of running safe, dependable, and successful hunts in the Arctic looks easy. Just as the people in the communities are led to believe that booking paying clients, at a decent price that allows for a quality trip, is just a matter of standing around the bar in Las Vegas.

Though no one will believe me, it simply isn't that easy.

The following facts, while general in nature, outline quite closely the situation as we near the end of the century.

There are probably two dozen Arctic communities that have access to polar bear tags. About half of these have enough tags to make it worthwhile encouraging the development and maintenance of dog teams. About half of this half are in areas where a good proportion of trophy-sized, big bears, are available and not subject to heavy hunting pressure by snowmobile for the fur trade and cultural uses. Out of these, how many have people interested, equipped, and prepared to offer safe, trouble-free and, successful hunts?

When the big rush is over and the lawsuits all laid to rest and when some community group, with reasonable expectations and good potential wishes to talk to us about a partnership, in which we provide both marketing and management, then we will once again be in the polar bear hunting business.

Until then, my advice remains the same: Study the situation carefully and take out trip insurance before handing over a big deposit to someone who may or may not be there when you arrive. And remember, you can survive a screwed-up deer hunt in Maine or Texas and laugh about it later. You might not be so lucky up North.

ICEBREAKERS AND ARCTIC EXPLORATION

F*rom the mid-1950s to nearly the end of the 1960s, I spent a great deal of my time away from the streams and forests of my native province. Guiding and trapping filled in my time at home.*

Working initially as a radio operator, both on ships and on shore stations, I gravitated to the jobs that were a bit more adventuresome than the ordinary, making good use of skills learned as a guide and in the military, in addition to being somewhat of a specialist in mobile communications.

Unfortunately, although the pay was good, this meant being away from home and family for many months at a time. One of my first postings was to a radio beacon station in the middle of the vast wilderness of subarctic Quebec and Labrador. This was followed by service in various places in the Eastern Arctic.

Tom Hennessey

For a while, in the late '50s, I was Radio Officer on one of the big ice breakers, *CGS Labrador*. We escorted grain convoys through Hudson Straits, across the bay to Churchill, and supply convoys up to the DEW Line Sites in Foxe Basin and on Baffin Island.

The Radio Officer, on most Merchant Marine Ships, also doubled as the Purser, and was universally known as "Sparks" or "Sparky," a holdover from the days of old spark-gap transmitters.

Although radio had been in existence for some time, the sinking of the *Titanic* in 1912 brought about the international requirement for ships at sea to carry radio equipment and stand watches according to agreements among all seafaring nations. The radio officer thus became an essential member of the crew.

As a bit of additional history, during two world wars the services of the men of the Merchant Marine went unrecognized to a great extent, despite the fact that without them the Allied victories in both Europe and the Pacific would have been impossible. It is a statistical fact that casualties, as a percentage, were higher in the Merchant Marine than any branch of the military.

Within this figure, more radio operators went down with ships than did captains.

It is a long and honorable record, and the fact that their job is to guard "safety of life at sea" overshadows the fact that like all sailors, a high percentage of us were either young hell-raisers or old drunks; devoted to duty at sea, but hard to manage in port.

In my day, before microchips and satellite communication, we worked in Morse code, keying high-power vacuum-tube transmitters. The development of a high-speed, but readable "fist" and the ability to copy and record the incoming messages, despite static, signal fading, high seas and hangovers, was the mark of the expert.

We communicated with local coast stations on medium wave frequencies. We stood watch on 500 kilocycles, the international distress frequency. For longer-range transmission, we worked the Morse key on high frequency bands and relayed messages around the world, through the international shortwave network and at times through military installations. Although less than forty years ago, it seems like the Stone Age, compared with present-day technology.

On one memorable trip I had the honor to sail with a legendary Arctic explorer, Superintendent Henry Larsen of the Royal Canadian Mounted Police. During the 1940s, Larsen and his crew of the little wooden ship *St. Roche* made history by traversing the Northwest Passage, first from west to east, and then reversing the journey a year later. This feat has never been duplicated.

The summer of 1958, breaking our way up the east coast of Ellesmere Island, tracing the route of earlier explorers, we became one of the very few ships to attain the region of 80 degrees north latitude, the entrance to Kennedy Channel. Beyond that point, with one of the world's most powerful ice breaking ships, we were unable to penetrate farther into the age-old Arctic ice barrier.

Later I transferred to another branch of government engaged in scientific exploration. We did everything from hydrographic survey, mapping and charting the Arctic archipelago, to oil exploration, biological surveys, and what came to be known as "gathering pertinent data" in defense-related projects.

Up until that time, in some areas of the Eastern and High Arctic, navigational charts were somewhat vague. It would take several summers of hydrographic work to more accurately position landmasses and to carry out soundings that could be relied upon. I have no doubt that some of this work is still being done in places, now thirty-odd years later.

On one ship, the Canadian hydrographic ship *Baffin*, for three years our season would begin with a couple of months on the coast of Labrador.

Most of the work was done ashore and from motor launches, running sounding lines controlled by transit shots taken on markers on the headlands. As we worked our way up the coast, places like Battle Harbor, Mary's Harbor, Black Tickle, Fox Harbor and Port Hope Simpson became our home for the summer.

Then we moved farther north, and for a couple of years worked in Lancaster Sound, Barrow Straits, and Viscount Melville

Sound, the legendary Northwest Passage. Here we did soundings both with the ship, running lines controlled by Decca Navigator systems that we set up on Devon and Cornwallis Islands, and with the motor launches and helicopters in the bays and inlets.

It was an interesting job, and part of it involved visiting sites well known to those who have studied the history of Arctic Exploration. One of the most famous mysteries of the North, surrounds the disappearance of the Sir John Franklin Expedition.

Over the course of more than a century, many expeditions had failed to find the fabled Northwest Passage to the Orient. During the brief summer of 1845, two British ships, *HMS Erebus* and *HMS Terror*, entered Lancaster Sound, and to all intents and purposes sailed into the pages of history.

As part of one voyage we visited Beechey Island, where the crew was known to have spent the first winter after leaving England. Beechey Island, during the summer of 1961 at least, was actually a peninsula at low tide, attached to the western end of Devon Island. Here we found the stone wall remains of a storehouse, and debris left behind by the explorers over a hundred years earlier.

In the near-desert of the High Arctic nothing deteriorates quickly. The wooden staves and metal hoops of barrels that had probably held salt beef and other foodstuffs were still well-preserved. Of particular interest were piles of tin cans, mostly about one-gallon size, all of which had heavy lead soldering around the rims, and a large lead "tit" in the middle of the covers. As far as we could figure this lead nipple must have had something to do with exhausting the air and then sealing the can; different from today's methods, for sure.

On the beach in front of the camp was a ship's mast, which we later learned was from the yacht *Mary*, one of the many vessels which over the years had engaged in the quest for the lost expedition. Behind the camp was a cairn and a monument left by Francis McClintock, another explorer involved in the long search.

Above the campsite, on a low ridge, were a number of graves, those of crewmen who died during that first winter. Some were marked by "grave stones" made from solid oak timber, with markings burned into them. The most legible reads: "Sacred to the memory of John Torrington who departed this life January 18 AD 1846, on board H.M. Ship *Terror*, aged 20 years."

One can only wonder at how this young man had set out from home, full of the hope of a heroic return, only to fall ill and perish in such an isolated part of the world.

Over the course of the years, many further traces of the lost expedition have turned up. Relics have been found on the Boothia Peninsula, on King William Island, and finally on the shores of the mainland continent. Here the last survivors expired as they strove to reach the Back River, which they hoped to ascend and travel south into known country.

There are many theories, but to date no one has found where the two ships actually came to grief. The grave of Sir John Franklin, leader of the ill-fated expedition, remains lost as well. While the voyage ended in disaster, the relief and search parties trying to solve the mystery were responsible for enormous gains in the knowledge of Arctic geography and the inhabitants.

The last year that I worked on this project, we accomplished the accurate positioning of many of the islands in the Passage, put a few more on the charts, and removed at least two that I can remember.

We sailed west to the area of the Magnetic North Pole on Bathurst Island, and continued on a voyage to eventually go into the history books. Before winter closed down the Arctic, we managed to be the first ship ever to completely circumnavigate Baffin Island. Whether such was originally intended or not, I don't know.

Having come up the east coast through Davis Straits and Baffin Bay, we had then turned west through Lancaster Sound. Now finished in that area, we headed south. Heavy, permanent ice prevented a passage down through Prince Regent Inlet, so that we were forced to reverse our course back up around Somerset Island. Heading south again, we were able, with much trouble, to force a route down through Peel Sound.

Turn of the century sporting in New Brunswick, courtesy N.B. archives.

Heading upriver. The way it was done when the author first started guiding.

Trapping in the middle of Labrador.

Eighty degrees North, Ellesmere Island. Fred and friends.

Fred and Irene. Married while on leave from the army.

Sandy Annanack

Sarah Gray and new addition to the family, Payne River, Nunavik.

Not exactly taken by B&C rules, but a nice bear anyway.

"Anybody home?" West coast, Greenland, late 1950s.

Charlie Bolt, Kugluktuk Guide

Traditional skills alive and well.

The author at the grave of John Torrington, one of only a few members of the Franklin expedition to be located. Beechey Island, High Arctic.

Evon Island,
Lancaster Sound.

High Arctic Survey Expedition

Time to leave again. Port of Halifax, 1960s.

A long way from the Arctic, some hunters still need guides.

Home is the
sailor,
Mamozekel
River camps,
1970s.

One that didn't
get away.

End of a long, hard day on snowshoes.

Derek, Martin, and pets, Nictau camps, northern New Brunswick.

im Rikhoff and Fred, one of the first of many annual National Sporting
raternity outings.

After one of many good days on the river. Were Hilly and I ever that young and good looking?

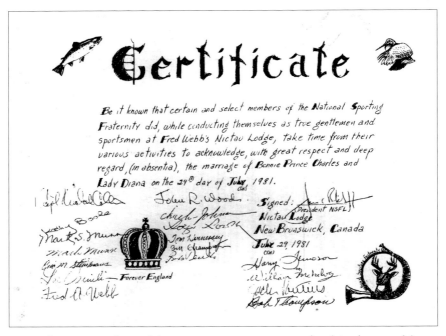

Certificate produced by Tom Hennessey on the kitchen table at Nictau Lodge in honor of the royal wedding.

Guiding the dean of professionals, Lee Wulff, Little Nictau Pool, Tobique River.

On the Koaksoak
River upstream from
Kuujjuag, in the
"good old days."

Norman Annanack
and Mary Jane,
Akuliak, Ungava
Bay.

Coleman
McDougall, chief
guide and
longtime friend,
Nictau Lodge,
1980s

Harry Tennison and
Jimmy Rikhoff, Helen
Falls at George River,
Nunavik.

Sandy Annanack and Fred Webb as guides, with Gene Hill, Sportsman at Helen Falls, 1985.

Toby Johnson, world record, since surpassed, Courageous Lake, NWT.

Derek Webb, on leave from the army, Courageous Lake, NWT.

Barren ground grizzly, head of the Rae River, after a long, hard chase.

Ron Pavlik from Florida, record book barren ground muskox, near Inulik Lake, east of the Coppermine River.

Ledgendary hunter and outdoor writer Col. Charles Askins, Fred Webb and Craig Boddington, on the way down from a Central Arctic hunt

With friends Bruce and Judy Keller, I received the SCI International Professional Hunter Award.

The only time in my life I wore a tuxedo. Awards banquet, Game Coin in San Antonio.

Bobby Snowball and Fred at the falls on the Tunulik River, Ungava Bay.

1994
Courageous
Lake, N.W.T.

Forty years
later, and we
still don't have
the Cadillac I
promised her.

Arrived in the Barren Lands in time for my sixtieth
birthday, a few weeks after undergoing open heart surgery.
One of our great crews: Peter Katiak, Martin Webb, John
Franklin Kaodloak, myself and Irene, Ricky Drygeese, Archie
Doctor, Louie Kokolak.

Friends Pauloosie and Kovenwaak, Hudson Strait.

Lee and Joan Wulff, with guides Fred Webb and Noah Ruff, at the Forks Pool, Tobique River, New Brunswick.

Getting rigged up to go. Fred with Blue Benny, client, guides Tom Everett and John Hancock.

Old enough to join the regiment, too young to go in the bars.

Left is Joe Herring, on the right is Martin Webb. Courageous Lake, NWT.

Tobique River salmon, taken by a fine angler, Bob Cook of Worcester, Mass.

We intended to visit the north coast of King William Island to search for more clues to the Franklin mystery. Despite extremely heavy ice, the ship got close enough to land some of us by helicopter. Here we made a brief but unsuccessful effort to find traces of the expedition. Others have had more luck fairly recently.

Unable to proceed farther south, we retreated back up the coast of the Boothia Peninsula, going ashore from time to time to search for evidence of either Franklin's party or other nineteenth century exploration. Various relics were found, including human remains of undetermined age, all adding to the belief that this must have been the route taken by the vanished party more than a hundred years before.

Returning to Peel Sound, we managed to traverse the narrow confines of Bellot Strait from west to east, stopping to visit the site of a long-abandoned Hudson Bay Company trading post. The only two vessels to have made this passage previously were Amundsen's *Gjoa,* and Larsen's *St. Roche*, the first and second ships to ever complete the Northwest Passage.

Continuing with some difficulty, we broke our way down through the Gulf of Boothia. Here we became hung up for a number of days. Finally, as plans were being made in case it proved impossible to escape, we were able to contact and request assistance from the most powerful icebreaker in the world.

The brand-new *John A. MacDonald*, had a chance to try out her enormous capabilities, in extracting us from the clutches of the ice pack. At last we broke free and bade farewell to our rescuer as she headed back north to complete her own program.

Cautiously working south, in totally uncharted waters, we managed a passage through Fury and Hecla Strait, into northern Foxe Basin. Taking a couple of weeks to do a biological survey in Duke of York Bay, on the north coast of Southampton Island, and make a brief visit to Coral Harbour, the major community on the island, it was time to head for home.

As we came out through Hudson Strait around the end of October, we had officially become the first ship to completely circle

Baffin Island. I don't expect that anyone will feel compelled to try it again, unless for some good reason.

Although I didn't know it at the time, this would be my last Arctic voyage. That winter I was offered a new job, in the international service. I would soon be sailing in warmer waters.

THE CHRISTMAS THEY KILLED THE COOK

As I sit in my comfortable room, in a modern hotel on the Arctic Coast, it is hard to believe how great have been the changes in the North. Arriving from down South in one day, enjoying the luxury of seven channels on the satellite television and instant communication with all the world, it is certainly not much like the old days.

With the holiday season almost upon us, I am reminded of another Arctic Christmas, one that was not all joy and peace. I can tell you the story, but of necessity, the names and situations must be somewhat rearranged. Probably the safest course is to state right up front that the following is pure fiction.

If anyone who was present remains alive and reads this narrative, they will know of which I write.

Shortly following World War II, Canada was rediscovering the North. There had been many expeditions, going back three centuries, but most of the "Whites" one encountered in the North were European missionaries and employees of the Hudson's Bay Company out from The Old Country.

The exceptions were the Mounties and the radio operators manning widely scattered posts across the immensity of the Arctic.

The aboriginal inhabitants lived much as they had since their long-ago ancestors moved into this part of the continent, traveling in small family groups as dictated by the game and the seasons. A few Inuit had begun to settle down around the trading posts and missions, some finding employment with the various government establishments including the radio stations.

Three of these outposts were known as the Straits Stations: Resolution Island, Cape Hopes Advance and Nottingham Island. Their purpose was to provide support to navigation through Hudson Strait and across the bay, assisting the grain ships bound for the railhead at Churchill. Before the opening of the St. Lawrence

Seaway gave access to Canada's heartland, Churchill was a major shipping point, through which the grain from the prairies flowed to feed the world.

At that time, a posting to one of the Straits Stations lasted about fifteen months, for which you were paid extra because of the isolation. To many young radio operators, the added pay was secondary to the quest for adventure.

The new crew arrived with the first ship, usually about mid-July. Most landed, after a three-week voyage from Quebec City, on the MJ *McLean*, one of the last of the coal-burning icebreakers. The outgoing operators would usually stay for the busy summer to train the newcomers, and then depart around the middle of October, when the last grain ship had been escorted out through the straits.

The season's supplies of food, coal, building materials, fuel oil, and gasoline all came north by ship. Everything, including the feed for the two dozen hens that would supply eggs until they ended up in the cooking pot, were brought ashore by barge and carried or hoisted on a wire line up to the station.

When the three blasts of the departing ship's steam whistle stopped echoing from the cliffs of Acadia Cove, you knew where you would be until summer returned to the Arctic.

With the closing of the shipping season, the stations dropped back to a restricted schedule, taking weather observations and maintaining watch on a couple of emergency frequencies, from which nothing but static was heard for most of the time. This left plenty of opportunity for reading, for hunting and trapping, or for brooding and worrying, depending on your personal nature. To those who like country living, it was the greatest adventure in the world; to those who missed the bright lights of civilization, it was the opposite.

On this particular year, the crew at one of the stations consisted of five *Kabloona* (whites) plus two Inuit families, the members of which spanned three generations.

George, while serving for the first time as officer in charge, was a veteran Arctic hand who had spent time on many of the stations in the Eastern Arctic. Jimmy, the second operator, came from a Newfoundland outpost with a population only about twice that of the station. Still, he worried about missing the city life.

Emil, the mechanic, was a French Canadian from the north shore of the St. Lawrence; he was an enthusiastic hunter and fisherman, who spoke very little English.

The third operator, youngest of the group, was looking forward to the Arctic adventure. He labored under the nickname "Sparky," a title traditionally awarded shipboard radio operators.

Hans, the cook, was the only jarring note in the outfit. The crew was not long in finding out that, like most cooks on bush jobs, he wanted to be the boss. About fifty years of age, he had a reputation as a bully when drunk, and a troublemaker in any condition. There were rumors, not only of drunkenness, but also of sexual abuse—habits apparently overlooked by head office, as cooks were hard to find for isolated locations.

The officer in charge was determined to make the best of things as there was not much choice in the matter. Once the ship has departed you were there, for better or worse.

Heading into the early winter the days rapidly grew shorter. Soon real daylight was almost totally submerged into the dusky gloom of the Arctic night.

Plenty of work remained to be done around the station, maintenance on equipment and buildings not finished during the summer rush. Diesel fuel from the big tank on the hill had to be transferred to the smaller tank beside the generator shack. Electricity was supplied to the radio transmitters and receivers, the station building itself, and the beacon lights on the antenna masts. Lighting in the staff building and the two cabins in which the Inuit families lived was supplied by naptha gas and kerosene.

Heating and cooking for the most part was by coal, supplemented parttime with fuel oil. One of the never-ending jobs was cutting ice from the freshwater pond and hauling it to the big tank above the kitchen, to melt down for cooking and drinking. Most of the outside chores were taken care of by Emil the mechanic and Sparky, working with the Inuit crew.

Mathewsee and his wife Alice were experienced station staff; they had one daughter, Pearlee, about sixteen, plus three younger children. Willy and his sister Annie, both in their twenties; Annie's boy Little Georgee; and their grandmother made up the other family.

As time went on Sparky and Emil, interested in the land and the life of the Inuit, became close friends, despite the difficulties in communication. They enjoyed helping Mathewsee and Willy get their dog teams trained, and looked forward to trapping and hunting, later in the winter when snow conditions made it possible to travel.

Everything would have been fine in the little community, except for one irritant: Hans the Cook. Starting with minor incursions, such as overruling the officer in charge in the matter of setting meal hours, he was soon making other moves to take over.

The Inuit families drew basic supplies from the station, as part of their contract with the government, to supplement their traditional fare of meat and fish.

While most cooks would have been glad to provide extra food left over from the station meals to people who could certainly use it, Hans considered it his duty to stick to the contract and supply only the staples such as flour, sugar, baking powder, and tea. He also became obsessed with organizing the times and conditions under which he would issue the food.

George the OIC attempted to handle the cook diplomatically, even if at the expense of some inconvenience to everyone else concerned. Any attempt at imposing authority over Hans was met with sullen withdrawal. He refused to speak to any of the station staff except George. His treatment of the Inuit staff was even more bizarre, alternating between cold disapproval one day and being overly affectionate the next.

Taken separately, most of the friction-causing problems were petty enough, but in isolation events take on a different perspective. George, with many Arctic winters behind him, but faced for the first time with being the boss, was apparently willing to go to any lengths to avoid confrontation. This might have worked with a reasonable and sane person; Hans took it as a sign of weakness.

On isolated stations, getting ready for Christmas and the celebration itself took on tremendous importance. Usually the cook is the center of such festivities, but in this case it was apparent that Hans had no intention of participating, much less doing anything beyond the ordinary routine.

When inquiries were made about cooking some Christmas fruit cakes, it was discovered that most of the dried fruit had disappeared, along with a good portion of the year's supply of sugar. The OIC might pretend to be blind to the truth, but everyone else knew that these were the main ingredients for home-brewed booze. In a happy and congenial crew, a bit of Christmas cheer would have been welcome. However, in this case it had the potential of causing nothing but trouble.

Two days before Christmas, while visiting for tea and bannock, the problems with the cook were being discussed when an embarrassed Alice brought up the subject that Hans had been making unwanted sexual advances to both the adult females and the children. He had also made it clear that such were connected to the issuing of the rations. Things had reached the point where they were reluctant to go up to the station unless the rest of us were present.

Sparky's first instinct was for immediate and violent confrontation. This was forestalled by the officer in charge, as he promised to take up the matter with the cook, and meanwhile surely everything would work out. This was, after all, the holiday season.

Christmas Eve brought it all to a violent conclusion. Hans had been well into the home brew all day and when supper was not on the table Emil and Jimmy had started to put something together. Suddenly a commotion was heard from the kitchen and a sobbing Pearlee, Alice's daughter, burst into the dining room in disarray, with a slobbering, drunken Hans still trying to pull her trousers down.

Initially stunned by the spectacle, Emil reacted in time to grab the cook and allow the girl to dart out the door into the cold night. Hans, enraged to the point of insanity and outweighing the mechanic by a hundred pounds, threw him onto the floor and proceeded to try to choke him to death. The fear-struck Jimmy, who had never handled a weapon before, grabbed the station rifle, kept loaded in case of polar bear visits. In a panic, he pointed it at the cook.

Dropping the gasping Emil, Hans lunged, grabbed the barrel of the rifle to wrench it away from Jim. It discharged, pointing straight into his groin.

Sparky, on watch at the station, was startled out of his dreams of Christmas at home by two of the younger kids bursting in the door. "Come quick Sparky, Jimmy shoot cook." Tearing down the icy path to the house, in slippery sealskin kamicks, he entered the living room to a nightmare of sound, sight, and smell.

Screaming and thrashing in a spreading pool of blood and vomit, the cook was rapidly bleeding to death. Emil and George, attempting to hold him down and tie a belt around his upper thigh, were drenched in blood as well. White-faced and useless, Jimmy still held in his hands the .303 Enfield, which usually hung above the door. Over it all hung the stench of blood, vomit, excrement, and cordite.

Passing through the upper right thigh bone, the softnosed 225-grain bullet had cut the major artery and blown away nearly the entire buttock. Despite every effort to staunch the flow of blood, shock soon took over, and in minutes no pulse could be found. The cook, surrounded by the entire crew, southern and Inuit, was very obviously dead. So much for having a Merry Christmas!

Sparky, unable to think of anything else to do in such a situation, returned to the radio station in a vain attempt to obtain medical advice from the nearest nursing facility, far away in Churchill. Although futile, he supposed rightly that it was legally required in such a situation.

Medium frequency Marine Band radio being the only possible communication, a relay was always required even at the best of times, via one of the other Straits Stations. To attempt such, on Christmas Eve especially, was asking for a miracle. A report would have to be transmitted later, but for now there were more pressing matters to take care of.

As can be imagined, everyone was in shock at what had happened. Sitting around the kitchen table, with only occasional glances at the blanket-covered body in the middle of the dining room floor, we began to formulate a plan.

First of all, George, as officer in charge, would have to write out in detail a record of what had occurred, while memories were still fresh. This would be signed by all present and forwarded to headquarters as soon as conditions made it possible.

Second, someone would have to go through and pack all of the late cook's personal effects, attempting in the process to find any mention of next of kin to be notified.

Finally, the body would have to be preserved in some manner as there was sure to be an inquiry when the ship came up the following July. After some deliberation, it was decided to wrap the corpse in the blanket, tie it up in good shape and place it in an empty corner of the coal shed where it would freeze within hours.

Sparky, Emil, and the two Inuit staff members would take care of this chore. As the corpse was still fairly flexible the wrapping job was soon accomplished, a bit messy but not bad for amateur morticians. Pockets contained nothing much but a cheap cigarette lighter and a package of condoms. The only other item was his wrist watch, still ticking away the way the Timex commercial guarantees.

All wondered at how such a big bully had shrunk so much. "Easier to handle dead than alive," was the opinion expressed by Sparky. Laid out on top of a couple of fuel drums in the coal shed, old Hans faced his first Christmas in Hell.

Back in the staff house, George and the still-blubbering Jim had gone through the cook's quarters and among other things had come up with a bottle of Scotch, smuggled up on the ship and undoubtedly kept to celebrate Christmas. Who says an ill wind doesn't blow someone some good? There was no mention of next of kin, perhaps something was on record at headquarters.

Christmas, although somewhat subdued, was a happy occasion, helped along by the cache of home brew discovered hidden in the pantry. With a message duly relayed along the line to headquarters, outlining the basics of the case and with no reply immediately forthcoming, the little community settled down to what should have been a routine Arctic winter.

Alas, it was not to be. Hans, who was a problem in life, continued to spoil the northern tranquillity even in death.

Groping his way up to the station one dark February evening, Sparky tripped over an object in the path. Going back with a lantern, his worst fears were confirmed. It was the somewhat worse-for-wear body of the late cook. Someone, one of the kids perhaps, had left the door open. The station dogs had managed to pull out poor old Hans and proceeded to eat one of his shoulders and most of his face.

Upsetting for sure, but hard to place any blame. Huskies are well known to be totally lacking in discrimination when it comes to any free lunch.

After turning down several alternate storage options, the little group, sort of spooked by this time, decided to wrap him up again, this time in double blankets and a wornout tent, and to hoist him partway up one of the antenna masts, where no dog could hope to get at him.

George, the officer in charge, had gained several white hairs in his beard by now. Jimmy, who was meek and retiring at the best of times, had become a shadowy presence, doing his shifts and retiring to his room. The rest of the crew, however, was enjoying the winter.

Emil had taken over the job of cooking and showed far more talent in that line than had his predecessor. Sparky was happily getting ready for an extended hunting trip up toward the northern end of the island. The Inuit staff, with Hans out of the picture, happily visited the station several times a week for tea and biscuits and card games.

Somehow everyone got used to seeing the bundle suspended fifty feet up the mast. As the weeks went by, Sparky began to view old Hans with some grudging fondness and would wave to him on the way up to the station to stand watch.

Going out during the midnight shift to take the weather observations, when everyone else on the island was asleep, it was somehow less lonely when one could look up and see Hans swaying in the breeze silhouetted against the moon. On dark nights, the creaking of the wire and the rattle of the chain shackle meant that he was still there, sharing the midnight watch.

For the young operator and the mechanic the winter passed quickly. Once the snow had firmed up for good travel, extensive trips were made up the spine of the island, and north along the sea edge fronting the cliffs. Trapping for white foxes and hunting for seals provided ample excuse to get away from the station.

George and Jim, on the other hand, never ventured out of sight of the buildings, spending most of their off-duty hours sitting at the table writing and rewriting the report that would be turned over when the ship arrived. Everyone went to great lengths to cheer up poor Jimmy, assuring him endlessly that the shooting had been an accident and that no one in authority could possibly attach any blame to him.

However, in those days before the liberal elite abolished hanging in Canada, and especially with months to brood upon the matter, it was weighing heavily on his mind. Being able to glance up, day or night, at the body swinging in the breeze undoubtedly did not improve his mental outlook. By the end of March, there were days he didn't venture out of his bedroom. Sparky and George were keeping the twenty-four hours of watch at the station.

As spring approaches and the open water of the Straits, caused by enormous tidal currents, brings the floe edge closer to land, unsettled weather is common. A warm spell and fog brought on by a southerly wind turned into a four-day blizzard, as the wind backed around into the east. Blowing snow would have made it impossible to travel between the buildings except for tunnels kept shoveled out by Willy, and a trip between the staff quarters and the radio station became a major expedition.

It finally blew itself out about four o'clock in the morning on Easter Sunday, enabling Sparky to dig out the thermometer boxes to resume the weather reports which had, of necessity, been suspended during the storm. For a while he could not figure out what it was, but he had a feeling that something was missing.

Finally, it struck him. Climbing out of the trench he looked down to the antenna mast, and sure enough, Hans the Cook was gone. The wire hung slack, half-wrapped around the mast; the shackle had worn through sometime during the storm. At the foot of the mast was unbroken drifted snow. No telling what had happened, or when.

A day was spent, shoveling and probing the snowdrifts, but no sign of the body was found. George was, by now, sunk in his own private depression. He and Jimmy were both convinced that the entire staff would be charged with the murder of the cook.

The rest of the crew went on about the business of running the station, bringing in the far-flung fox sets, and taking advantage of the increasing open water-hunting for seals and polar bears.

About the middle of May, the puzzle of the disappearing cook was finally solved. Sparky and Mathewsee, hunting along the shore a mile away from the station, came to an area where snow had blown away, leaving the unmistakable impressions where a large polar bear had traveled quite some time previously. Idly following along, as the track appeared and faded, they were shocked to come across part of a tent, frozen into the ice. Chopping it out, they encountered pieces of a gray wool blanket, beyond any doubt part of the shroud that had contained the body.

Two hours of searching revealed nothing further. That night, with an onshore wind, a large section of ice broke away from the land and when the wind shifted, it moved out into the current. The search for Hans was thus concluded.

Talking it over with the Inuit guides later, it was apparent that sometime during the big storm, when the human inhabitants were sticking close to the buildings, and when the dogs were all buried in the snow as they do to wait out a blizzard, the chain shackle had worn through and the body had dropped.

Annie's grandmother, sleeping the light sleep of the elderly, now remembered that something had disturbed her slumber the third night of the storm. Was it some of the dogs who had awakened with bear smell in their nostrils, some disturbance made by the bear, or simply some change as the wind shifted? No one will ever know for sure, but old Nanook, as bears often do, carried away his prize to deal with at leisure, away from the habitation of man and dogs.

An inquest was held, somewhat complicated by the absence of a body, when the ship arrived in July. After nearly three years, a conclusion was reached when the entire incident was declared a tragic accident.

Thankfully there were no next of kin to complicate the matter further.

By the time the final judgment was rendered, George, the officer in charge, had passed away and was buried where he had spent a good portion of his life, in the Arctic. Jimmy was retired as being unsuitable for further northern posting, after some months spent in the psychiatric hospital in Dartmouth, Nova Scotia. Following the conclusion of the hearings, Emil apparently returned to the north shore of the St. Lawrence and has not been heard from since.

Of the native members of the staff, Mathewsee and Alice are gone. Some of the children probably still live in Nunavik. Years later, Sparky was reunited with Annie, spending her last years in a wheel chair, still a wonderfully warm and cheerful lady. Willy died in Kuujjuaq in the late 1980s.

Sparky looks back upon the "good old days" when all were young and free in the land of the Inuit.

NANOOK

T aking up nearly an entire wall in my office is a rug made from the hide of a truly tremendous polar bear. I did not myself shoot this particular bear. It was killed by a late and dear Inuit friend, Sandy Annanack, on a trip to the ice edge off Killiniq, the northernmost tip of Labrador. It is certainly as valuable to me as if I had personally pulled the trigger.

One might assume, having had ample opportunity over the past forty years of travel in the North, that I would have filled a trophy room with bears. The truth is that there has only been one occasion that I am definitely sure of when mine was the only bullet to hit the bear. In the course, however, of traveling and hunting with Inuit friends, during the 1950s and 1960s, my old Winchester featured fairly prominently in several bear mix-ups.

I hesitate to admit, to hunting clients in particular, that despite being a guide all my life, I have never actually been what is termed a "sport hunter." Simply too busy trying to make a living out of hunting, I have not had much time to indulge in it for fun.

I saw my first real live polar bear from the deck of an old coal-burning icebreaker, stopped for the night in the ice at the entrance to Hudson's Bay. Nose in the air, he was coming right up the wind toward the ship, attracted I suppose by the ever-present smell of rotten meat and burned grease coming from the galley exhaust fans.

We had on board a couple of Inuit families; four of the male members quickly produced rifles of various sizes and conditions and lined up along the rail. In those days, if there were any game laws most of us traveling in the Arctic were unaware of them.

The dogs chained out on the foredeck were still fighting over their supper and hadn't seen or winded the bear, or there would have been an uproar as he kept getting closer by the minute. I ran below and brought up my .30-30 Winchester, figuring they might need some back-up. The bear kept coming and it was easy to see he would soon be within dependable shooting range when, all of a sudden, the mate, an excitable Frenchman, cut loose from the wing of the bridge.

He managed to strike the ice about halfway to the bear. It was just enough to make the bear think the matter over, dive into the water between the ice pans, and make off at a great rate of speed.

That was my first encounter with Nanook, the Great White Bear of the North. I didn't know it at the time, but I would have the chance to see many more of his kind, some at much closer range.

I was employed then as a radio operator aboard ships and as a guide and communications man ashore on various survey and scientific expeditions. In almost all cases we worked with native Inuit helpers.

In the 1950s most Inuit still maintained a fairly traditional life; traveling mostly in small family groups, they lived from the land and the sea. About the only cash economy was the result of trapping white foxes and hunting seals, for which there were good markets, before the whims of the fashion world and the development of the animal rights industry killed this important part of their livelihood.

Some other wage employment was just becoming possible. Working around the small communities, on the isolated radio stations, and with various seasonal survey and scientific projects.

In the case of the radio stations and on some of the scientific trips, whole families were employed. Without the ladies who gathered and prepared food and made most of the skin boots and clothing, nothing much would have been accomplished.

Aside from the prohibition on killing muskox, mostly present only on the High Arctic islands and scattered across the barren grounds west from Hudson Bay, very few restrictions were placed upon hunting for subsistence. Sport hunting had not yet become an issue and quotas, season, or methods of hunting had no application to a people who had survived in the Arctic environment for centuries by hunting.

Simply as a matter of life, everyone went armed and in most cases killed anything that was encountered, if it was required to feed people or dogs, or the fur was useful. Didn't matter if it was a loon, a seal, a caribou, walrus, narwhal . . . from owls to whales and everything in between, including polar bear.

Incidentally, if you have ever heard the saying, "tougher than a boiled owl," be assured that like most old sayings and stereotypes, it is well founded in fact. One serving of half-boiled *ookpik* was sufficient to last me a lifetime, right up there on my list of favorites with a good mature stewed loon.

In those days, large-caliber magnum rifles were unheard of in the Arctic. Aside from shotguns and the ever-present .22s, most Inuit hunters favored the .22 Hornet; later the .222 came into its own. Firearms were universally banged up and rusty, to the dismay of some southern visitors. Rifles in the North are used as tools, not generally treasured as art objects. Later, when we began dealing with sport hunters, I used to tell them that if their fancy thousand-dollar rifle was out there 365 days a year, lashed on sleds, bouncing in the bow of a motor canoe in the ocean, or standing in a snow bank outside the tent, it would probably show some signs of wear also.

I always carried my Model 94 .30-30, primarily because it was the only rifle I owned at the time. It was listed in the Sears catalog then at $59.95, and I couldn't have afforded to buy one, but a grateful Yankee deer hunter I had guided who left it with me.

In the present era, with strict game laws and enlightened attitudes by all of us toward conservation, not to mention the idiots of the antihunting movement, one hesitates to tell tales from the "good old days." However, I will admit that, in addition to the ordinary prey such as deer, moose, and caribou, that old .30-30 killed everything from a weasel to a three-quarter-ton walrus, and was involved in the assassination of at least a dozen polar bears. As a tool of survival, it killed rabbits for stews, and shot the heads off many a grouse and ptarmigan; I even shot a salmon one time in a brook in Labrador. That rifle has put a lot of meat in the pot!

Over the years I have been the grateful recipient of a number of expensive and high-powered rifles from appreciative clients, writers, and manufacturers. However, that old .30-30, though derided at times by the Magnum Boys as the "Red Ryder Special," still holds a special place in my arsenal. Someday it will belong to one of my sons, or grandsons . . . that is if some teen-aged burglar, or some government bureaucrat, doesn't manage to steal it from me.

Hunting as we did it, in the context of that day, had absolutely nothing to do with hunting as a "sport" or the Boone and Crockett Code of Ethics. We were simply working and traveling and our Inuit companions pursued with a vengeance any bear that was unlucky enough to cross our path. They were killed by chance encounter among the ice ridges, and in the water from boats. Some were chased by dog team and *komatik*, cutting the dogs loose at the proper time to bring them to bay. With the arrival of the snowmobile, it is a good thing that quotas were established.

One of the most interesting hunts, and perhaps the closest to a "traditional" hunt that I witnessed, occurred one bright early June day, off the southeast corner of Baffin Island. Out mainly for seals, we had been quite successful and had four laid on the ice when Mathewsee spotted a medium-sized bear far out among the shifting ice floes. The bear was hunting seals himself.

It was not the type of situation where one could take off in pursuit with the sled, so we would have to try to lure the bear within reasonable range. The dogs were taken back up among the rocks, out of sight, and anchored securely.

We had been successful in crawling out to within range of the seals sunning themselves on the ice, despite the discomfort of getting half-soaked in pools of melted water. Now my companion was going to try the same with the bear, except that he first had to entice it to come closer, onto the solid shorebound ice. He knew I wanted to help, but even though we were about evenly covered with seal guts and gurry, he convinced me that, "Bear maybe no like smell *Haloona*, maybe only *Inuk*."

Tom Hennessey

So I was persuaded to remain a spectator, but could at least contribute in other ways. Mathewsee had previously killed three out of the four seals with his old rusty Cooey single-shot .22, but he gracefully accepted the loan of my "Really Big Gun," the .30-30 lever action.

To approach the sunning seals, we had crawled along behind a two-foot-square frame covered with white canvas, sneaking ahead when they were relaxing and freezing in place when they looked up . . . about every minute it seemed. Now, from around the side of a big chunk of shore ice, I watched as Mathewsee tried a variation of the same plan on the bear. I was equipped with half of a pair of binoculars, the other side having met with some misfortune. We had agreed that as he moved out, keeping low, he would look back at me for direction if the bear got out of his sight.

The bear by now was about a mile out, in and out of sight in the loose ice just off the floe edge. The wind, slight though it was, blew pretty well across the scene, so that until the hunter was actually spotted, the bear would be unaware of his presence.

Partway out, to my surprise, Mathewsee abandoned the white screen and simply began sort of humping along, trying to avoid the deeper pools of water, while moving ever closer to the bear. I began to understand the strategy at last: When hunting seals you try to look like the snow and when hunting bears you do your best to look like a tasty seal. The hunter thus becomes the decoy.

For what seemed like a long time, this drama continued, the bear and the hunter getting closer together, but neither seeing the other, while through the spyglass I had a grandstand view of the arena. At last, the bear, sensing something out of the ordinary, clambered up over the edge of the ice. Spotting the strange object, now about two hundred yards away, he must have thought it was his lucky day. To his limited vision, probably old Mathewsee looked just like "*utjuk*," the big square flipper seal.

I was now watching an age-old performance, one that had undoubtedly been played out many times, since the days before rifles, when a harpoon or lance would have been the weapon. The hunter would stay still for minutes, then wriggle ahead, not directly toward the bear but at a tangent that brought him ever closer. The bear by now was practically crawling on his belly also . . . stalking the "*utjuk*."

Tense with suspense and excitement, I knew that something had to give. Although looking through a telescope shortens up the perspective, I know the bear was within thirty feet when he started to rise, and then, in an instant, lurched over backward, a red spot centered on his chest . . . "*Ka-pow*" the sound at last reached my ears. The hunt was over.

Trying to run in sealskin boots over wet ice is always a challenge. By the time I slithered out there, it was time to start the skinning. Mathewsee solemnly handed me the rifle and the remaining two cartridges. We had only had three. He expressed his satisfaction, "Really Big Gun, killing bear only one shot!"

For the millionth time, I wished that I had a decent camera and some film, but alas we just couldn't afford such luxuries.

Over the course of the years there have been many more "bear stories," enough to fill a book. All different and all exciting; the time the bear tried to clamber into the boat, the time when, wakened by the dogs, I crawled out to find an enormous bear about twenty feet away standing astride the meat-laden *komatik*—and many, many other incidents, most of which resulted in the demise of old Nanook.

The fur market at that time was fairly good. I remember one season when white foxes sold for seven dollars, blues for four, and the very rare black fox for nearly a hundred. It must be remembered that this was in the era of four to six dollars a day wages, so at these prices the hunter made out very well indeed. Polar bear skins, if well handled, brought anywhere from twenty to eighty dollars or so, a far cry from what they were to reach a few years later.

Few of us, myself included, had the foresight, or the money, to hang onto any of these "bargains." In fact, I can tell you of one trade we made, to illustrate that we were not very smart traders in those days.

On a calm August evening, a rust-covered old tramp steamer, flying a flag we did not recognize, anchored well up in Acadia Cove, off Resolution Island. I managed to raise her on the radio, to find out she was the SS *San Carlos*, headed in to Churchill for a load of grain to transport around the world to India. We were invited to come out and visit, an invitation eagerly accepted by myself and our Inuit staff.

A half-hour later, fourteen of us, including women and kids, all loaded aboard a freighter canoe and went out to find that they had already lowered the gangway so we could scramble aboard. Met at the rail by the skipper and the radio officer, both of whom spoke passable English, I was invited to the captain's cabin for a drink. It was my introduction to cognac, certainly a cut above the vile-tasting home brew with which we had been poisoning ourselves for months.

226

Meanwhile, my Inuit friends were escorted down to the galley, where the cook and his helpers laid on an enormous feed of codfish and rice. Despite the difficulty in communication between Spanish and Inuktitut, someone brought out an accordion and a party was soon in progress.

Sometime during the festivities the subject of trading came up, so a couple of our guys went ashore to return with a bunch of fox and sealskins, some stone carvings, and a really good big polar bear which immediately took the captain's eye. Cash money, especially in Spanish currency, wasn't of much use to us, but the ship was a veritable treasure trove of articles useful in the North. We ended up loaded to the gunwales with food, carpentry tools, yards of white canvas, miles of rope . . . lots of good stuff. Willy, one of our younger guides, went ashore in his stocking feet after he bartered his sealskin boots for a handsaw and a ten-pound bag of flour.

As the polar bear was the top item, we held that out to the last, and then swapped it for a full three gallons of cognac, in jugs wrapped in heavy twine and wax. The captain, in a fit of generosity, threw in a pack of pornographic playing cards. We were satisfied that we had got the best of the deal.

The cognac, though tasting like varnish remover, lasted a long time as we rationed it out for special occasions. The playing cards were something else again. This was in the days before every newsstand featured glossy magazines full of bare-naked people, so they were quite shocking. They were especially intriguing to our native friends, who couldn't quite figure out some of the things these white people were doing.

The photographs must have been shot in the 1920s in a portrait studio, as they all featured the same background. The ladies involved were big huskies with high-topped boots and combs in their hair, while the lone male participant was a well-endowed but skinny little runt with a Charlie Chaplin mustache, wearing only his black socks, held up by garters. Masterpieces for sure, I should have kept them as they would undoubtedly be museum material today.

Fond memories, a few pictures, and one polar bear rug, are all I retain to remind me of long-gone journeys and companions.

Cliché though it may be, I cannot but think that these were the "good old days." Bridging the gap between Stone Age and Atomic Age, these were the last of the days of space and freedom in Arctic Canada.

NORTHERN LIGHTS

Courageous Lake, Northwest Territories, 1990s

*C*old, calm and clear; a beautiful Northern evening. As I step outside to check the camp before turning in, I can see that the guides and guests have gone to bed in anticipation of an early morning launch to hunt the shores of Courageous Lake. We are now into the third week of our caribou season; so far it has been an enjoyable one, with many fine trophies taken.

My son Martin, the camp manager, cuts the diesel generator. The land drops back to primeval silence, broken only by the music of the loons, tuning up in the bay behind the camp. To the southeast the full moon rises from behind the esker. So strong, so near—the hunter's heart feels drawn to answer the call from beyond the hill, to run with his brother, the wolf.

Suddenly the sky is lit with roving bands and swirls of palest green. Across the entire arc of the heavens, aurora borealis, the northern lights of mystery and legend. I rouse my wife, Irene, from the tent, my partner in a lifetime of wilderness work and travel. No strangers are we to the land beyond the trees, but here we stand, as much in awe as the first-time visitor, as waves and billows, with flashes of rainbow colors, march across our line of vision.

The oft-quoted lines of Robert Service run through my mind: "The Northern Lights have seen queer sights, but the queerest they ever did see . . . " I recall with fondness how these northern lights have illuminated a lifetime of Arctic journeys.

Eastern Arctic, 1950s

We had been stuck for two days in a hastily built igloo. The blizzard had stopped in the night. Now within a good, long day's sledding of our home base, my two Inuit companions were eager to get going. I had lost track of the days, but for something approaching two weeks we had been hunting and traveling. From caches along the coast, we were now bringing back two *komatiks* loaded with seal and fish, food for a couple of large families and about thirty dogs.

A mug of heavily sweetened tea helped wash down the few bites of bannock and frozen char that passed for breakfast. Turning off the primus stove reminded me that we were nearly out of fuel. Maybe enough left for another mug-up on the trail, but we had better get in tonight. Bedding skins and sleeping bags were bundled up, last minute toilet chores taken care of in the soon-to-be-abandoned igloo. With outside clothing on, I started to crawl out through the entrance tunnel. With a laugh, Pauloosie provided a shortcut by the simple expedient of a few swipes of his snow knife. One more lesson in Arctic travel for the *Kabloona*.

The wind had quit around midnight. We stepped out into a dead calm, a landscape of sculptured wonder, lit by every star in the universe and the Aurora rolling and flashing from horizon to horizon.

As I paused to view the spectacle, the beliefs of the Old People came to mind; here indeed were displayed the spirits of the long departed, sent to light the way of the traveler.

With a pan of melted snow water and a piece of polar bear skin, Isaac, the younger Inuk, worked at putting a new surface on his runners, while Pauloosie and I stacked everything in preparation for loading the *komatiks*.

One after another, twenty mounds of snow erupted; two teams of dogs staked and chained apart. Now stretching, pissing, leaping and howling, they knew they wouldn't be fed until evening, but always hopeful that we would be careless enough to leave something edible within reach.

Breath stood frozen in the air from men and dogs alike, as we finished loading and hitching up to travel. Far to the south the faintest glow reminded me of a sun not due to top the horizon for at least another couple of weeks. Overhead to light our trail, the vast array of aurora borealis. With any luck, tonight we would eat and sleep, with friends around us, in a warm cabin.

Barrow Straits, High Arctic, 1960s

Working on a geographic and hydrographic survey on the Canadian government ship *Baffin*, we had spent the summer charting the waters of the Northwest Passage. Now in early September, with the approach of winter threatening to close down the operation for another year, we had placed a lone surveyor on top of Prince Leopold Island by helicopter. He was there to take telurometer measurement shots across the strait to Cornwallis Island. Within a few hours, a snowstorm had descended, not severe but persistent enough to bring helicopter operations to a halt.

Twenty-four hours later it was still snowing. When last contacted, before the failure of his radio batteries, the surveyor reported that although in no danger, he was indeed uncomfortable and hungry.

Employed as an expedition guide and communications operator, I was paid for this kind of job. Examining the chart, the navigator and I decided that if we could get ashore safely on the narrow beach at the foot of the cliffs, we could probably work our way up the edge of a small glacier that filled a steep valley coming down to the shore. The ship approached the island on radar, and with a couple of seamen volunteers, I was able to get ashore by motor launch. Despite the light snow and fog restricting visibility to a hundred feet or so, we soon started to pick our way up the glacier.

Partway up I came across the fresh tracks of a good big polar bear. Abandoning the more traditional route along the water's edge, he had stopped in several places to dig into the hill, possibly for bird nests, which were numerous. Having brought along my .30-30, mostly intended for signaling as we tried to locate the stranded surveyor, I chambered one, just in case. The tracks kept heading in the direction we were traveling, and I couldn't help but wonder if we were going to have some competition in picking up our stranded companion.

From where we finally reached the top of the cliff, it was only about a half-mile to where the survey point had been established.

Visibility was by now nearly zero, and the compass worse than useless this close to the Magnetic North Pole. However, guided by the steady wind, we walked right up to within hollering distance of our lost friend. Needless to say, he was glad to have company, especially as we had brought a primus stove, a tent, and food.

Contact was soon established with the ship and Captain Kettle agreed with my decision to await better conditions before attempting the return trip.

Late in the evening the storm ended and the skies cleared. A million stars and awe-inspiring Aurora shining upon the new snow provided plenty of light to travel. Camp was swiftly broken and the glacier descended without incident or injury.

Pacing the shore to keep warm, waiting for the motor launch, I once again ran across the fresh tracks of our fellow traveler. Far down the curve of the beach I thought I could make out the form of Nanook, the great white bear, going about the business of patrolling his island. With the rifle under my arm, I couldn't help but think that perhaps it was best for both of us that we did not meet in person.

Turning back I could see that the launch was rapidly approaching, soon we would be back aboard ship with a hot coffee in hand, talking over plans for the next day's operation.

Once more the Northern Lights had brought me to my destination.

UNGAVA BAY, NUNAVIK, 1970S

Bill Tait and I, with a group of Inuit friends from George River, were headed up the coast to evaluate a new hunting ground. The local people wished to open a caribou hunting camp. They had the ambition and the caribou, and it was my job to figure out if the logistics were reasonable and whether the trips could be marketed successfully. For this trial run we had brought along a small party of visiting hunters.

Once around the headland at the mouth of the river, it becomes quickly apparent that you are traveling on the ocean. The big freighter canoes favored by the people of the area can handle

232

fairly heavy seas, but only when driven by people who have spent their lives hunting and fishing on this coast. The shorelines are rockbound and constantly changing, depending upon the state of the tides, which are recognized as the highest in the world. I was glad to be in the boat belonging to Stanley Annanack, a true old-time Inuk hunter and traveler. If anyone could get us there safely it was Stanley, and if we did decide to open a new camp, he would be my partner as the local manager.

Our destination was about sixty-five miles east, beyond the Korok River, an area in Keglo Bay known to Stanley and his people as "Akuliak." Here we eventually built a camp, which became famous as the many happy clients and the record books can attest. For now, we were told that a couple of families were camped there awaiting our arrival, looking forward to the employment and excitement that visitors would bring.

As travel had to be timed so that the tide was high enough to get into the bay, it was early in the evening when we came in through the outer string of islands. Shivering in the boats, Bill and I were looking forward to a hot cup of tea and a shot from the bottle of vodka that he had carefully packed in his knapsack when leaving Montreal.

The tea was forthcoming immediately after our arrival at the tents, but, alas, the vodka toddy was not to be. Upon reverently opening the wrappings, all that remained were some shards of broken glass and Billie's sweet-smelling but very damp underwear.

Disaster for a couple of guys who believed then that the proper end to any good day was a relaxing drink around the fire. It was, however, the only disappointing moment of the trip.

We were standing out later in front of the tents; the display put on by the Northern Lights brought cries of wonder from our southern guests. It was a fitting omen and the start to a wonderful association with our Inuit partners of George River.

Before that week was over we knew that we had indeed come to an area that was home to the big bulls of the Torngat Mountains. We laid out plans for the eventual camp, paced out the tundra for an airstrip, and returned to George River secure in the knowledge that at "Akuliak" we had a winner.

Many memories of that era compete in my mind, but the first evening on the shore, with the aurora borealis winding high above the offshore islands in Ungava Bay, defines forever my feelings for the People and the place . . . "Akuliak."

ON THE GEORGE RIVER, ARCTIC QUEBEC, 1980s

For years I have celebrated my birthdays in the North and the milestone fiftieth was no exception. Helen Falls, or Kanniq as the Inuit term it, is one of the finest locations in the world for an Atlantic salmon camp. Owned and operated, at that time, by my late friend Sandy Annanack, the crew consisted of Inuit from George River Village and Nain, Labrador. My son Martin, guiding there for his third year, was the only non-native in the crew. He was considered part of the family anyway, having been adopted by Sandy and his wife, Maggie.

After a month spent with caribou hunters up on Ungava Bay, I had traveled by boat a hundred miles down the coast and nearly seventy miles up the George River to meet a special incoming party of guests. I arrived just in time to welcome Jim Rikhoff and members of his National Sporting Fraternity. Known affectionately as "Rikhoff's Rangers," they were always one of the season's most enjoyable parties to have in camp. They had hunted and fished with me many times before, in New Brunswick, Newfoundland, and northern Quebec.

This time, the group consisted of many longtime friends: Gene Hill, Tom Hennessey, Harry Tennison, Whit Smith, Bob Devito, and one of my favorite couples, Wayne and Donna Grayson. We were in for a happy week, highlighted by some of the finest salmon fishing any of us had ever experienced.

Each evening before dinner the gang would congregate in Rikhoff's cabin, to enjoy what he termed a "small refreshment." At that time, having tamed a downright destructive craving for alcohol, I had remained resentful, but sober, for somewhat over ten years, to the dismay of all who had known me in the good old days. I stuck to Tang, ice water, and tea.

The evening of my fiftieth birthday provided more than enough incentive for Jim and the gang to lay on a record breaker of a party. Amongst the guests was a more than ample supply of liquid refreshment. Martin was kept busy chipping ice from blocks that had been stored the previous winter, hoarded for just such an occasion. Maggie and her helpers, Minnie, Annie, and Jessie, had prepared snacks of caribou liver *paté*, alderwood-smoked salmon, and caviar made from salmon roe.

With the eight visiting sports and the thirty-odd men, women, and children of the camp crew all participating, it was the kind of celebration one often hears about but seldom witnesses. Not wishing to be an unappreciative and sulking guest of honor, I was convinced to accept a couple of drams of good Scotch whisky and George River water. Surprising to no one, it tasted just as good as I had remembered.

The cabins making up the Helen Falls camp are lined up on the edge of a high esker, overlooking a major rapids, the sound of which becomes part of your life. Wooden walkways snake along the top of the cliff, with railings more to warn the unwary than with any pretense of protecting you from falling to your death in the rapids below.

Later, as the party wound down, keeping in mind an early start to fishing in the morning, I was happy to have the company of my son, as I carefully navigated the walkways back to the tent. With a nightcap of Tang, we toasted my birthday, and the regret that Irene and the rest of our family couldn't have shared it with us.

Sometime after midnight, perhaps in a dream, I left my sleeping bag and stepped outside. The entire dome of the valley was ablaze with sheets and strings and waves of changing color; the world seemed awash in cascades of aurora borealis.

I stood transfixed, filled with the eerie feeling that I had been here before, maybe had been here forever. Wisps of wind-blown spray, and the rumble of the rapids seemed to fill the universe, adding to the knowledge that life is fragile and man is but a mere speck poised on the edge of time and space in this northern wilderness.

The hint of woodsmoke, drifting across the clearing, brought me back to the reality of sleeping comrades. I sensed that I was not alone; in the flickering ghostly light, on the edge of the walkway, I made out the form of a companion.

Jimmy Rikhoff, the evening's final drink in hand, stood on the brink of the cliff, arcing a steaming stream into the abyss, pissing joyfully and defiantly into the roar of the rapids. The spell was broken: man is supreme in nature after all.

Kindred spirits, brothers in our love of the world's wild places, we saluted each other and the heavens; without a word, we went our separate ways.

I dreamed of the morning, a fresh run of salmon, bright fish leaping in the falls, a fine beginning to my next half-century in the land under the Northern Lights.

LIES I HAVE TOLD THE CLIENTS

T he Webb family is known, among other things, for being totally "No Bull" operators. We tell the truth, whether the
clients want to hear it or not. However, once in a while
circumstances just seem bound to make a liar out of me, despite my best
of intentions to the contrary.

NEW BRUNSWICK BEAR HUNTER

On a Sunday evening I would outline to the guests just exactly what to expect when bear hunting on a baited stand. Then
I would answer all questions, at least the ones that had answers.

It would go something like this: "Your guide will put you on
a stand, some of them tree stands, overlooking an area where we
know with certainty that a good bear has been feeding regularly.
You should wear camouflage and paint your face. Take nothing
to the stand that makes noise, sit extremely still and stay alert. Do
not expect the bear to show up the first evening; sometimes it
takes a few days. Just about all the bears coming to baits will be
male bear; the females, just like our own species, are usually smarter.
You will never see anyone in the woods except your guide. After
he places you, he will remain a couple of miles away from where
he can hear you shoot and come to your assistance immediately.
Good Luck!"

On Monday morning rifles were sighted in and after lunch
all the crews headed out to their remote stands. I was scouting out
some new areas, down south of the Renous Game Refuge, and
came across Larry, one of our younger guides, camped out beside
the road. As it was far too early to expect anyone to shoot, I told
him to jump in with me so I could take him to look over a new
location for the following week.

"We're going to drive right past the end of the trail I put that fat guy on. I don't imagine he will hear the truck going past anyway, and we know it doesn't bother the bears. He went in there with that bright red teddy bear suit on and a knapsack full of toys to keep himself occupied, so I don't have much hope he will kill anything."

"Typical, first time bear expert," I fumed.

"Tried to tell him to follow your advice, but guess he had ideas of his own."

"OK, to hell with him . . . if he wants to do the guiding, he's paying the bill," was my reaction.

We came around a corner in the road and there sat our hunter in the ditch.

Hauling up in a bit of a fit, I demanded, "What in hell are you doing out here this early? The hunting hasn't even started!"

"Oh, Mr. Webb," he replied, "I have had a wonderful hunt and the bear is right here in the bushes, and now I am ready to go fishing."

He went on to tell us that despite all of our good advice, he had gone up in the tree stand in the bright red suit, got out his supply of glossy skin magazines, set up his portable radio, fired up a cigar, and sat back to wait for the bear.

"I wasn't halfway through my cigar when I looked up and there came the bear. Took me awhile to get my gun down from where I had hung it on the tree, but when I shot, the bear fell down dead. While I was taking pictures of it, a man and his wife and two kids showed up. They took my picture and then helped me drag the bear out here to the road."

"Just wonderful, congratulations," old friendly me . . . thinking that now we were stuck with baby-sitting him for a week fishing.

"Only one thing," he went on in a hurt tone of voice, "You told me that I would never see a female, but the man looked at it and told me it was a mother bear."

"Jesus Christ!" I exploded, "every single thing I told you was a goddam bald-faced lie, so that may as well be one of them too!"

GEORGE RIVER, ARCTIC QUEBEC

Three of us were lying out on the side of a high ridge, over-looking the George River, a few miles below the Helen Falls salmon camp. Having taken a day off from fishing, we were glassing for a good trophy bull caribou for our guest.

Breck had come up from Maryland, one of the gang from the National Sporting Fraternity. The other guide was a young Inuit, Georgee Kooktook, from Fort Chimo. Georgee didn't talk much English, but was game for anything to do with hunting, a welcome change from watching the client endlessly casting for Atlantic salmon.

Half asleep in the early autumn sun, I was looking over the caribou trails winding down the mountain across the river from us, when . . . "Hold it, there's a bear eating blueberries up there. Looks like a pretty nice one. Too bad it's so far away."

I was about at the end of a two-month season, traveling and hunting constantly, and was just about worn out. To add to my problems, a week before I had twisted a knee and was barely getting by, just hobbling from the boat up to the hills to glass.

"Gee, I'd really love to get a bear. I've killed a couple of small ones, but never a real trophy. Is he really a big one?"

"Yes," said I, the expert, "I can tell because of the way he waddles and his belly nearly touches the ground."

After a half-hour of wishful comments from our guest, I figured what the hell, he was young and agile, Georgee was eager to go, so why not.

"All right," I told them, "this will pretty well blow the rest of the day, so we will concentrate on caribou again tomorrow. You've got to get down off this mountain, cross the river, and climb the other one. I will stay here, where you can look back and see me, so I can direct you once you get over there and start to climb."

Two hours later, having crossed the river, gone through a mile of flat woods and started to climb the mountain, the boys were right on course. My eyes were beginning to water by now, and the heat haze and shimmer made it nearly impossible to make out the bear. All of a sudden I realize that I am looking at two different bears; one is still eating blueberries and, higher on the slope, what must have been the original bear I was watching, had stretched out on the rocks to sleep. The one asleep was definitely a good-sized bear; the one pulling and thrashing in the bushes looked somewhat smaller, but with the mirage in the glasses it was hard to be absolutely sure.

Two tiny figures were now making their way up a shallow gulch and I could see that they would come out close to the feeding bear. It would be impossible for them to see the larger one in the rocks considerably farther up the slope.

I had the blueberry picker in the glasses when he hurled himself backward and I heard the delayed sound of the rifle shot coming across the valley. Frantically glassing for the other bear, I caught the rear end of him scooting over the top. Gone.

Three hours later, having skinned the prize, they slid back down the hill, crossed the river and toiled up to where I was boiling the kettle for a cup of tea. Georgee dumped the bear skin out of his knapsack, about the size of a Newfoundland dog.

"Boys, isn't he nice and black and shiny," I offered, trying to find something nice to say about the pitiful little thing.

"Well," said Breck, worn out, bedraggled and disappointed, "I thought you said he was real big because his belly was so close to the ground."

"I'm sorry, but goddammit, I didn't know his legs were only eight inches long!" was all I could think of to say.

Thought it was better to have him think I was a poor judge of bears than to tell him about the bigger one that went over the hill. Sure as hell, he would have thought I was an even bigger liar.

MUSKOX HUNT, *KUGLUKLTUK NUNAVUT*

Pamela and Stan from California became two of our favorite friends and clients, after we straightened out all the lies I had told them before booking.

Trying as always, to provide frank and accurate answers about the perils encountered in Arctic hunting, I had pretty well stated that of all the uncertainties involved, there were a few things I could almost guarantee.

1. The airline would get them to Coppermine on time.
2. We had never had anyone lose their luggage or rifle.
3 We had the proper tags for a hunt to Victoria Island.
4. They would be absolutely guaranteed to travel together, sleep together, and hunt together.

Naturally, as always happens when we attempt to "guarantee" anything in the north, it all turned upside down.

1. The airplane did *NOT* get them up to Yellowknife in time to make the connection to Coppermine as it was supposed to do.
2. Their rifles ended up in Cambridge Bay, so we only received them in time to go home. Fortunately, we were able to borrow one.
3. The tag quota had inexplicably been altered for Victoria. Fortunately, we had tags for a better area open at the last minute.
4. The worst was yet to happen. I had planned for a month in advance that they would hunt with an excellent Inuit father and son guide crew, Charlie Bolt and his son, Jorgen.

After the delay over the lost rifles, after changing the tags and getting dressed for the trail, they left town in bright sunshine about four in the afternoon, headed east for the hunting area.

At seven o'clock in the evening Jorgen radioed us back at base. They had been in a total white screaming blizzard for two hours. He had not only lost sight of Charlie, but had lost the trail as well. He was going to stop and camp until the storm blew out. Best decision possible. That is why we work with Inuit guides: they know the land, the weather, and how to survive in it. Stan, of course, must have been worried about how his wife was making out.

Half-an-hour later, Charlie called in. He and Pamela were camped on a lake, probably twenty miles distant from Stan and Jorgen. The storm was raging and no one was going anywhere. Martin and I went to bed knowing that at least everyone was tented down and safe; probably the storm would quit in the night.

Sure enough it did. By noon the next day they had gotten back together. A day later, using the borrowed rifle, they were both successful in taking high-scoring trophy muskox

At least I hadn't lied about that part of it.

ARE WE LOST?

One question a guide is occasionally required to answer is, "Have you ever been lost?" This comes, quite often, from an uneasy client, to whom ten acres of woods is an awe-inspiring wilderness. Having been required to visit a few down south cities while on promotional tours, I can sympathize with the feeling.

My usual comforting reply might be, "Well, I've been confused a few times, for a couple of days, but never really lost."

There is a lot of truth in that statement, and any guide who has ever gone out of sight and sound of the highway knows what I am talking about.

When we were guiding deer hunters in the northern interior wilderness of New Brunswick, back when it *WAS* a wilderness, it was common practice for the guide to allow his guest a certain amount of freedom. Still-hunt stalking, and sitting, is best accomplished by a person alone, just as long as you can trust the guy to be where you put him. The guide would scout around and sometimes circle the area in which he placed the client, in hopes of moving game in the right direction.

My welcoming address to the clients would go something like this: "Your guide may put you on a trail or advise you where to go. Listen to what he is saying! Forget all your Boy Scout training, just listen and do it! If you have a compass, okay, keep it in your pocket for company. A compass is not a hell of a lot of good if you don't know where you are, and you don't know where you want to go. Just do what the guide tells you, and in all probability, you will be sitting here tomorrow night eating dinner.

"However, if you do disregard our advice, do not worry. You will be sitting out there all night under a tree with the snow dripping down your neck, while we are home sleeping, but nothing will eat you. If someone comes along in the night, do not bother saying 'Hi, Fred' because it will *not* be me. In all probability you will think you are *lost*, but you are *not* because I goddam well know where you are, and sometime before the end of the week we will come and bring you in. You are never *lost* to the extent that we can't track you down and drag in your carcass so that your wife can collect your insurance."

This was usually sufficient deterrent to even the most enthusiastic Davy Crockett fan, but there were a few exceptions.

One hot-shot from Philadelphia arrived, complete with survival equipment, compass, and maps enough to cover most of eastern North America. He decided to ignore my advice. His guide, Coleman, came in three hours late for supper to report that the guy had walked out of the country on him.

About midnight I was awakened by a phone call from the guy's wife wanting to wish him a happy birthday. "Well," I said, "Joe is camping out tonight."

"Oh goody," was the reply, "I know he is enjoying himself immensely."

Glancing out the window at the freezing rain slanting across the dooryard I opined, "Oh yes, I am sure he is."

He was damn glad to see Coleman and me when we tracked him down about noon the next day.

On another occasion, we had a group of Italians from Montreal, only a few of whom spoke English. No problem, communication was accomplished by means of sign language and a smattering of French. Leigh Everett and my sons, Rick and Martin, took the six of them over into the Sisson Branch country. As the crow flies this was only about fifteen miles away, but required a drive of some thirty miles to get there by vehicle.

Two hours late for supper, just about when the snow started coming down in flakes as big as quarters, the boys arrived with a distraught gang of hunters. Uncle Giovanni had been placed on a little round knoll in the hardwood ridge, where there was plenty of evidence of deer and bear pawing for beechnuts. He was to walk back down a hundred yards of spotted trail, hit the main trail, turn left, and walk a half-mile out to the truck.

He did not turn up. The boys went in and scoured the ridge, shot and whooped to no avail. Fine way to start a new week.

We went out after breakfast, drove clear over there and arrived just as it became light enough to see. By this time there was a foot of snow covering everything. Enough, as I told the boys, out of hearing of the clients, to "cover the old sonofabitch up if he is lying dead in a blowdown."

Leigh and I built a good big fire and insisted that the rest of the family either sit there and leave us alone, or better yet, go across the road and up on another ridge and try to shoot a deer. They chose to sit by the fire, drink coffee, whine, and worry.

Leigh and I went in to circle the ridge for any fresh sign, while Martin and Rick went up the road another five miles, then in on a trail that cut across the area to the north.

Back at the fire in a couple of hours, we were trying to calm the increasing anxiety when the boys arrived back. They cut his track but had a mystery on their hands. He had evidently blundered onto one of the main trails in the evening. Having whittled down half the woods with his jackknife with a great fire going, he had nothing to worry about. But for some unexplainable reason, instead of staying there, he got up sometime after the snow stopped and headed right back into the woods in a southerly direction.

"Jesus," said Leigh, "we've got a runner on our hands boys, be lucky to find him before Christmas."

Moans and hand wringing from the clients as this was translated.

From where he spent the night, Leigh and I took his track and again sent the younger guides to cut around to another ridge and run down it, in case he went in that direction. Four hours of blundering through the woods, by now dripping snow water down our necks, we tailed old Giovanni right out to where he crossed a major trail without stopping, and headed southeast.

The boys came in again; they had swung way out around and crossed his track five miles farther to the southeast.

Back to the fire for some much needed late lunch and a change in plans. Fighting off the by-now-blubbering family members, I instructed the boys, "We've got him corralled now, he is going right down toward where Broad Brook comes into Sisson Branch, he will cross the brook and then he is headed down to where the Branch comes into Little Tobique. He can't cross either without swimming. We've got him into a corner; all we have to do now is run him down."

Leigh and Rick would take his track and stick with it; Martin and I would take the gang back to camp, load a canoe, drive up to Little Tobique and get ready to pick them up.

Leigh, who was carrying his rifle for signaling, asked, "What will we do if we catch him before he hits the river?"

"Shoot the old sonofabitch in the leg and slow him down!" was my reply.

Big moans and whimpers from the family spokesman, "Oh, please, Fred, don't shoot Uncle Giovanni!"

I never dreamed anyone was taking all of this seriously; it was pretty routine to us.

When Martin and I unloaded the canoe hours later, we could see a fire across the river. The boys had run him down, wet and tired, but nothing a good supper wouldn't fix.

I can only imagine the story told when they got back to Montreal.

I was seriously "turned around" myself one time forty years ago, in the middle of Labrador, and might have become truly "lost" if the weather hadn't cleared at the right time.

Emil Champagne, a north shore of St. Lawrence Frenchman, and I were running a trapline out of a post called Lake Eon. We had started out to tend the line, this section usually taking only one day, when we ran across fresh trails made by a band of caribou.

Needing both camp meat and trapline bait, we set off in pursuit.

That country is all flat spruce woods and interlocking lakes. During the whole day we would catch up when they were wading snow and pawing for moss in the woods, then they would hit one of the lakes several miles long and gain ground on us again. Dumb thing to do, but we kept at it until we gave up thinking about getting back to camp by dark.

By this time it had started to snow. Fortunately it was staying fairly warm. We would camp out with just what we carried, a bit of food, boiling kettle and tea, a rifle, and an ax. We made up our mind that if we didn't come up with the caribou by a few hours after daylight we would quit and hit the back trail.

As soon as we could see we were on the track again. It was snowing harder but we were still able to make out the caribou trails easily enough.

Finally giving up—by now it was snowing harder—we started on the back trail, but lost it when we struck a long stretch of inter-connected lakes. We headed in what we thought was the right direction and kept pushing on.

Around noon, we came across a snowed-over trail; maybe some of the animals had split off. The trail led directly onto a lake about three miles wide. Crossing that in the by-now-blow-ing snow, we found the snowed-over trail again and followed it into the woods.

Once inside the woods where it hadn't blown the snow around, we immediately found, surprise of surprises, snowshoe tracks!

"*Mountainais*" (Indians), said Emil.

"Bullshit," said I. "See that track right there? That's my goddam snowshoe!" And I turned up my left shoe to show him that the crossbar was spliced with a piece of birch wood wrapped with rabbit wire, so that it made a distinct impression.

We were now really and truly in a mess if we couldn't shorten up the back trail. Another night out in sweat-soaked and frozen clothes, without tent or sleeping bag, with no more food or tea, would not be fun. Beyond that, it could become a real pain in the ass!

Emil made it known that he knew which way to go, so giving him the chance to lead, we traveled for another four hours. We then had to pick out a good spruce thicket where we could get wood easy to spend the night.

By now I had thought the situation over. Remembering the look of the country, gambling on the wind having stayed fairly constant once it had started to snow, I figured that Emil was leading us in exactly the wrong direction.

Dozing on and off—it is difficult to keep a decent fire going for long with dry spruce—I awoke shivering about midnight. It had almost stopped snowing. The trees in that country were not very high, but I beat the snow off and climbed the biggest one I could find.

What a surge of relief! Through a break in the clouds, I found the Big Dipper, leading straight up to the North Star. We were no longer lost, simply slightly confused. I was right, Emil was leading us south instead of north where we should have been heading.

Taking no chances, I threw my hat down from the tree to mark true north. When I lit on the ground I tramped out an arrow in the snow, and axed three spots in a line toward our correct course.

Too impatient to sit any longer, with the storm almost over anyway, we hit the trail, this time with me leading. Each time we hit an open lake we adjusted our course by the Star. By full daylight, we were in country we knew, and by noon we were back at camp cooking up some long-delayed breakfast.

Lost? I would have to admit we were damn near lost! It would have taken a walk of about 250 miles to bring us to the Gulf of St. Lawrence if we had followed Emil's directions.

Over the course of the years there have been many occasions when in fog, or clouds, or blowing snow, I have indeed become confused and even occasionally turned around. One of the first things that one learns is that a so-called "sense of direction" simply does not exist. On some expeditions, where I was required to travel accurate straight lines or arrive at a pinpoint destination, sometimes even in the dark, by map, compass, and dead reckoning, I soon learned to forget any ideas about a mythical "sense of direction."

To confuse the matter, there are many experienced wilderness travelers, especially aboriginal people, who will display a truly amazing ability to get where they are going. Many people attribute this ability to some inborn sense of direction. However, when it is analyzed, this "sense" comes from having a finely tuned sense of staying oriented. Keen observation and good memory of the skyline allows the expert traveler to read the country like a map. Add to this the ability to use such aids to navigation as the sun and stars, wind direction, wave action, snowdrift patterns, and other natural phenomena, and one doesn't need a "sense of direction."

It also helps to remember when traveling with our Inuit and Dene wilderness hunters, that their attitude is, "everyone has to be some place so it doesn't really matter whether we are here or there." Most *Kabloona* get "lost" because they cannot put away the white man's habit of insisting upon being at a certain place at a certain time.

They are slaves to the clock, to arrangements they may have made, and most of all to the ego that would be shattered if they had to admit that they have become turned around. Native guides, unless convinced that they must stick to the white man's time schedule, do not have any such hangups.

Two incidents involving bad weather travel out of our "home town" of Coppermine, in the Central Arctic, illustrate what I mean.

A few years ago a legend, of sorts, was born when a local white guy jumped upon his snowmobile one warm May afternoon, for what was supposed to be a couple hours hunting up the coast. As happens commonly at this time of year, fog rolled in and he lost the trail. A native Inuit at this point would have pulled up, rolled a cigarette, or if it persisted, simply dug in and waited for the fog to clear. Not so of the white man. He didn't have proper camping gear, indeed no gear at all. He had someone at home waiting supper for him, and most of all, he didn't want anyone to think he could get lost so easily. So he drove around in the fog until he ran out of gas, then started out walking. To make a long story short, a couple of weeks later, after a horrendous and death-defying journey, after the official search was abandoned, on the day they were holding a memorial service for him in town, he came staggering in. Fine story, may even be made into a movie someday. It illustrates once more why most of the tales of Arctic heroism and suffering involve white men.

In contrast, during the muskox hunts in March of 1995, a couple of our Inuk guides, with their guests, got stuck out in a string of blizzards sixty miles from town. They had left their base camp to scout for muskox, during a few hours' break in the blizzard and could not get back to it. In this kind of blowing snow, trails are obliterated in seconds, and blundering around in country where there are cliffs a hundred feet high is definitely not a good policy.

For four days and nights the two guides and two guests hunkered down and waited it out. Uncomfortable for sure, but alive.

When it cleared enough to travel, they spent some hours attempting to find their base camp, a white tent stuck down in a sheltered hole in a white landscape.

Unable to find their camp, but before exhausting their gas, they headed in and arrived in town about the time we would have sent out a search and supply party.

Jokingly I asked Peter Katiak, "Were you guys lost?"

"No, not lost," was his smiling reply. "I don't know where the tent is, but I know where Coppermine is."

No worse for wear, and with stories enough to do them a lifetime, the guests were back safe in the hotel.

With non-native guides, there is at least a fifty-fifty chance that they would have exhausted their gas during the first day of the storm, had no fuel to put in the little stove and would have been in some very serious trouble.

Our Inuk guides, with centuries of Arctic survival in their genes, will travel when they can and sit when they must; they know it is useless to battle nature.

These two stories, out of the same community, point out the difference between being turned around, confused, and delayed, as opposed to being well and truly lost.

TOO LATE TO BE A COWBOY

COME TO THINK OF IT, I NEVER REALLY LOVED HORSES.

In the days of my youth, during World War II and for a decade thereafter, in our part of the country farming and logging were still pretty much dependent upon horse power. Most members of my family were horse fanciers, but with me, the relationship was always a matter of necessity, rather than choice.

At one time or another, I have been kicked, stomped, bit, and crowded against the wagon tongue. When riding I've been bucked off, scraped off on a convenient tree limb, and rolled upon at least twice. Some men yarding logs in the woods had horses that were a joy to work with. I was always stuck with some high-strung sonofabitch that would lunge ahead every time you attempted to hook the chain into the grab on the whiffletree, trying to cut off a couple of fingers.

Oh yes, I have heard it said of horses, that: "At least they make good bear bait." To which I would reply, "Yes, that may be so, but a pig makes better bait and has a higher IQ to boot!"

With such an attitude it is hard to figure out how, in the early summer of 1985, I found myself, along with my son Martin, headed up into the majestic Rockies, destined for a week's vacation horseback riding. I can only plead that I was probably drunk, at the Sheep Convention in Hawaii, when I bid on this donated vacation trip.

Martin and I were on our way from coastal BC to the Northwest Territories to open the caribou camps, so at least we did not have to drive too far out of our way.

We had arranged to meet the horse outfitter in Nordegg, Alberta, a picturesque little town nestled in the mountain forest. My enthusiasm dimmed a notch or two when I found out it was the site of the Provincial Penitentiary and when the owner of the motel advised us to take all valuables into our room, just in case our truck got stolen in the night.

Late the next morning, about the time we had given up waiting and decided to head out for the NWT, the outfitter arrived in a well-used pickup truck.

He gained our confidence at once. Here was a guy who looked like the genuine Alberta Mountain Cowboy: slim hips, broken nose, rodeo belt buckle and all. Years later, we learned he was really a school teacher on summer vacation.

Short on conversation, he informed us that we would drive about thirty miles into the mountains to meet up with the packstring, somewhere near the head of the Bighorn River.

Bighorn River . . . the name alone excited our imagination!

Incidentally, he added, we had better bring along our Toyota 4x4, as he was having trouble with his truck.

This was the year of the big rains in Alberta. Streams were out of their banks, bridges washed out, but, as he said, "don't worry," the weather had been fine the last couple of days, the roads at least were dried up. He took off with gravel flying and Martin and I followed along in the dust.

Fitting revenge for my years of being the guide, I now found myself in an awkward position. Like all "dudes," I had a couple of thousand questions I wanted the guy to answer, but as an outfitter myself, I didn't want to look like too big a pain in the ass.

Three hours rough going brought us to the end of the road, where we met the rest of the outfit. The wrangler turned out to be the outfitter's ten-year-old kid, and the cook a nice young lady from England. She was obviously in love with horses, and quite possibly the outfitter as well. She appeared to enjoy it all, happy to be along as unpaid camp help. About a dozen saddle and packhorses completed the outfit.

Sticking to his strong and silent mode, the outfitter bustled about getting packs made up, while we dudes could only stand around trying to decide what went where. Fortunately, being people who make our living in the woods, we had some idea of what to bring for clothes, rain gear, and sleeping bags.

I had quizzed the outfitter by phone about whether or not we should bring camping gear, special boots, etc. His reply had been, "don't worry," that he would supply everything.

Fortunately, as it turned out, I had tucked a small nylon tent, minus the poles, along with a nylon ground sheet, into my pack. Luckily again, being on the way to our own camp, we had our sleeping bags in the truck, as apparently the ones promised by the outfitter had somehow been mislaid.

Getting closer to the time when we would have to approach the horses, I wondered if anyone planned to give us a bit of advice and instruction. I had at least been around the beasts, but Martin, having done all of his guiding in the North where airplanes, boats, and snowmobiles supply the transportation, was far from an expert around horses. Aside from understanding that you put hay in one end and got horseshit out of the other, he was an absolute novice.

As the senior member of the party I was assigned the most senior-looking steed, a big draft horse-type named Mack. Martin was introduced to a buckskin gelding—wall-eyed, ears laid back, not resigned to his status. For reasons which would later become apparent, his name was "Stormy."

With no instruction whatever, not even the basics about adjusting stirrups, how to hold the reins, or where the gear shift and emergency brake were located, we were off on our great adventure. The outfitter's only comment being, "Don't worry boys, just follow me!"

Two minutes into the trip, we rode over to the brink, slid down a fifty-foot sheer bank, and lunged into the river. Full flood and muddy, with trees, roots, and all riding the current, it was icy cold and awesome. By some miracle, unexplainable to this day, we all emerged on the other side. Soaking wet, scared shitless, but across the river.

"Jesus," I managed to croak, "I'm sure glad that is over with."

"Don't worry," was the response, "we are almost to the Base Camp."

Six hair-raising hours later, having crossed the same river a total of seven times, we arrived in a foggy mountain meadow, on the far side of which was the long-awaited Base Camp.

Never have two dilapidated tents and a rough log hitching rail looked so welcome.

After a fine supper of beans and bacon, with fresh hot biscuits miraculously produced by the young lady, on hands and knees over a little tin stove, it was time to have coffee around the fire. Campfires, in any part of the world, are great at breaking down the barriers between the guides and the guests. Our host at last opened up sufficiently to explain our trip schedule.

In as few words as possible, he informed us that we were headed for the high country, a couple days of riding, up toward the boundary of Jasper Park. We would follow the streams and cross over the mountain spines and passes, at times following game paths and traces of ancient Indian hunting trails, with which he was familiar.

Not wanting to be a nagging client, but figuring that we had better catch our guide while he was in such a talkative mood, I mentioned that this all sounded fine, but maybe some basic pointers on the horse part of the deal would be helpful. "Don't worry, you'll soon get the hang of it," was the extent of the advice and instruction.

Always interested in how the other guy makes a living, Martin and I were up early to watch the horses being brought in by the young wrangler. He let us know that he had been exceptionally lucky in that all of the horses had been content to stick around for the night, that sometimes they took off for the home ranch, hobbled or not. We were learning all the time, and quite fascinated to watch as everything was packed and made ready to hit the trail.

Trying to help, without getting in the way too much, reminded me of how our own clients must have felt over the years, as they watched us loading gear into everything from canoes to *komatiks*, trucks to airplanes.

Mostly by trial and error, we managed to get our own horses geared up and ready to go. As no advice seemed to be forthcoming from the experts, I felt compelled to at least advise my son to adjust the stirrups so that he didn't have his knees up around his ears. I told him as well to take up a couple yards of slack in the reins, so that old Stormy couldn't walk along munching the blossoms off the dandelions. By the looks of the buckskin gelding, sooner or later Martin would need some leverage.

Strung out behind the outfitter, we headed off into lowering gray skies and the occasional rumble of thunder. "Great," I was thinking. "Just what we need, a stampede in the middle of a lightning storm." Once I had found a convenient stump from which to mount old Mack, he was easy enough to handle, just sort of plodding along, happy to stay in line on the trail.

Thinking about the difficulty involved in getting aboard such a tall horse, I finally concluded that blue jeans and saddle broncs are just not made to fit short-legged, fat-assed cowboys.

All of a sudden the clouds opened up; lightning lashed the ridges around us. In an instant, all was in turmoil. Packhorses scattered; our wrangler and the cook were plunging off in one direction, Martin and I in another. The outfitter actually became quite vocal as he scrambled around getting us all together again.

Soaked to the skin, we dismounted and tied up the horses in a thicket. Now it was time to dig our rain gear out and lash it on behind our saddles. At this rate, I thought, in another hundred years or so, we will be experienced trail riders.

After some cold beans eaten straight from the can with a whittled-out spoon, we were off again, clothes drying on our backs, steam coming off the horses. As the skies cleared everything began to look better. The beautiful mountain scenery, the horses strung out on the trail, the romance of it all; just like being in the middle of the tourism department's brochure.

I was really starting to enjoy myself, and to become resigned to the fact that if you are going to go on a horse trip, you have got to put up with the horses.

Old Mack and the rest of the string settled down and trailed along nicely—all except the one ridden by Martin. Half of my time was spent trying to haze his unruly mount back into the trail. Wall-eyed and prancing, he seemed to think his proper place was farther up toward the head of the line.

I told Martin once again to keep the slack out of the reins and to start letting the hard-headed nag know who was the rider and who was the critter. Attempting to crowd past on a narrow trail, he tried to dump old Mack and me over a hundred-foot cliff. A good cut across the face with a branch I had broken off for just that purpose got his attention. Now I knew he could be educated, hard headed or not.

Saddle-worn and weary, we camped that night in an enchanting Alpine meadow. All signs of civilization, including the seismic lines and claim markers, had been left behind. Only a few old blaze marks and traces of ancient campfires bore witness to the fact that long ago hunters had traveled this route.

Although a sober look at the map revealed that a couple days' ride to the west would bring one into the National Park, with its highways and condominiums, it was easy enough to dream that here indeed was the mountain paradise first seen by Europeans during the days of the fur trade.

In the middle of the night, I crawled out of the tent, for the reason that most middle-aged cowboys get up to look at the moon. Across the star-lit meadow lay writhing layers of fog. The looming shadows of the surrounding peaks, and the tinkle of horse bells put me back in time to a simpler age. I could sense the presence of long-gone aboriginal hunters and smell the lingering smoke from their fires. No jet trails crossed the vault of the heavens. Above the northern horizon loomed the Dipper, leading up to Polaris, the North Star, confirming my place in the universe.

The next few days were almost an anticlimax. Certainly we had some thrills and, almost, some spills. In one spectacular runaway, leaping blowdowns and ducking branches, Martin finally became a proper bronc buster and Stormy reluctantly became adjusted to his role in life. Runaways, packhorse rollovers and horse-wrecks, became as routine as the problems that we face every day in our own areas of operation.

Delivered eventually back to the trailhead, if we weren't exactly seasoned cowboys, we at least had lost the feeling of being total aliens. Against my better judgment I had become somewhat of a horse fancier. In the mountain wilderness it is easy enough to believe in reincarnation. Maybe next time around I will be an Alberta Mountain Cowboy.

BURIAL AT SEA

*O*ften enough life is lost at sea, through illness and other means. Usually it is possible to return the body to the family for burial ashore. This was done, for instance, on an extended Arctic voyage, when the chief cook, old "Ptomaine Tom," expired from the effects of his own cooking, we were sure. Placed in one of the galley freezers, he made the trip back to Montreal in nearly as good shape as the rest of us.

On another trip overseas we had a tragic accident. A flash fire in the engine room killed our seventh engineer and an electrician. Two other members of the black gang had fairly severe burns and suffered as well from smoke inhalation.

Fortunately for the safety of the ship, the CO_2 automatic extinguisher systems had worked, although having blown off in the closed space of the control room probably accounted for the two fatalities.

The two injured men were treated by our ship's doctor, who was fairly sober for a change, and we headed for Londonderry, the nearest port with British Navy facilities. The winds of the late winter gale were in our back, and we steamed into Loch Foyle, to land the injured men and the dead electrician, within about thirty-six hours of the explosion.

It turned out that the seventh had left documents in the care of the captain so that if anything ever happened to him, he should be buried at sea. Apparently the captain had gone into the matter in depth, to the extent of having on file a letter from the man's lawyer attesting to the fact that he had no known family. There was also a signed and witnessed will, naming as sole beneficiary the Mission to Foreign Seamen. So burial at sea it was going to be.

After a three-day around-the-clock effort by dockyard workers, enough temporary repairs were accomplished for us to sail for Halifax. The weather, as usual at this time of year in the North

Atlantic, was absolutely atrocious. Each evening, as I received the signals by Morse code and plotted the weather map, it was the same story. Winter storms making up along the coast of North America, and the deep low pressure areas swinging in an arc to the northeast across the ocean. With everything lashed down, we made slow but steady progress westward, although we were taking an incessant pounding.

A week later, within the time that we should have made the crossing in decent weather, we were approaching the Grand Banks. Tomorrow, the captain informed us, we would be passing over the spot where the *Titanic* had gone down in 1912, with such horrendous loss of life. As I recall the position is around fifty degrees north, forty-five degrees west, although I may have it backward. Anyway, it was a fitting place to lower the remains of our ex-shipmate, the seventh engineer.

Talking it over later, it occurred to us that the silent little man had so kept to himself, not even leaving the ship while in port, that we had to ask the skipper his real name. We had all simply called him the seventh. His body had been taken care of by the doctor, the carpenter, and the bosun, and he waited patiently in a freezer on the hangar deck aft.

Next morning, around eleven o'clock, we hove to in the thirty-foot swells, on the position of the *Titanic*. With only the helmsman and the fourth mate in the wheelhouse, and two of the black gang keeping watch in the engine room, the rest of the ship's company were mustered aft to the hangar deck to honor our comrade. Upon two sawhorses and a sheet of plywood, lashed to the starboard rail and held in place against the pitching motion, lay the canvas-wrapped and weighted remains.

If I live to be a hundred I will never forget the scene. Wind-whipped gray North Atlantic swells, flag at half-mast beating against the standard, shivering as my pant legs drummed against my shins; watching as the master struggled to keep the pages from being torn out of the Bible, while he read a brief passage.

A ragged attempt was made to sing two verses of the old hymn, "Abide With Me," till we ran out of words and petered out into an embarrassed silence. At a nod from the captain, struggling against the wind and the ship's motion, the bosun and carpenter raised the end of the plywood and the body began to slide over.

Just at exactly the wrong moment, with hardly any way on, the helmsman let her drop off to port into the trough of the swell.

"Good God!" shouted the captain, "Grab the seventh!"

It was too late. As the ship lurched on her side, the body dropped down, hit the rail of the quarterdeck below, and fell back on board.

Shocked immobility. Then a mad dash for the ladder. The first three men to arrive grabbed the corpse and dumped it over the side.

Back on course again, some of us gathered in the officers lounge for a bit of a wake. All agreed it had been somewhat of a botched job, but after all you don't get much practice at that sort of thing. The navigator summed it up pretty well when he said, "The seventh didn't have any home except this old ship. I guess when it came time to leave, he tried to change his mind."

Aside from the final legal paperwork, the matter was closed.

Although none of us could even remember what he looked like in life, I doubt like hell if we will forget his funeral.

L ike everything else in the hunting business, *Sports Shows* have certainly changed over the last forty years or so. It used to be that the public could expect to talk to the guides who were actually going to take them hunting. Nowadays, in plenty of shows, the majority of booths are manned by salesmen and representatives, sometimes agents selling for agents . . . several layers removed from the mud and the blood and the guts of the hunting operation.

Over the years we have seen some great shows come and go. The ones that failed invariably took the attitude that the guides and outfitters were lucky to be allowed in the door, and that the public would come to see the flea market salesmen, the wood splitter, personalized monuments, and the computer dating service. As we tried to tell them, without the guides and outfitters, it is like trying to run a rodeo without the cowboys.

When I first started attending shows the guides often put on competitions . . . wood chopping, kettle boiling, canoe poling, log rolling, and such. Among the "salesmen" attending the present shows, you wouldn't find three out of fifty who could make you a cup of tea in the middle of a spruce thicket. Of course, if you are looking for a seminar on Electronic Fish Finding, GPS Satellite Navigation, or How to Lobby Your Congressman, then you are in luck.

Older, perhaps smarter, and definitely more sober, I now look back with nostalgia at the good old days when we went to shows for the fun and excitement. The bookings, it seemed, came automatically.

SOMETIMES A GUIDE NEEDS A GUIDE

Henry was a fine guide and woodsman, but a stranger to city life. At a show in New York, the boys were staying in one of the big hotels right down in the guts of the Big Apple. A policeman observed Henry standing for a long time watching people streaming down the stairs leading to the subway.

Figuring he might be a stranger, the cop went over and inquired if he needed any help. Henry replied, "No, I ain't lost . . . staying in that great big building right there. What I been thinkin' though is that some feller must have a hell of a big cellar. People been going down there all morning and not one sonofawhore has ever come back up!"

HIGHLIGHTS IN HARRISBURG

Having done the biggest show in the Northeast for over two decades, there are literally a million stories one could tell. One of them involves a legendary Alaskan guide and pilot, now tragically gone the way of so many others in the profession.

Most of his friends will remember Clark Engle, not only as one of the great Alaskan guides, but also because of his delight in pulling off practical jokes.

Back when we did the Harrisburg Sports Show, known by exhibitors as "the Meat Grinder" for its long hours and immense crowds of people who seemingly paid the price of admission simply to harass the guides, we occupied a booth across the corner from Clark. During a period of extreme boredom he started a string of jokes which finally led to us nearly closing the show.

The initial moves were innocent enough. Whenever Clark got a real "clinger" stuck to the front of his booth asking a million dumb questions, he would refer him to us across the aisle, explaining that despite the fact that our sign said "Newfoundland," we were really experts on Alaskan hunting. To counter this we posted little signs with arrows, saying "This way to sign up for the FREE Alaskan Hunt," which eventually landed the pilgrims, looking for something for nothing, in front of poor old Clark. He wasn't long in striking back.

Upon arrival next morning, we found that an indecency had been committed against the mounted black bear which was the highlight of our booth. Someone, we could only guess who, had gone out to the "Adults Only Toy Store," purchased a truly impressive anatomically perfect object termed the "Ladies' Home Companion," and had attached it to our poor old Smokey the Bear.

Needless to say this caused us some embarrassment and before long the show management came out and requested that we remove the offending appendage. We spent all day plotting revenge.

That evening, one of our local groupies went out to a specialty shop called "Art and the Alternate Lifestyle." He purchased two dozen of the most gross and explicit images from their considerable selection of pornographic color slides.

The next morning it was but a few minutes work to install the tray of slides in Clark's Ektographic automatic slide projector, the screen of which faced the public. Coming in a bit late after being out the night before, he put his booth in order for serious business and switched on the projector.

Watching from across the corner, we were truly amazed at what we had brought about. The aisles filled up, as a record audience gathered from all around the hall. Clark couldn't believe the great reception he was getting and started frantically handing out hunting brochures and attempting to sign up all the interested prospects. They kept pushing him off and crowding around for a better view of what was happening on the screen.

Before long it turned into a near riot. Clark finally caught on when he saw us across the way nearly rolling on the floor. He gave up handing out brochures and joined the audience.

Despite the fact that security came and closed him down, we all agreed it was the best response we had ever witnessed in the Harrisburg Sports Show.

DEALING WITH THE ANTIS IN A SENSITIVE MANNER

A long time ago, in the Boston Show, the Old Outfitter had a booth right across from an authentic duck pond, set up by the Massachusetts Game Department.

After a few days of answering questions from the natives of the combat zone, the smell of mud and duck excrement added just the proper touch. Being stuck in between the guy selling electronic organs and the girl from New Jersey with the computerized dating system had not improved his attitude toward the show and Boston in general.

Up to the booth came two Joe College types, the white liberal with the Kennedy accent, and the black college activist in the Che Guevara beret. Despite all efforts, the outfitter was soon drawn into the same old stupid discussion on why we guides make a living in the "blood sports." Attempting to be diplomatic, the outfitter explained the basic facts of wildlife management, sustainable renewable resources, and Man's place in the food chain since Adam and Eve.

All to no avail. The critics were not to be reasoned with, and by this time the dialogue had attracted a cheering section of like-minded urbanites to back them up. The poor old outfitter was badly outnumbered and on foreign soil.

Things finally reached the inevitable conclusion.

The white liberal with the educated air declared, "I don't know how you sleep nights with the blood of all those animals on your conscience."

The black activist made his pronouncement for the benefit of the audience even more condescendingly:

"You Canadians are barbarians! I am proud that our efforts helped to end the slaughter of those innocent baby seals up there in your backward country."

"Well," observed the outfitter, "It's a goddam good thing that those seals were snow white, cute, and cuddly. If the sonsofbitches had been black with short kinky hair, you couldn't have raised a dollar in the entire United States of America to save a goddam one of them!"

This served to end the philosophical discussion and the outfitter was left in peace, to figure up his losses from attending such a show, and to enjoy the refreshing smell of the duck pond.

Skin 'em Alive

One day, years ago, in a show in New Jersey, the Old Outfitter was showing a pretty decent hunting film about black bear hunting in Eastern Canada. As the films were made deliberately to

263

show the country, the guides, the culture of our people, and not simply shooting critters, one of the sequences showed the guides skinning a bear and properly preparing the trophy for taxidermy.

As the film progressed, the hunters in the audience expressed their enjoyment, but in the crowd, two well-dressed, middle-aged women with briefcases under their arms were not too impressed.

After several minutes of enduring their disparaging comments, the outfitter had about reached the boiling point when one of them said in a loud voice, "There they are torturing that poor animal, skinning it alive, just like they do those poor seals up in Canada!"

Although his sensitive nature was injured by such a comment, the outfitter attempted to be diplomatic. Mildly he observed that: "You have undoubtedly been listening to the propaganda of the antihunting industry. They put a well-known evangelical preacher in the slammer for taking money away from stupid people. Why do they not do the same in the case of the crooks duping the public in these phony rights causes?"

"Oh, well!" said the dominant partner of the pair, and here she quoted a well-known hippie movie actress and anti-war activist, "Ms . . . says that all hunting is barbaric and should be abolished."

"For Christ sakes," blurts the poor old outfitter, now fully out of his depth, "that bitch skins more meat in a year than do all the guides in this goddam building!"

An hour later a representative of the show management dropped by to advise that a complaint had been lodged in the office by two ladies from a well-known anti-everything organization. His advice was to keep up the good work.

WILDERNESS ENCOUNTER

Doing a show one time on a college campus in New Jersey, Jack Hegarty and I were in his booth talking over business as usual.

The show was a slow one. It didn't take any genius to figure out that a hunting show held in such surroundings, in the middle of the liberal elite, was going to be a dead loss. The reception from most of the audience made us feel about as welcome as the village whore at the Baptist picnic.

Up to the booth strolled a couple who appeared vaguely interested in the fact that the sign said "adventures in the Maine woods."

Professional students, in their mid-thirties, undoubtedly studying for a doctorate in something guaranteed not to produce a job, they personified the tail end of the Vietnam protest era. The lady apparently was used to doing all the talking.

"Oh, you're from Maine," she observed brightly. "I was up in Maine once!" Jack and I nod politely.

"Yes," she continued, "me and my boyfriend . . . not this one!" and she points to the guy rolling his eyes as if he had heard this story before.

"We were going up to the University of Maine to help in an antiwar demonstration, so we took a few days and toured up around Rangely Lakes, sleeping in our Volkswagen van."

Jack interjected, "Yes, that's lovely country, we have cabins and run a hunting business up in Jackman and get lots of people coming through in the summer."

"Well, I'll tell you what happened one night up there in the campground," and the lady disclosed a story to amaze the most experienced guide in the woods.

"It was a lovely warm evening. After supper we had a bottle of wine, and smoked a couple of joints before going to bed in the van. It was so warm that we left the door wide open, and as my boyfriend was afraid of the woods, I slept on the outside. Sometime in the middle of the night, I woke up and could see the gigantic full moon lighting up the campground. Just then a shadow fell over the van, I heard a snorting noise, and against the light of the moon, I see that it is an enormous moose. He came right over and stuck his head into the van and sniffed me."

"My goodness," exclaimed my friend, "you never know when a moose can turn dangerous!"

"Well, I was so petrified that I didn't think about being afraid. That moose smelled me all over, then he started with his big hot slobbery tongue and he licked me from head to toe. He licked and licked until my sleeping bag was clear down around my feet!"

By this time Jack and I were trying to look everywhere but at her, and could not think of a thing in the world to say.

"Yes," the lady continued, "he just kept licking me all over. It was the most erotic thing that has ever happened in my whole entire life!"

Feeling I had to say something, and trying to sound as if I knew something about moose, I came out with, "maybe he was attracted by the smell of your perfume."

"Well maybe," was the rejoinder, "but not the kind you put behind your ears, *IF YOU KNOW WHAT I MEAN!*"

As they wandered happily away, with their free brochure and the map of Maine, we could only agree that of the million sports show stories, this one simply had to be told someday.

LET'S TRY IT ON FOR SIZE

This story is too good not to tell, but it is too current to use the actual names of the participants. Suffice it to say it happened during the last couple of years at one of the major U.S. club conventions.

A friend and I were sitting in a booth across the aisle from a gentleman who made high-quality, custom-made cowboy boots. The boot maker is a serious and sensitive person. He attempts to put his prospective buyers at ease while making the necessary molds and measurements to properly fit their new boots.

Up to the booth came a somewhat mismatched, but apparently loving couple. He was at least eighty, well turned out and obviously of sufficient means to support a lifestyle that we all might admire. The lady looked about twenty-one, extremely attractive; she could have stepped from the pages of any fashion magazine. In addition to enough gold jewelry to buy out all the outfits in the Yukon, she wore an obviously expensive buckskin "cowgirl" dress, tight as a coat of paint and extending nearly to her ankles.

After the discussion as to which type of exotic leathers would be used, and a deal struck on several styles selected, it came time to take the critical measurements.

After the molds were made, the lady was asked to step up onto the little elevated throne, so that the craftsman could put the tape measure around her calf to ensure a snug fit.

Constrained somewhat by the tight leather dress, she nonetheless managed to seat herself on the chair, while our friend knelt with his tape measure. "Madam," he inquired politely, "could you just raise your skirt a bit so I can pass the tape around your legs?"

"No problem!" Grasping the garment at the hem, she jerked it up, somewhat farther than necessary and spread her legs to facilitate the operation. Total shock to all concerned!

It was glaringly apparent, especially to the cobbler, who promptly dropped his tape, that the young lady had neglected to put on her underwear that morning!

The boot maker was struck totally dumb, not so her husband.

"For goodness sakes, Honey, the man is trying to fit you for cowboy boots, not a goddam diaphragm!"

WATCH WHERE THAT GUN IS POINTING

Of all the hazards associated with the guiding profession, the unsafe handling of firearms is at the same time the most serious and the most preventable.

Despite all the claims to the contrary, and all the courses in firearms safety, one was only to attend a sports show or convention where guns are exhibited, to glance down the aisle and be looking into a gun muzzle. True, they are unloaded; that does not detract from the instinctive aversion and the cold sweat that I experience.

One always hesitates to create a scene. After all we live by the myth that all North Americans were born with guns in their hands, and to question their expertise in handling them is somewhat more personally insulting than asking their wives how they stack up in the sex department.

The reluctance to confront is natural, but any guide who does not take charge and see that the client is acting in a prudent manner is only waiting for the inevitable tragedy to occur. Over the years, I have been much closer to death by accidental discharge while guiding than I ever was when in places where we were paid extra for getting shot at.

All of these experiences have been deadly serious, but like anything else in life, some of them have had their comic aspects.

I have had holes shot in boats, trucks, camps, and once in an airplane. I went three years without an incident happening, then in one fall deer season had the following occur. A client shot through the hood of his Cadillac. With four men in a Volkswagen bug, an "unloaded" .300 magnum discharged out through the roof. A supposedly expert gunsmith let the action of a supposedly semi-automatic rifle slam shut, and it went off around our feet four times with no finger on the trigger. The final week of the season, gun shy by now, I made the hunter walk ahead of me in the woods, even though he would wander off a path as wide as Interstate 80 without constant teaming. As we paused to look over a ridge, he fiddled with the action and the rifle discharged, shooting a hole through my knapsack, boiling kettle and our lunch. That was the end of his outing.

One time I had a judge from Ellicott City, Maryland on a bear hunt. Returning to my truck, he tossed his pack in the back, started to struggle out of his rain gear, laid his .444 Marlin on the front seat with the muzzle pointing toward me standing at the driver's side door. I jumped back. "Boy," he laughed, "you sure are gun-shy!"

Reaching in he worked the lever. The rifle discharged, cut across my brand-new seat, hit the armrest and damn near blew the door off. Had I been standing there it would have been all over with. My reaction caused me the loss of a client. He was surprised that I didn't want him back again next year.

At Akuliak on Ungava Bay, Stanley Annanack and I were guiding a young man from West Virginia. Going ashore to have a closer look at two big bull caribou, the young man became unhinged. The minute I jumped ashore to hold the canoe, before I could stop him, he slammed a shell into the 7mm magnum and squeezed one off. It went through the bow of the boat, missed me by about three inches and scared both Stanley and me damn near to death. He then sat down and cried, while I threw a screaming fit and the caribou walked away over the hill.

Stanley, normally a fairly dark-skinned Inuk, had turned white. "What the matter, crazy *Kabloona* shooting boat, no double shovel on boat!"

Although my left hand was numb for an hour and I was picking specks of lead and slivers of fiberglass out of my skin, I couldn't help but laugh at Stanley's amazement.

In various times and places I have had a bobcat dog grazed by a .222 and a Brittany spaniel peppered with bird shot. We damn near lost a good friend, Jim Rikhoff, when an overeager client swung on a grouse and forgot the man beside him. Tragically, at an Inuit camp in Ungava, we had a four-year-old kid pick up a .22 carelessly left on the rocks and shoot his seven-year-old brother through the liver. He didn't live an hour.

I had a retired U.S. Army ordnance officer set off his rifle, which was supposed to have been unloaded, while climbing down out of a tree with it slung over his back. The bullet went straight up through the brim of his cowboy hat. When I demanded just what in hell he thought he was doing, I got the typical army answer: "I was simply clearing my piece!"

"Sounded to me like your goddam gun went off!" I replied, not overly impressed with proper military terminology.

If close calls can have a humorous outcome, such happened one late evening as I picked up a bunch of Good Ol' Boys from Georgia, strung out on bear stands along a high ridge. In the dark and drizzling rain, with five men already inside the truck camper, I loaded the last client. As always, I demanded, "Before you put that rifle in the truck, make damn sure it is unloaded."

I had just swung in under the wheel and started to pull out when, *BOOM*, a rifle went off in the back of the truck.

Jumping out I rushed to the tailgate. All was silent. "What in hell happened?" I yelled. "Is everyone okay?"

A few seconds silence then a small quivery voice answered, "Oh, man, if blood smells like shit, I been shot!"

I could never quite express myself that eloquently, but that is exactly the feeling I have experienced too many times. So please, unloaded or not, don't point any guns in my direction.

CIRCUMSTANTIAL EVIDENCE

O ne time a prominent local businessman and supporter of the current governing party was apprehended under very suspicious circumstances.

Two rangers had observed the suspect's fancy Jeep Wagoneer coming out from a private salmon pool, which was scheduled for fly fishing only. As a matter of routine they attempted to stop the vehicle. When the red light went on the Wagoneer took off with sufficient speed to get a considerable head start.

Following a speeding vehicle on a crooked woods road in a cloud of dust is not an easy matter. By the time the suspects were stopped, five miles down the road, it was apparent that the main evidence had been disposed of, thrown into the woods on one of the blind turns. There was still plenty of cause to lay a charge and proceed to court.

Trials involving fish and game laws in northern New Brunswick in those days took a certain course. Politics was involved, as well as culture and historical animosities. With the defendants being Acadian, the judge and the two opposing attorneys the same, the English-speaking arresting officer, to say the least, started out with a considerable handicap,

The facts were fairly straightforward. The vehicle had come up from one of the most productive salmon pools on the Kedgwick River. After a dangerous high-speed chase, which alone was sufficient to lay a charge for failing to stop and obstruction of a peace officer, two occupants were placed under arrest.

In the back of the Wagoneer was a landing net, and a heavyweight spinning rod, complete with treble-hooked lure, gear that was prohibited on a scheduled fly fishing river. On the carpet in the vehicle were fish scales, which proved to have come from a salmon, a wet and bloody spot, and as the young ranger described it, the definite odor of salmon! Pretty strong cir-cumstantial evidence.

On cross-examination of the ranger, the defense attorney felt he had the case won. "Now, Mr. Ranger," he demanded, "do you not concede that the rod itself is insufficient evidence, because my clients could have been fishing on another river?"

"Yes," admitted the ranger, "I guess that is possible."

"And must you not admit that the salmon scales could have come from a legally purchased fish that came from the Newfoundland commercial fishery?"

"Well, yes, that is unlikely but possible, but the carpet in the Wagoneer was wet and smelled of fresh salmon."

"Now Mr. Ranger," bored in the attorney, "surely you must admit that the water could have come from my client's beer cooler, and certainly we all know there can be other explanations for what you thought was a fishy odor."

"Now hold on right there!" exclaimed the Ranger, turning to the Judge, "Your Honor, I know what he is talking about, and as a newly married man, I have smelled lots of it. *And it does not smell the least bit like a salmon!*"

"I agree," declared the judge, after he quit laughing. "Six hundred dollars or sixty days, confiscation of all equipment!"

Chalk one up for conservation and an expert witness.

H*aving managed, mainly by pure accident, to pass my sixtieth birthday, I now realize that a great many of the people I shared the trail with are no longer around. I could not possibly name them all; in some cases I cannot use their real names anyway. Mutual friends will know to whom I refer.*

Sandy Annanack from Ungava

Sandy and I were sitting on the shore watching a bunch of George River Inuit arriving in several canoes. Up over the rocks came hobbling a poor twisted-up Inuk, actually pulling himself along on his hands and knees.

"Jesus, Sandy, what happened to that poor guy, polio or what?"

"No, no," replied my friend, "was screwing!"

"My God, I never heard of sex affecting anyone like that before."

"Oh, yes! With lady in tent, Coleman lantern lighting, husband outside, 16-gauge shotgun slug . . . shooting!"

So much for the old myth about northern wife-sharing.

Bob Milek, Outdoor Writer

Having come in off a hard muskox hunt, Bob and I were sharing a room at the Coppermine Inn. Bill Backman, Huck Spaulding, and Ric Martin were across the hall. The other party, which we had named "The Odd Couple," included a doctor from France and a guy I will call "Joe" from Pittsburgh. Joe was a forthright businessman who had made his money the hard way, and he was somewhat of an expert in foreign affairs.

Joe finished cleaning his rifle and was putting the rod back in his duffel, when the French gentleman asked if he might borrow it for a moment. He thought this over a bit, and then replied: "Hell, no! You can't borrow it! You French sonsabitches wouldn't let Reagan refuel the airplanes when he went to bomb Gadahfi! So you can all just plumb go to hell!"

Milek and I agreed that Joe should be put in charge of foreign policy. Unfortunately, Bob didn't get around to forwarding the recommendation to Congress, so perhaps this will get the ball rolling.

BLAKE AND THE TRAVELING PREACHER

Although not a fanatic about attending church, Blake was always ready to lend a helping hand and believed in hard work and living by the Golden Rule. One day a traveling preacher came through the country. Down at my place, hard-bitten sinner that I am, I set the dog on him. Blake, always courteous, invited the guy in for tea. The preacher launched right into the hellfire and damnation scenario, apparently to be avoided only by purchase of the pamphlets and other forms of bribery.

"Just a minute now," observed Blake, "I have tried my best to lead a good life, and I have read the Bible from cover to cover, and to tell you the truth, I just don't believe this stuff about burning in hell forever."

"Well," came back the preacher, "that's surely a comforting thought for someone who is probably going there!"

The preacher maybe won that round, but I'd still rather take my chances and go along with Blake when the chips are down.

THE NAVIGATOR

We were coming in off a long trip one time and the evening before entering port, the talk got around to the joys of homecoming. One of the mates, although he looked forward to spending time with his three young children, remarked about how difficult it was to get any time alone with his spouse.

Archie the navigator, with many years of experience had figured this problem out long ago.

"Boys, when I was younger, I could barely stand to be parted from the wife. After a long separation, we could hardly wait to be alone. Most guys when they hit port, the first stop they would make was at the liquor store or tavern. Me, I went to the corner candy store. I always bought fifty cents worth of green jelly beans. When the kids rushed out of the house, I would give each of them a big hug and a kiss, then I would toss the green jelly beans out across the lawn. That's how the wife and I always had the first hour alone together."

Nowadays the kids probably wouldn't leave the TV long enough to give the old man the time of day, jelly beans or not.

ALL IN THE FAMILY

Two old horsemen, I will call them Henry and Jack, were not only longtime friends, but brothers-in-law, having married two of the Jones sisters.

One day they made a trip over into the French country to buy horses for a logging operation. They had looked over and arranged to purchase about a dozen, but needed just one more to fill out the order. Culling out several, for one reason or another, their choice had come down to a half-broke, heavy-set, chestnut mare. Trying to figure out her lineage, Jack observed, "You know, Henry, she's mostly Alberta bronco, but she may have a dash of Arab, and by the size of her feet, maybe a good bit of Clydesdale as well."

As Henry approached for a closer look, the mare raised up her tail and began to make water, splashing the leg of his new pants.

Hastily jumping back, Henry declared "Well, Jackie boy, by the looks of that, she's got a good bit of Jones in her for sure!"

A fine judge of horse flesh and matters pertaining to pedigree, one of the last in the country.

WASTE NOT, WANT NOT

John was about thirty years older than me the spring we trapped muskrats. Of a long line of famous Micmac trappers, he

275

taught me a lot about rats, including the fact that as he put it, "some old ladies down on the reserve would throw a turkey out of the oven to put in a good mess of rats."

John's rat soup always smelled inviting when bubbling over the fire, but the buggy little eyes and the big yellow teeth staring up at you through the steam might put off the more finicky diner.

Although a professed Christian, John had retained many of the beliefs of his forefathers. He told me about how the Great Manitou had fashioned the earth, and at first it was covered with water. Then Beaver was created, and he dove down to the bottom and with his front paws brought up mud which he made into an island.

Muskrat then appeared and brought green shoots to plant in the mud, and eventually the whole world became as we know it today. And the People were told to take the animals and the fish; and to use them but wisely and with respect . . . and never to waste any gift from land or sea. This was pretty deep stuff, but lying around a fire, drinking black tea liberally laced with Demerara Rum, brings out the spiritual in many of us.

That summer old John and his wife Rachael, as they had done for years, moved out to the coast, where it was traditional to set traps to harvest the millions of fresh water eels returning from the ocean. There was good money in eels, bound for the markets in Boston. It was told to me afterward that this season my friends, always hard drinkers, were into the booze even while working.

On some days John never left the tent, while Rachael did the best she could to manage the eel traps. It is dangerous for one person alone in a canoe to pull traps, especially in the current, and tragedy resulted. The canoe was found anchored out, with a trap buoy line wrapped around the middle crossbar; of John's partner there was no sign.

At first John helped with the search, as the Mounties, other fishermen and most of the community turned out to look for the body. After five days he retired to the tent to grieve, fortified by nearly a full case of Captain Morgan's Dark, supplied by his many friends and relatives. Some were concerned that he might do harm to himself in his grief, but the elders knew that he would never waste his life, as that was a gift like any other.

He told me a year later that he had consumed the case of rum, over three days and nights with no sleep. He had entered a kind of trance in which he saw visions from the days of his youth, and tried to figure out where he had gone wrong. It must have been some gift from the Creator that he and Rachael had thrown away or wasted.

In the middle of his vision, in the rum induced haze, the local Mountie appeared all wet and excited. "John! You will have to come to the dock, we have found the body, but she's all full of eels!"

"Oh Thank god!" cried John, now knowing what the vision meant. "Don't throw them away! Bait her up and set her again!"

....

On Earth they never met, but all have crossed the Long Swamp, to gather, I am sure, at the Hunters' Campfire, where we will all meet again one day. They just don't make them like that anymore!

" **B**y God, *Jim*," I observed, "*it's always a pleasure to host the Fraternity. It gives us yokels the chance to meet some real high class drunks for a change.*"

It was near midnight on 29 July 1981. I was sharing a toddy with Jimmy Rikhoff, president of the National Sporting Fraternity, a group sometimes known as Rikhoff's Rangers. As dedicated colonials, here at Nictau, a far-flung corner of the empire, we were celebrating the marriage of Charles, Prince of Wales, and Lady Diana.

We had gotten a head start a day earlier. Col. John Woods, fellow member of the Royals, my own old regiment, and a friend of Prince Philip, had suggested that we simply must prepare to properly pay homage on this historical occasion.

As we could receive one channel in that area, but alas did not have a television, Harry Tennyson solicited donations from among the members, and Jimmy and I were off to town forty miles away to make the purchase. No sense in wasting a trip, so additional refreshments would be acquired at the same time.

Allowing for the crossing of several time zones, it was necessary that all gather for bloody Marys and huevos rancheros, in the dining room, at five o'clock in the morning. There, courtesy of the brand-new TV, we would miss no moment of the pomp and pageantry being played out in Britain, half a world away. It was marvelous in the extreme.

A couple of hours of this, however, and a few of the less than ardent Monarchists among us, decided to get geared up and go salmon fishing.

Irene, with helpers Willa and Eleanor, planned to produce a feast of fresh Atlantic lobster with all the fixings for some time in

Tom Hennessey

the early afternoon, so all the fishermen were warned to be back to camp in plenty of time for pre-dinner refreshments.

Tom Hennessey and I figured to sail down the Right Hand Branch from Rocky Bend to Grassy Island at the mouth of Tom Pole Brook. Martin and Rick would haul us up and then meet us for the pickup later. Just in case we had to cross any burning deserts, we took along what our Cajun neighbors term a "Van-cat Molson." To those who don't savvy frog lingo, that's a twenty-four-pint case of Canada's finest beer

As we unloaded the big twenty-foot canoe from the top of the truck, I instructed the boys to be sure and take it easy going back up the Riordan Gulch road, and to meet us at noon on the log landing at Grassy Island. It was a beautiful summer morning, big fluffy white clouds over the Serpentine Mountains, just enough of an upriver breeze to keep the midgets ashore, while not enough to work me to death poling.

Rocky Bend, as one might imagine, is a curving, hard downhill run, through boulders from the size of basketballs to bulldozers. Fun enough at any time, with a five o'clock start and beer before breakfast, it can be a bit tricky.

Canoes on Tobique are poled. They are launched with the bow upstream, snubbed up at the stern, a push as the bow swings out and downstream. Nothing to it . . . done it a million times, daylight and dark, rain and shine, drunk and sober. Only this time the pole gets snagged between the rocks and breaks in two, nearly dumping me into the river.

Fortunately Tom is a good friend, a woods wise old Mainiac as we call our cousins across the border in Maine. He is not some fearful city dude, but one who appreciates a chuckle at the perils of being a guide. I manage to run the rest of the Bend, fending off the rocks with the broken end of the pole.

Not to worry, just a nice pitch of water, I can cane her along with the abbreviated pole. We'll be anchored fishing much of the time anyway.

Funny how nice that cold beer goes down, just seems to be the right thing for such a lovely morning. Across from the mouth of Rocky Brook and at the foot of the log sluice, we anchored while Tom worked over the pools. Fish raised and missed at one, a couple grilse landed then released at the other; great morning, as anyone who knows Atlantic salmon fishing can appreciate.

It came time to sail on down and meet the boys, and the beer was almost gone anyway.

Coming down the stretch I could see Martin had backed the truck out on the landing, ready to help us load.

As we slipped alongside the shore, I pulled the classic Tobique maneuver. You scull around until the bow now points upstream, snub her at the stern and gently glide against the bank in a professional manner. Only this time, when I was snubbing, the short pole slipped on the rocks. Just as I reached for another purchase, Tom threw himself around to see what was happening. Instantly we were upside down, in two feet of water! In panic we both grabbed for the last two pints of beer floating away in the box, and completely forgot Tom's expensive camera sitting on the river bottom. One must never forget one's priorities.

Arriving at camp, soaking wet, I attempted to put a good face on things. "Jesus, boys, did we ever get a bad thunderstorm up the branch! Did it hit down here?" Of course Martin, with the honesty of the young, could not keep his mouth shut.

After dinner, after the evening's fishing, the group came back to camp still in a celebrating mood; after all, Royal weddings do not happen every day. Sometime during the festivities the talk got around to traditional sports as played in the Old Country, and Jim got the bright idea of demonstrating the ancient Scottish tradition of "tossing the caber." In this strenuous and somewhat hazardous undertaking, one attempts to lift vertically a solid wooden log of about twelve feet, then heave it in the air to supposedly come down on a target.

Not to disappoint my guests, I hauled the chain saw out of the truck and whacked a reasonable replica of the famous caber, out of the railing protecting one of the wife's flower beds. We would have to deal with that later.

Rikhoff, always the innovator, tottered out into the dooryard, urinated copiously, and said "Okay, boys, now here is the target."

While some of the more athletic lovers of tradition somewhat unsteadily attempted to emulate the Highland warrior of a bygone era, Jim and I reflected on what a success the day had been.

Looking back now, realizing that a number of our compatriots are no longer with us, one can only hope that they have gone to the land where bright fish are rising, where the beer is always cold and the days never ending.

While some of them are gone, and the rest of us no longer young and crazy, we have at least outlived the Royal Marriage.

EPILOGUE

Irene and I were driving over the mountains from our winter base in interior B.C., heading for Vancouver, where I was slated for heart surgery. We had been talking about some of the changes in our life and in our hunting business, which in great part is our life. The suggestion came up once more that I should put some of these recollections down on paper before it was too late.

While I had written short articles strictly related to the hunting and fishing sports, the very idea of even thinking about a *book* put me into cold sweats. To begin with, to my way of thinking, I had led a fairly routine existence and was simply too *young* for any attempt at an autobiography.

Besides, there is my well-developed inferiority complex. After reading many books by professional hunting friends from Africa, my meager adventures seem fairly tame. They always seem to be sitting around the fire with the client's beautiful wife, resting up from having been trampled by elephants and torn to shreds by leopards all day. Black bear hunting in New Brunswick in comparison, looks fairly routine.

"Who in hell," I wondered, "would read any book that I wrote?"

"Well," said my spouse and partner, "You know we are not getting any younger, and you have led a pretty free and exciting life . . . especially for someone who has been *married* for just about all of it."

The way she studied my face for reaction when she emphasized the word "married" made me believe that I had at least one guaranteed sale.

A week later, as I lay in the hospital full of tubes and wires, the cardiac surgeon told me they had done five bypasses on major coronary arteries. He went on to explain that although there was certainly no warranty on the job, with any luck I would live long enough to die of something else.

Two principal subjects on my mind were getting well enough to join Irene and Martin in the barren lands caribou camp in time for my sixtieth birthday in September, and finding time to gather together enough reminiscences to interest a publisher.

One of the problems in writing about personal experiences, before all the people in the story are dead, is that some nitpicker will surface to say that the author doesn't know what in hell he is talking about. Usual complaints are that some obscure incident didn't happen in just the way, on the very day, that the writer has indicated. The obvious and the most personally rewarding way to avoid this happening is to outlive all the bastards. However, if this is impractical, the author must use some sort of disclaimer.

One of the best "disclaimers" I have ever heard came from a veteran outdoor author, Col. Charles Askins. We were sitting around in an Arctic airport, on our way back from a muskox hunt on Victoria Island, when the colonel was approached by a young hunter who had read his book describing a lifetime's experience of guns, hunting, and adventure.

Questioned on one amazing episode regarding his early years as a patrolman on the Texas border with Mexico, the colonel replied, "Son, there *may be* lies in that book, but THAT ain't one of them."

That, I guess, is as close to the truth as one should require from guides and professional hunters, in their tales about critters, clients, and life in general. To that I can only add: This narrative reflects the experiences of a lifetime spent primarily as a guide, in one context or another, in various times and placed. I hope it has entertained you in some small measure.

Fred A. Webb
Pritchard, B.C.
Winter 1996